CHINGIS KHAN RIDES WEST

Chingis Khan Rides West

The Mongol Invasion
of
Bukhara, Samarkand,
and other
Great Cities of the Silk Road, 1215–1221

Don Croner

Polar Star Books
Ulaanbaatar

ISBN 978-0-9852880-7-5

Photographs by Don Croner

Polar Star Books

books@doncroner.com
www.doncronerblog.com

Contents

CHAPTER I

CHINGIS KHAN CONFRONTS UIGHURS, TANGUTS, AND JURCHENS

BY THE CLOSE OF THE YEAR 1215 Temüjin, the Mongolian chieftain known to the world as Chingis Khan, was sitting pretty. Nine years earlier, in 1206, he had defeated and brought under his rule most, if not all, of the nomadic peoples of the Mongolian Plateau, and in a great assembly of the tribes on the Onon River he had been confirmed as Chingis Khan, the Great Khan of the Mongols. He then cast his gaze to the south, to the great sedentary civilizations of China which, for over a thousand years, had been the plundering grounds of the nomads to the north. As early as 1205 his forces had raided the borderlands of the kingdom of Xi Xia, centered upon the modern-day Ningxia and Gansu provinces of China, and returned with huge hauls of camels and other livestock. In the autumn of 1207 a more ambitious raid raked in more plunder and even managed to capture the town of Wulahai, near current-day Tingyuan, in the Alashan region. Still not ready for a full-scale assault on Xi Xia, the raiders returned to their Mongolian homeland in the spring of 1208.[1]

Meanwhile, the people known as Uighurs, who occupied many of the oasis cities to the north and south of the Tian Shan Mountains in modern-day Xinjiang Province, China, were alerted to the rise of the Mongols and decided to make a strategic alliance with them. The Uighurs had originated in Mongolia (the extensive ruins of their old capital of Ordu Baliq ["Royal Camp Town", also known as Karabalgasun], can still be seen in Arkhangai Aimag, north of the town of Kharkhorin), and in the 840s they had migrated en masse to the Zungarian and eastern Tarim basins in what is now Xinjiang. Since the 1130s they had been under the thumb of the Qara Khitai, the remnants of the old Liao Dynasty (907-

1125) in China who had migrated westward and set up a powerful con-federation centered upon current-day Uzbekistan, Kyrgyzstan, and the western Tarim Basin.[2] The Uighur ruler Barchuk, who held the title of *Idikut* ("Sacred Majesty"), may have sensed that the Mongols were the ascendent power in Inner Asia. If Chingis Khan succeeded in defeating Xi Xia, immediately to the east of the Barchuk's domains, he would no doubt soon turn his armies on the Uighurs themselves. By aligning him-self with Chingis early, Barchuk may have thought he could free himself from the Qara Khitai and at the same time avoid a devastating attack by the Mongols. He was of course gambling that the suzerainty of the Mon-gols would be less onerous than domination by the Qara Khitai.[3]

In the spring of 1209 Barchuk dispatched an embassy to the court of Chingis Khan with an offer to accept the suzerainty of the Mongols: "If you, Genghis Khan, show me favour, I will be your fifth son and will place all of my strength at your disposal." Chingis agreed and even offered one of his daughters, Altun, as a bride for the *Idikut*. Chingis stipulated, however, that Barchuk must come to the camp of the Mongols and make obeisance to him personally, adding that the *Idikut* should bring with him gifts of "gold, silver, small and large pearls, brocade, damasks, and silks."[4] (Here was an early indication of the Mongol fascination with fine fabrics—brocade, damask, and, silks—which later motivated Chingis to turn his attention westward, to the Islamic realms of Inner Asia, a major source of these rich materials.) Barchuk agreed to accept Mongol suzer-ainty in 1209, making the Uighurs the first sedentary people south of the Mongolian Plateau to come under Mongol rule. Still, just to be on the safe side, Barchuk bided his time until 1211, awaiting the final outcome of the Mongol war against the Xi Xia, before finally appearing in person at the court of the Mongols on the Kherlen River in central Mongolia.

In any case, Chingis had by 1209 gained a valuable ally in Barchuk and the Uighurs. He could now invade Xi Xia without fear of an attack from his western flank, and he could utilize the administrative and intellec-tual abilities of the much more cultured Uighurs. Plundering a sedentary culture was one thing, but ruling it and successfully collecting taxes was another. The Uighurs would provide much of the expertise needed to gov-ern the lands that Chingis would conquer, and they would provide the hitherto illiterate Mongols with a writing system adapted from their own Uighur vertical script. (This Uighuro-Mongol vertical script would re-main in use in Mongolia until the adaption of the Cyrillic alphabet in the 20th century and since the early 1990s has enjoyed a modest resurgence.)

As important as the Uighur's intellectual acumen was the location of the land they occupied. With their summer capital of Qocho (also known as Gaochang, Qarakhoja, and Houzhou,) near current-day Turpan, on the south side of the Tian Shan Mountains, and their winter capital of Beshbaliq, near current-day Jimsar, on the north side, and controlling a host of other oasis cities strung like beads on a necklace from Hami in the east to Kucha in the west, the Uighurs sat directly astride the main trunks of the Silk Road between China and the great Islamic civilizations of Inner Asia and the Mideast. Uighuristan at this time was still largely Buddhist, but Islam was inexorably advancing eastward by means of both conquest and ostensibly peaceful Muslim traders on the Silk Road. By adding Uighuristan to his domains without a battle, Chingis gained an invaluable window to the West through which he may have gotten a tantalizing glimpse of the fabulously rich and cultured Islamic civilizations shimmering like mirages on the horizon, a world totally unlike anything the rude nomads from the steppes of Mongolia had hitherto imagined possible.

With the Uighurs securely in his corner Chingis was ready to launch a full-scale invasion of Xi Xia. The people of Xi Xia, known as Tanguts, founded the Xi Xia Dynasty, or "Great State of White and High", in 1038. The Tanguts were a people of Tibeto-Burman extraction who had developed a prosperous agrarian and livestock-breeding culture and occupied well-fortified towns and cities. They aspired to some level of culture and soon developed their own writing system, based on Chinese ideograms, which they used to translate both Tibetan Buddhist texts and the Chinese classics. While espousing Chinese culture, they also practiced Tibetan-style Vajrayana Buddhism. They also maintained a large army and, at their height, were one of the strongest military powers in Inner Asia. Like the Uighurs, they sat astride the Silk Road, controlling the vital Gansu Corridor, a narrow strip of land between the rugged mountains to the south and the inhospitable deserts to the north through which Silk Road caravans had to pass.

The intertribal warfare in Mongolia at the beginning of the thirteenth century had decimated the herds of the nomads, and the early Mongol raids into Xi Xia in 1205 and 1207 were mainly attempts to capture livestock which was then driven back to Mongolia.[5] These raids, however, were enough to alert the Tanguts to the danger of the nomads to the north who like wolves swooped down on their herds. The failure of the Xi

Xia ruler at the time, Li Chunyu, to protect his domains may have led to the palace revolt that deposed him in late 1207. The new ruler Li Anguan, perhaps hoping to placate the Mongols and buy time, gave Chingis one of his daughters as a bride. At the same time, he strengthened the country's defenses in anticipation of another Mongol attack. He didn't have long to wait. Having subdued the Uighurs to the west without a battle, Chingis was now ready for a full-scale onslaught upon the territory coterminous with the North China plain controlled by the Chin Dynasty, his ultimate target.

In early 1209 Chingis himself led an army 650 miles south to the domains of Xi Xia and soon captured the border town of Wulahai. The Xi Xia armies rallied, however, and a stalemate ensued until the end of summer when reinforcements arrived from Mongolia. The Tanguts were soon driven back to their fortified cites, including their capital of Ningxia, current-day Yincheng, on the Yellow River. A weakness of the Mongols was soon revealed. Although masters of horseback warfare on the open steppe, they had very little experience in besieging fortified cities. Having surrounded the Xi Xia capital, Chingis attempted various stratagems to capture it, including diverting the waters of the Yellow River in an attempt to flood the city, but by the end of 1209 none had succeeded. In the meantime, the Xi Xia ruler had sent messengers to the Chin ruler in Zhongdu (current-day Beijing), asking for assistance against the Mongols. His advisors recommended sending an army to relieve the besieged city, arguing that if Xi Xia fell, the Chin themselves would be Chingis's next target. The emperor responded, "It is an advantage to my state if its enemies attack each other. What grounds do we have for concern?"[6] No relief army was sent, and the Xi Xia were left to their own devices. This proved to be a fatal miscalculation on the part of the Chin emperor.

In January of 1210 the Mongols themselves suffered a setback when the waters of the Yellow River, perhaps diverted by the Tanguts themselves, flooded their own camp. Faced with a stalemate, negotiations began between Chingis and the Xi Xia ruler. Control of the countryside by the Mongols was a *fait accompli*, but Chingis offered to let the Tanguts keep control of their cities as long as they provided auxiliary troops for the Mongol army. The Xi Xia ruler declined, pointing out that "We are a nation of town-dwellers. We would not be in a state to fight as auxiliaries in the event of a long march followed by a heated battle."[7] He did offer to provide the Mongols with herds of camels and other livestock, trained falcons, wool garments, silk cloth, and, as a final sweetener, another one of his delectable daughters as a bride for Chingis Khan himself. Although the Tanguts were allowed to remain as figureheads in their own country, most of their territories were now effectively controlled by the Mongols. For the moment Chingis Khan was satisfied with the outcome, but he would never forgive the Tanguts for refusing to provide him with troops. Before he died he would return to Xi Xia and exact a terrible revenge.

The defeat of the Xi Xia served a number of purposes: the campaign was good training for the upcoming war with the much stronger Chin Dynasty, and it had revealed weaknesses in the Mongol army—namely their ignorance of siege techniques—which would have to be corrected before any further campaigns against fortified cities. A western spring-board for the invasion of the Chin Dynasty domains had been secured, and the Mongols now controlled the Gansu Corridor, the bottleneck through which most of the caravan routes that originated in Xian and other Silk Road terminuses had to pass.[8] The Mongols now sat astride the Silk Road from the boundaries of the Chin Dynasty domains in the east to the western edge of Uighuristan in the Tarim Basin. The road had been cleared for Chingis's attack on the Chin Dynasty, the rulers of northern China, still considered to be the richest source of plunder and the ultimate prize by the nomads from the Mongolian Plateau.

The people known as Jurchens who eventually founded the Jurchen, or Chin Dynasty, originated around the timbered basins of the Amur, Ussuri, and Sungari rivers in Manchuria, in what is now northeast China. They spoke Tungusic, an eastern extension of the Altaic language family closely related to Manchu, the language of the people who would later create the Qing Dynasty.[9] It was completely different from the Chinese language and thus, from the Chinese viewpoint, marked the Jurchens as an alien people. Almost nothing is known of their history prior to the tenth century A.D. Apparently they began to use iron only in the early eleventh century. One tribe of the Jurchen, the Wanyan, began making farming tools and weapons from iron and on the basis of this new technology soon dominated their neighbors. Under the leadership of a chieftain known as Wugunai (1021–1074), the Wanyan soon assumed leadership of a confederation of the various Jurchen tribes. Wugunai, according to contemporary histories, "was addicted to wine and women and could outdrink anyone," but he was also a warrior of legendary stature.[10] His sons and grandsons emulated his military exploits, and by 1114 his grandson Aguda and a horse-mounted army of some 10,000 men had defeated a 100,000-man army sent north to the borderlands by the emperor of the Liao Dynasty (907–1125), then in control of much of northern China. Based on his military exploits, Aguda audaciously claimed the Mandate of Heaven and, at the beginning of the first lunar month in the year 1115, proclaimed the commencement of the Chin (Gold) Dynasty with himself as emperor. He then launched a full-scale assault on the territories of the Liao Dynasty. The various Liao capitals fell one-by-one, culminating with the Southern Capital (current-day Beijing) in 1122.[11]

In 1125, the last of the Liao rulers, the Tianzou Emperor, was captured while trying to escape westward through the Ordos Desert. This signaled the end of the Liao Dynasty. The same year the Jurchens attacked the Song Dynasty, which controlled much of middle and southern China. The Song capital of Kaifeng quickly fell, followed by Taiyuan and other strategic Song cities. On January 16, 1127, the Song Emperor Qinzong personally surrendered to the Jurchens. Intermittent fighting between the Jurchens and hold-out Song forces would continue for years, but by the 1140s the southern boundary of the Chin Dynasty would be fixed roughly along the course of the Huai River, about two hundred miles south of the Yellow River, where the wheat and millet fields of northern China graded into the rice paddies of southern China. South of here the reconstituted Song, known as the Southern Song Dynasty (1127-1279), would continue to rule.[12]

With the defeat of the Liao Dynasty in 1125 the Chin had turned their attention north to the Mongolian Plateau. While still engaged with the Song Dynasty, they had no desire to confront their potentially dangerous neighbors to the north and sought instead to court their friendship or at least neutrality. Thus it was that they invited to their court Khabul Khan, the great-grandfather of Chingis Khan. Khabul Khan was the leader of the Khamag Mongols, a loose confederation of the various Mongol tribes, and thus one of the most powerful men on the Mongolian Plateau. The details are hazy, but some sources suggest this meeting took place during the coronation of the Chin emperor Xizong in 1125 at the Chin capital of Zhongdu.[13] During the meeting Khabul Khan reportedly got roaringly drunk and in his intoxicated state even dared to tug on the emperor's beard. Not wanting to antagonize the capricious Mongol ruler, Xizong apparently shrugged this off as the playful antics of an uncouth barbarian. He even loaded down Khabul Khan with generous gifts of gold, precious stones, and rich fabrics when he left the capital. The emperor's courtiers took a dimmer view; infuriated by what they perceived as insults to the emperor, they dispatched troops to capture Khabul Khan and bring him back for punishment. Khabul Khan managed to escape, but the seeds of ill will were planted between the Chin Court and the Mongols.

Although various treaties sought to maintain trade and tribute relations between the Jurchen and the Mongols, their alliance continued to deteriorate. War broke out between the two parties in 1139, 1143, and in 1147, and the Jurchen suffered some humiliating defeats. After the latter conflict, the Jurchen agreed to sent the Mongols yearly gifts—essentially bribes—of livestock, grain, and silk in an effort to secure peace along the borderlands. The gifts of fabrics alone amounted to 300,000 bales of fine silk and 300,000 bales of coarse silk a ÿear. When his cousin Ambakhai became khan of the Khamag Mongols after Khabul Khan's death, the Jurchen decided that it was finally time to rein in the unruly nomads. They contrived with the Tatars, their erstwhile allies and hereditary enemies of the Mongols, to capture both Ambakhai and Khabul Khan's own son Ökin Barkhakh and take them as prisoners to the Chin capital, where they were executed by nailing them onto a wooden donkey, a traditional punishment for rebellious tribesmen. Before he died, Ambakhai managed to dispatch a courier, a man named Balaqachi, back to Mongolia with a message for Khutula, one of Khabul Khan's sons, and his own son, Qadaan-taishi: "I became the Khan of all, Lord of the Nation . . . I have been captured by the Tartar people. Do not follow my example. Strive until the nails of your five fingers splinter and your ten fingers drop from you hands to avenge me."[14]

For the moment Ambakhai's supplication would go unanswered. The Jurchen and Tatars renewed their attacks on the Mongols, and by the time of Chingis Khan's birth in 1162, the confederation of tribes ruled over by Khabul Khan and later by his son Khutula had collapsed. Anarchy reigned among the Mongols. According to the Persian historian Ata Malik Juvaini (1226–1283):

> They had no chief or ruler. Each tribe lived separately; they were not united with one another, and there was constant fighting and hostility between them. Some of them regarded robbery and violence, immorality and debauchery as deeds of manliness and excellence. The Khan of Kitai [the Jurchen emperor of the Chin Dynasty] used to demand and seize goods from them. Their clothing was of the skins of dogs and mice, and their food was the flesh of those animals and other dead things . . .[15]

Temüjin, the future Chingis Khan, although the great-grandson of
Khabul Khan, ruler of the Khamag Mongols, was born into straitened
circumstances, and after the murder of his father at the hands of Tatars
his family was reduced to outright poverty. At one point, according to the
thirteenth century *Secret History of the Mongols*, the entire family had only
nine horses and was reduced to eating marmots and mice.[16] Temüjin's rise
to power has been oft-related elsewhere and will not be recounted here.
Suffice it to say that by 1189 he had been recognized as Khan of the Mongol tribes at a convocation held at Khökh Nuur (Blue Lake) in what is
now Khentii Aimag, and, according to some accounts, it was at this time
that he was given the title of Chingis Khan. By 1206 he had defeated most
of the other tribes who had opposed him, and at a convocation on the
Onon River his title of Chingis Khan was affirmed. From this point on,
he was the undisputed ruler of the Mongolian Plateau.

During Chingis Khan's rise to power he had sought the patronage of
Tooril, the powerful ruler of the Kerait Tribe who was headquartered in
the valley of the Tuul River, not far from current-day Ulaanbaatar. Tooril
had recognized the nominal suzerainty of the Chin and apparently paid
tribute to them. In return he was awarded the title of Wang (or Ong)
Khan. As one of Tooril's vassals, Temüjin also received a minor title from
the Jurchens of the Chin Dynasty and may have also paid tribute to them.
There are also hints that Temüjin sought refuge among the Jurchens during low points in his early career when he was being hounded by more
powerful tribes in Mongolia.[17] Chingis Khan and the Wang Khan would
later fall out, and the Keraits would be defeated, calling into question the
Chin title Temüjin had received as one of the Kerait ruler's vassals. The
Chin, for their part, still believed that Chingis Khan owed them loyalty
and tribute, even after he had been confirmed as leader of all the Mongols
at the 1206 convocation on the Onon River. The Jurchens were no doubt
aware that, having become the most powerful ruler on the Mongolian
Plateau, Chingis now posed a direct threat to themselves, but at the time
they were embroiled in a war with the Song Dynasty in the south of China and could not confront Chingis directly.

In 1208 the Chin Dynasty finally sought to clarify their relationship
with Chingis Khan. The Chin emperor Zhangzong sent his uncle Wanyan Yongji, the Prince of Wei, north to reaffirm their suzerainty and re-
ceive tribute from Chingis.[18] The Mongol Khan met with the prince but
refused to make the proper signs of obeisance. It soon became clear the
Chingis no longer recognized the Chin as his overlords. No mention was

made of tribute. The infuriated Prince returned to China and began mo-
bilizing troops to attack the Mongols. In late 1208 Emperor Zhangzong
died and Wanyan Yongji became the new ruler of the Chin Dynasty. The
attack was postponed, and instead Wanyan Yongji sent an ambassador to
Chingis with the news that he was now the Altan Khan (Golden Khan),
as the Mongols called the Chin Emperor, and that Chingis should declare his loyalty to him. Chingis, however, apparently had not been to
impressed by Wanyan Yongji at their previous meeting. According to one
account, when Chingis was asked by the ambassador to make obeisance
to the new emperor, he "flew into a rage" and stormed: "'Is an imbecile like
[Wanyan Yongji] worthy of the throne and am I to humble myself before
him?'"[19] He answered his own question by turning to the south and spit-
ting in the direction of China. The ambassador was dismissed and Chingis rode away to the north. The import of these actions was clear to the
Chin Emperor: Chingis Khan was declaring war on the Chin Dynasty.[20]

Chingis Khan's disdain for the Chin Dynasty was not based on mere
bravado. He had been receiving intelligence about the weakness of the
Chin even before his affirmation as Khan of the Mongols in 1206. Muslim
merchants who traded in both northern China and Mongolia had kept
him apprized of the various internal disputes in the Chin court and of
the grumblings of discontented peasants. One Muslim merchant, a man
named Jafar, was an early stalwart of the Mongol Khan, and Chingis eventually sent him to the Chin court fishing for information. Chin officials
quickly surmised that he was a spy and dismissed him, but during his
travels in northern China he gathered much information that would later
prove useful to the Mongols.[21] Then in late 1206 and again in 1208 dis-
sidents and defectors from the Chin brought Chingis brought more news
of political upheavals and social disturbances in northern China, but he
was still not ready to be drawn into a conflict with his powerful neighbors
to the south.

His confrontation with the Chin ambassador seems to have marked a
turning point in Chingis's altitude toward the Chin. In early 1211 Chingis
summoned his followers to a convocation on the Kherlen River where
the subject of an attack on the Chin Dynasty was broached. Moreover,
the Uighur *Idikut* Barluk appeared in person as he had earlier promised
and cemented his allegiance to the Mongols. With the Tanguts of Xi Xia
already neutralized and the Uighurs firmly in his corner, Chingis now
controlled the western approaches to the territory of the Chin. The pieces

were falling into place for an invasion.

Still, before riding south, Chingis climbed to the top of a high mountain—local people to this day claim it was 7,749-foot Khentii Khaan Uul, also known as the Burkhan Khaldun of the Khamag Mongols, in current-day Khentii Aimag (the president of Mongolia is still required to go to a pilgrimage to the summit of this mountain at least once every four years)—and sought the guidance of Ikh Tenger, the Great God of the Eternal Blue Sky.[22] According to the Persian historian Rashid al-Din, Chingis proclaimed:

> O Eternal Heaven! You know and accept that the Altan Khan [Chin Emperor] is the wind which fanned the tumult, that it is he who began this quarrel. He it was who, without cause, executed Ökin Barkhakh and Ambakhai Khan, captured and delivered over to him by the Tatars. These were the elder relatives of my father and grandfather and I seek to avenge their blood.[23]

The Persian historian Minhaj al-Siraj Juzjani (b. 1193) relates the same episode, but with differing details. According to Juzjani, after learning about the situation in the Chin realm from the above mentioned Jafir, Chingis:

> determined upon the design of rebelling, got his forces ready, and first directed so that the whole of the Mughal [Mongol] families assembled together at the base of a mountain. He enjoined that all the men should be separated from the women, and the children from their mothers: and for three whole days and nights all of them remained bare-headed; and for three days no one tasted food, and no animal was allowed to milk its young. The Chingiz Khan himself entered [a felt tent], and placed a tent-rope about his neck, and came not forth from it for three nights and days, and during this period, the whole of the people . . . were crying out, Tingri ![Tengri], Tingri! After three days, at dawn, on the fourth day, the Chingiz Khan issued from the tent and exclaimed, "Tingri hath given me victory. Now we are ready to wreak our vengeance upon the Altun Khan!"[24]

As is clear from these accounts Chingis attempted to justify his attack on the Chin Dynasty as revenge for the deaths of his relatives. There were, of course, other considerations. In his struggle to attain supremacy on the Mongolian Plateau, Chingis had mobilized large armies, and these men were traditionally paid in plunder. With their enemies on the Mongolian Plateau already defeated there was little left to loot. Once again the no-

mads of the steppe turned their attention south, where the rich and fattened cities of China glittered on the far horizon.

The invasion began in May of 1211. This was no small move on Chingis's
part. The Chin Dynasty, despite the symptoms of dynastic decay that had
been reported to Chingis by his various spies, was still one of the five or
six great sedentary states of Eurasia. The Chin state had a population
of perhaps 40,000,000, although only around 3,000,000 of the populace were Jurchens, descendants of the original Jurchen tribesmen from
Manchuria, the rest being Han Chinese and other indigenous peoples.
The Chin state could muster approximately 150,000 cavalrymen, most of
them Jurchens, and 300,000 to 400,000 infantrymen, most of them Chinese. The loyalty of the Chinese infantry was, of course, in question. Still,
according to one modern historian, "the Chin army retained a reputation
as the most powerful military state in the known world."[25] Chingis had
under his overall command one army of perhaps 50,000 cavalry led by
himself and another army of 50,000 cavalrymen led by his three sons. His
ranks would soon be swollen with discontented tribesmen and deserters
from the Chin.

The Mongols first confronted the Onggut, a tribe of nomads that
guarded the southern rim of the Mongolian Plateau on behalf of the Chin
Dynasty. Their leader Alakush quickly defected to Chingis along with
many of his troops, demonstrating just how tenuous a hold the Jurchens
had over many of their subjects. Loyalists along the Onggut reacted by
assassinating Alakush, but at the urging of his nephew and heir the rest
of the Ongguts soon fell in line and joined the Chingis's forces. Several
towns near Kalgan (present day Zhangjiakhou) on the very edge of the
Mongolian Plateau quickly fell to advancing nomads, and more border
troops deserted. Liu Bailin, the Chin commander of the town of Wein-
ing defected and would go on to play a leading role in the defeat of the
dynasty.

With the Mongols, their ranks now swelled with former Chin auxiliary troops, poised on the very edge of the great ramparts overlooking the
farm lands of northern China and within a couple days ride of the Central
Capital of Zhongdu (Beijing), the Jurchen court panicked and put out a
peace feeler, apparently thinking that this was just a another Mongol raid
in search of quick loot and that Chingis could be bought off with some
suitable bribes. When this initial overture was rejected, a senior envoy, a
Khitan man by the name of Shimo Mingan who knew the Mongolian

language and had earlier met with Chingis in Mongolia, was sent north with more serious peace proposals. Shimo Mingan promptly defected to the Mongols and was made a commander of both Mongol detachments and of native Chinese troops who had now turned on the Jurchens.[26]

The now-augmented Mongolian forces swept down upon the North China plain and by the autumn of 2011 they had invested the Chin Western Capital (modern-day Datong, in Shanxi Province). The Chin commander of the Western Capital, a man named Hushahu, who one modern historian describes as an "irascible ruffian," abandoned his post, allowing the Mongols to take over the city (there were rumors the Mongols had bribed him), and another Chin general, the commander of Chin armies in the west, also turned and fled with most of his troops to the Central Capital, even though they far-outnumbered their Mongol opponents. The official history of the Chin Dynasty would later declare that the desertion of their posts by these two commanders was an foreboding sign: "The spirit of resolution was lost and could not be regained. The collapse of the Chin was foretold by this event."[27]

With the approaches to the city unguarded, the Mongol armies quickly moved eastward, and by the end of the year had invested the main capital of Zhongdu, where the Chin court was headquartered. In early 1212, after laying siege to Zhongdu for a month but failing to take the well-fortified city, the Mongols decided to return back to the Mongolian Plateau. Chingis himself had been wounded by an arrow in the battle for the Western Capital and his injury may have contributed to his decision to withdraw. Chingis had by no means been defeated. On their way home the Mongols even detoured eastward to loot the Chin Eastern Capital (current day Liaoyang in Liaoning Province). The Mongols were simply retiring to the fastness of the Mongolian Plateau to enjoy their loot, let their horses fatten on the steppe over the summer, and regroup for their next assault. The weaknesses of the Chin Dynasty had been exposed, and Chingis intended to exploit them.

In early 1213 the Mongols again descended onto the plains on North China. The Western Capital was quickly retaken and the main capital of Zhongdu again besieged. While many Chin troops were tied down in the capital, Mongol troops spent the summer and fall rampaging across the North China plain, looting and plundering much of current-day Shanxi, Hebei, and Shandong provinces. By early 1214 the armies had converged on the Central Capital and Chingis himself was bivouacked in the northern suburbs. The noose around the city was tightened, and his sons and generals urged him to attack the city and to put an end to the Chin Dynasty once and for all.

Inside the city walls the Chin Court was in shambles. Hushahu, the same man who had abandoned the Western Capital in 1211, had made his way to the Central Capital where he made a bid to seize control of the Chin Dynasty himself. First, he killed the governor of the city and then seized the sitting Chin Emperor, the hapless Wanyan Yongji, whom Chingis had earlier dismissed as an "imbecile". After ordering court eunuchs to kill Wanyan Yongji, he connived to put the aging Wanyan Xun, the older brother of Emperor Zhangzong, who had died back in 1208, on the throne as the new Chin emperor. Hushahu himself hoped to rule as the power behind the throne. But the backstabbing was not over. Shuhu Gaoji, a Chin general who harbored his own ambitions, seized Hushahu and had him executed. Now Wanyan Xun, who Hushahu had intended only as a figurehead, was ruling the Chin as the Emperor Xuanzong. Whether he would be able to right the tottering Chin State and defend it against the Mongols camped outside the walls of his capital was open to question.[28]

Chingis, with his well-developed spy network, must have been well aware of the turmoil in the inner circles of the Chin. Yet, when pressed to force the walls of the Central Capital and overthrow the dynasty, he hesitated. Plundering the countryside was one thing; actually overthrowing a dynasty and assuming the responsibility for governing its subjects was quite another matter. He had seized control of the Xi Xia Empire to the west while leaving the Tanguts to govern under his suzerainty, and perhaps he envisioned the same relationship with the Chin. And there were very immediate, practical considerations to take into account. The siege had already dragged on for months, and more months might be required to finally take Zhongdu. The Mongol forces drawn up around the capital were desperately short of food. The Christian missionary Carpini, who would later visit the Mongol court, claimed that the Mongols outside Zhongdu were so starved that they resorted to cannibalism, killing their own comrades for food. One out of every ten died to provide sustenance for the others, he claimed. This may have been a slanderous exaggeration, but numerous other sources attest to the dire straits of the Mongol troops. Rashid al-Din reported that "things were so bad they ate the corpses of their dead companions and of fallen horses; they even ate hay."[29] To make matters worse, an epidemic of some unspecified disease soon raged among the Mongol troops, and with the onset of spring the legendary heat of the North China plain would be debilitating to both the nomads, who were used to their cool highlands on the Mongolian Plateau, and to their horses. It was not clear how much longer the Mongols could hold out.

Chingis decided to make peace overtures. The Muslim merchant Jafar, a long time camp follower of Chingis who years earlier served as his envoy to the Chin and whose knowledge of the geography of the north China plain had proved invaluable during the invasion, was chosen to negotiate with the Jurchen court. The embattled Jurchens quickly came to terms, offering huge material inducements to persuade Chingis and his men to return to Mongolia. As part of the settlement, according to one source, Chingis received a Chin princess as a wife, 500 boy and girl slaves, 3000 horses, and large quantities of gold and expensive fabrics.[30] The *Secret History* maintains that Chingis himself got only a princess named Qiguo but that his soldiers received vast qualities of gold, silver, satin, silk, and other expensive goods: "Our soldiers loaded as much of the satin and other goods as they could carry, tied the loads with silk, and left."[31] Thus Chingis and his troops returned to the cool steppes of Mongolia laden with booty, and there was no doubt great rejoicing among the Mongolian women when they saw the luxurious silks, satins, and brocades their men had brought home for them.

The Mongols would not have long to enjoy their plunder. In July, while they were fattening their horses on the steppe, came the disturbing news that Emperor Xuanzong had abandoned Zhongdu, the Central Capital. On 30,000 carts, and accompanied by 3000 camel loads of treasure, the Chin court and government had left Zhongdu and was on its way to the Southern Capital (current-day Kaifeng), hopefully out of reach of further Mongol incursions. Many Jurchens viewed this apparent refusal to face the Mongol threat head-on as abject cowardice on the part of their leadership. Mutinies broke about among Jurchen troops and even more units defected to the Mongols. The Southern Song Dynasty, sensing the impotence of the Chin, refused to cough up the tribute it had previously promised to pay them. Chingis Khan, after the humiliating terms he had earlier imposed on the Chin, considered them to be subordinate to the Mongols, effectively part of the nascent Mongol Empire, and he viewed the move south as a treacherous attempt on the part of the Chin Emperor to regroup and continue the fighting, despite the treaty agreements of early 1214.[32] Obviously the war with the Chin was not over.

In the autumn of 1214 Mongols armies again poured off the Mongolian Plateau, and by the end of the year Zhongdu was once more invested. The court and government may have fled, but the inhabitants of Zhongdu, including the army units that had remained, were by no means ready to surrender their walled and well-fortified city. In their earlier battles with the Xi Xia, the Mongols had failed to take any major fortified cities due to their ignorance of siege techniques. This weakness again manifested itself. The walls of the city refused to yield, and a brutal war of attrition played out through the winter and spring of 1215. Food supplies within the city were soon exhausted and according to the *Secret History*, "the remaining soldiers, who began to grow thin and die, ate human flesh."[33] When a relief train sent to the beleaguered city was captured by the Mongols, the defenders knew they were doomed. The commandant of Zhongdu, Way-en Fuxing, committed suicide, and in late May or early June of 1215 troops led by the Khitan Shimo Mingan, who had defected to the Mongols back in 1211, forced their way into the city. A month-long orgy of looting and mayhem ensued. According to one account, 60,000 women and girls committed suicide by throwing themselves from the city walls in order to avoid capture by the Mongols.[34] This was no doubt an exaggeration, but after huge amounts of loot had been seized a large part of the populace was massacred and much of the city burned.

Chingis then ordered an inventory of the gold, silver, fine fabrics, and other valuable goods that had been plundered in the city and sent three men, Öngur, Arkhai Khasar, and Shigikhutug to take control of the looted goods. The vice-regent of the vanquished city, a man named Khada, met them, in the words of the *Secret History*, "face to face, taking with him some gold-embroidered and patterned satins." There are hints that near the end of the siege this man had opened the gates of Zhongdu to the Mongols, apparently in an effort to save his own life.[35] Now it appeared he was offering gifts—bribes—to the three Mongols, in an effort to ensure their good will. Shigikhutug, a member of the Tatar tribe who as a small boy had been captured by the Mongols and adopted by Chingis's mother, refused to take the gift. Pointing out that the city of Zhongdu and everything in it belonged to Chingis Khan, he said, "How can you steal Chingis Khan's goods and satins and bring them here and give to us behind his back? I will not take them."[36] The other two men took the gifts. Later, Chingis Khan, perhaps expecting that Khada would attempt to bribe the three men, asked them if they had been offered any gifts. Shigikhutug replied that Khada had offered them "gold-embroidered and patterned satins," adding he had refused the gift but the other two had taken it. Chingis "angrily rebuked" the two other men but praised Shigikhutug for his honesty. He asked Shigikhutug, "Will you not become my seeing eyes, my listening ears?"[37] This might be construed to mean that Chingis was asking him to become a spy and informer; in any case, Chingis later appointed him as a judge, and he would play an increasingly important role in the Mongol court. For our purposes, this incident shows the importance the Mongols attached to satins and other luxurious fabrics.

Meanwhile, the Eastern Capital (current day Liaoyang in Liaoning Province) had also fallen to the Mongols. No siege had been necessary. By means of various subterfuges the nomads had entered the city "without firing a single arrow."[38] One hundred thousand soldiers threw down their arms and surrendered, and vast amounts of loot were seized. Thus by the summer of 1215 Chingis Khan again occupied much of North China. This time he had no intention of allowing all of his troops to return to Mongolia and handing nominal control of the conquered areas back to the Chin. He demanded that Xuanzong, still cowering in the Southern Capital, cede to him outright the lands the Mongols now occupied plus additional areas in current-day Hebei and Shandong provinces that were still claimed by the Chin. Henceforth, Xuanzong would rule over only a small rump state in the middle Yellow River Valley (modern-day Henan Province) with Kaifeng as its capital.[39]

The Chin would not be totally extinguished until 1234, but by the end of 1215 Chingis Khan had at least nominal control of most of Northern China and ruled as suzerain over Xi Xia to the west and Uighuristan still farther west. The great trade routes which Occidental peoples would later call the Silk Road were now open from its various eastern terminuses, including the old Chin Central Capital of Zhongdu, through the Gansu Corridor to the great oasis cities of Uighuristan at the foot of the Tian Shan Mountains. News of these monumental events quickly spread beyond the Tian Shan, and soon ambassadors of the great Islamic empires of Inner Asia were wending their way eastward to learn what they could about the great conqueror who seemed to have appeared out of nowhere and now stood astride one the world's most ancient civilizations.

CHAPTER 2

AMBASSADORS, TRADE MISSIONS,
AND THE CATASTROPHE AT OTRAR

ONE RULER WHO COULD NOT HELP but take note of Chingis Khan's sudden rise to power in the East was Ala ad-Din Muhammad II (r. 1200–1220), the Sultan of the Khwarezmian Empire, also known as the Khwarezmshah. At its height, the empire over which he would reign was the most powerful state in Inner Asia. The Khwarezm Empire was centered upon the ancient province on Khwarezm on the lower reaches of Amu Darya River and its delta where it flowed into the Aral Sea. By 1215, the Khwarezmshah's burgeoning domains included Transoxiania (also known as Mawarannahr, Arabic for "that which is beyond the river"), located between the middle stretches of the Amu Darya and the Syr Darya River, in current-day Uzbekistan and southern Kazakhstan, and much of ancient Khorasan, comprised of what is now western Afghanistan, Turkmenistan, and northeastern Iran. By 1217 his empire would include Iraq-i Ajam, in current-day central and northwestern Iran, and the rest of western Iran south to the Persian Gulf. Strictly speaking, Khwarezm refers to the core territory of the empire that straddling the lower Amu Darya. Henceforth, we will refer to the Khwarezmshah's domains collectively as the Khwarezmian Empire or just Khwarezmia.

In the far west, at the edge of the Iranian Plateau, the Khwarezmshah's territories abutted Mesopotamia and its capital of Baghdad, home of the long-reigning (since 750 A.D.) Abbasid Caliphate headed by Caliph an-Nasir (r. 1180–1225), the Commander of the Faithful in the Islamic geosphere. An-Nasir had managed to restore the military power of the Caliphate after its subjugation by the Saljuq Turks and in the late 1190s clashed with the Khwarezmshah's father, Ala ad-Din Tekesh (r. 1172–

1200). There was still bad blood between the Khwarezmshah and an-Na-sir, but in 1215 the former was not yet ready to directly challenge the Ab-basid Caliphate. Instead, the restlessly ambitious Khwarezmshah turned his attention eastward. The Muslim traders from Khwarezmia who did business in China may have informed him of the fractures in the Chin Dynasty and unrest among the peasantry in North China. This intelli-gence had given the Khwarezmshah ideas, and there are some indications that he considered attacking China himself. Rashid al-Din asserts that the Khwarezmshah, as far back as 1205, entertained visions of invading China.[1] The Persian historian Juzjani claimed to have heard straight from the lips of a secretary to one of the ministers of the Khwarezmshah:

> that the ambition to appropriate the countries of Chin had become im-planted in the heart of Sultan Muhammad [the Khwarezmshah], and he was constantly making inquiry respecting those states, and used to ask the comers from the territories of Chin and the extreme limits of Turkistan about them. We [his servants] used to make representations in order to lead him from entertaining that resolution, but in no man-ner was that thought removed from his mind until he despatched the Sayyid-i-Ajali, Baha-ud-Din, the Razi, for that important affair."[2]

His informants from the "extreme limits of Turkestan" also may have apprised the Khwarezmshah that the Uighurs, whose territories came close to his own eastward boundaries, had several years earlier recognized a chieftain known as Chingis Khan, the leader of a little-known people from the Mongolian Plateau, as their overlord. Now came the perplex-ing rumors that this same Chingis Khan had swept into North China and, after shouldering aside the Chin Dynasty, had taken the reins of the country into his own hands. The Khwarezmshah decided it was time to find out more about Chingis Khan and the Mongols. In late 1215, he dispatched eastward an embassy led by the above-mentioned Baha al-Din Razi with instructions to meet Chingis Khan, find out if it was true that he now controlled North China, determine the extent of his forces, and divine what his further intentions were. Juzjani claims that his account of the embassy passed straight from the mouth of Baha al-Din Razi into his own ear. According to Baha al-Din Razi:

> "When we arrived within the boundaries [of the Chin territories] and near to the seat of government of the Altun Khan (Chin Emperor] from a considerable distance a high white mound appeared in sight, so distant, that between us and that high place was a distance of two

or three stages ... We [members of the embassy] supposed that [the] white eminence was perhaps a hill of snow, and we made inquiries of the guides and the people of that part, and they replied, 'The whole of it is the bones of men slain.' When we proceeded onwards another stage, the ground had become so greasy and dark from human fat, that it was necessary for us to advance another three stages on that same road, until we came to dry ground again."[3]

Beneath the walls of the city itself were more huge heaps of bones; some of these, according to Baha al-Din Razi, were the remains of the afore-mentioned 60,000 Chin women who had allegedly committed suicide to avoid falling into the hands of the Mongols. The stench from the decaying bodies made it nearly impossible to breath, and an epidemic caused by the unburied corpses had broken out, causing several members of Baha al-Din Razi's own party to fall ill and die.

Where Baha al-Din Razi and his party finally met up with Chingis Khan is unclear. Perhaps to escape the insalubrious environment, Chingis had left the capital even before it fell, leaving the final assault to subordinates. Some accounts suggest he was camped on the Mongolia Plateau at the time, north of the Great Wall, and it was here, perhaps in the neighborhood of current-day Anghou Lake, that Baha al-Din Razi finally caught up with him. If Baha al-Din Razi told Juzjani where the meeting took place, the otherwise estimable Persian historian failed to report it.[4]

Wherever it occurred, the meeting was by Baha al-Din Razi's own account congenial. Chingis did parade some Chin prisoners before the members of the embassy, including a captured son of the Chin emperor, in an apparent attempt to further demonstrate his domination of the Chin Dynasty, but he soon got down to the business at hand, which was the promotion of trade relations with his Muslim neighbors to the west. According to Juzjani, the Mongol chieftain told Baha al-Din Razi to relay the following message to the Khwarezmshah:

> "Say ye unto Khwarezm Shah, 'I am the sovereign of the sun-rise, and thou the sovereign of the sun-set. Let there be between us a firm treaty of friendship, amity, and peace, and let traders and karwans [caravans] on both sides come and go, and let the precious products and ordinary commodities which are in my territory be conveyed by them into thine, and those of thine, in the same manner, let them bring into mine.'"[5]

Rashid al-Din puts the following speech into Chingis's mouth:

> "We should undertake and support each other in times of need and

to ensure the security of the caravan routes from disastrous incidents in order that merchants, on whose flourishing trade the welfare of the world depends, may move freely hither and thither . . ."[6]

There is no reason to believe that Chingis Khan was not sincere in these declarations. The nomads of the Mongolian Plateau had always oriented themselves south, and the plundering and defeat of sedentary China was their age-old goal. This, Chingis was well on his way to accomplishing. But trade was also of utmost importance to the nomads of the North. Fabrics, clothes, grain, iron, and other metals were all in high demand and could be acquired only through exchanges with sedentary societies. Much of the commerce between Mongolia and China was already conducted by Muslim merchants, and Chingis was well aware that the Muslims merchants of Khwarezmia controlled much of the trade on the Silk Road stretching from northern China, which he now controlled, to the Mediterranean Sea.[7] By establishing trade relations with the Khwarezmshah, he would be able utilize the skills and experience of these traders. Moreover, although the Chin capital been taken by the Mongols and the Chin had retreated south, they were still at this time staging furious rearguard actions and were threatening to retake a few cities previously conquered by Chingis's generals. Other Mongol troops were tied down in Mongolia itself to guard against revolts by the various tribes already subjugated by Chingis. Thus he may have sincerely wanted to encourage trade with the sedentary societies to the west in order to secure his own position in the east, which may not have been quite as secure as he let on to the Khwarezmshah.

The Khwarezmshah had a different agenda. He had dispatched the embassy to China mainly to ascertain the strength of Chingis, who he considered a potentially dangerous rival, and was not interested in promoting trade, which in his view would only make Chingis Khan and the Mongols stronger and more of a threat to himself. In this he was at odds with the powerful mercantile class of his own state, which very much wanted to establish trade relations with the Mongols now controlling the eastern end of the Silk Road. This fissure between the Khwarezmshah's ambitions, which centered upon increasing the extent of his empire by conquest, and those of many of his subjects, who were more interesting in fulfilling their millennia-old role as trade intermediaries between the Orient and the Occident, would continue to widen and eventually have disastrous consequences for the Khwarezmshah and Khwarezmian Empire as a whole.

ↀ

Since at least the second century B.C., the people known as Sogdians, inhabitants of the oasis cities of Mawarannahr, the land between the Amu
Darya and Syr Darya rivers, had been trading with China far off to the
east. Sogdian merchants around this time were familiar with Chang'an
(the current-day city of Xian), which would later become perhaps the
most important eastern terminus of the Silk Road, and they also initiated trade with the Xiongnu (Hunni) peoples of current-day Mongolia.
According to Chinese sources, "At birth honey was put in their mouth
[so they would be adept at the sweet talk often needed to seal a deal]
and gum was put on their hands [so that any money they touched stuck
to them] . . . they learned the trade from the age of five . . . and at twelve
were sent to do business in a neighboring state."[8] To the west they eventually extended their trade networks into Iran and across Asia Minor to
Constantinople, capital of the Byzantine Empire.[9] Such was their business acumen and the reach of their commercial contacts that their very
name—Sogdians—became synonymous with "merchant", and their language, an early form of Persian, would serve as the lingua franca of the
great trade routes that connected the Occidental and Oriental worlds.
With the incursion of Arab-speaking Muslims into Mawarannahr starting in the late seventh century and the later invasions of Turkic peoples,
the Sogdians were slowly subsumed and by the tenth century had largely
disappeared as a distinct people. Yet the more than thousand-year old
tradition of far-reaching trade networks that they had established lived
on in the thirteenth-century Muslim traders of Khwarezmia. According
to Juvaini:

> wherever profit or gain was displayed, in the uttermost West or the
> farthermost East, thither [Muslim] merchants would bend their steps.
> And since the Mongols were not settled in any town and there was no
> concourse of merchants and travellers to them, articles of dress were a
> great rarity amongst them and the advantages of trading with them well
> known. For this reason three persons, Ahmad of Khujand [in current-
> day Tajikistan], the son of the Emir Husain, and Ahmad Balchikh,
> decided to journey together to the countries of the East, and having
> assembled an immeasurable quantity of merchandise—golden embroi-
> dered fabrics, cottons, zandanichi [an exotic fabric produced only in
> Zandana, a village about fifteen miles north of Bukhara, in Mawaran-
> nah], and whatever else they thought suitable—they set their faces to
> the road.[10]

It is not exactly clear when this trade mission occurred, nor where its members finally encountered Chingis Khan. The Russian Orientalist V. Barthold (1869–1930) suggests that the three merchants accompanied the fact-finding mission of Baha al-Din Razi. Trade, diplomacy, and spying were inextricably linked at the time (as they still may be), and it is possible the traders finally met up with the Mongol Khan when he was camped north of the Great Wall in the autumn of 1215. Juzjani does not mention the traders, however. On the other hand, Juvaini, who gives an account of the trade mission, does not mention the embassy, nor does he enlighten us as to when and where the traders met with Chingis Khan.

In any case, by the time the three merchants from the realm of the Khwarezmshah arrived, Chingis Khan was already actively encouraging trade. Merchants arriving at the borders of his domains were given safe conduct passes and their merchandize carefully examined. If officials determined that their wares might be of interest to Chingis himself they were sent to his court for an interview. The wares from Khwarezmia were deemed to be of sufficient worth for the merchants to be sent directly to Chingis's camp, wherever he may have been at the time. According to Juvaini, the Muslims were warmly welcomed: "For in those days the Mongols regarded the Moslems with the eye of respect, and for their dignity and comfort would erect them clean tents of white felt."[11]

Perhaps the friendly reception they received made the merchants overconfident. The merchant Ahmad Balchikh was the first to offer his merchandize directly to Chingis. Unwisely, he set an exorbitant price on this wares, demanding three *balish* of gold coins for pieces of fabric which sold for twenty or thirty *dinars* in Khwarezmia. One *balish* was probably equal to about seventy-five *dinars* at the time, so the merchant was asking 225 *dinars* for a length of fabric which sold for twenty or thirty *dinars* in Khwarezmia.[12] This was an exorbitant markup even by Silk Road standards, and Chingis was understandably outraged. "'Does this fellow think that fabrics have never been brought to us before?'" he bellowed.[13] In order to demonstrate to Ahmad Balchikh that he wasn't dealing with gullible rubes and country bumpkins, Chingis ordered that he be shown a storehouse bulging with similar fabrics already procured by the Mongols. He then confiscated all of the merchant's goods and put him under house arrest.

His two companions were called in next. Chary from of the treatment of their fellow trader, they refused to set a price on the their goods, saying simply that they brought them for the Khan's delectation. Mollified by this approach, Chingis then offered them a *balish* of gold for each length of gold and silk brocade and a *balish* of silver for each length of cotton and *zandanichi*. This still represented a handsome profit for the merchants. Chingis then released Ahmad Balchikh and bought his confiscated fabrics at the same price. Obviously he wanted to remain on good terms with these merchants who could provide him with the luxurious fabrics that he and his fellow Mongols valued so highly.

In the account of the three merchants from the Khwarezmian Empire it is perhaps significant that only fabrics were mentioned. The Mongols were in need of much else from sedentary societies, including metals for weapons, tools, and utensils, pottery, and grains, but these utilitarian items were seldom discussed. The foremost among trade items, or at least those which attracted the most comment, were silks, satins, damasks, brocades, and other fine textiles. There is no doubt that Mongols loved luxurious fabrics. As shown by the incident in which Chingis showed the three Khwarezm merchants a warehouse stuffed with expensive textiles, the Mongol upper-crust was by 1215 already well-supplied with these expensive trade items. Clothes made from luxurious fabrics were status symbols, and on ceremonial occasions Mongol leaders liked to drape themselves in gold brocades that "would gladden the heart of a Liberace," as textiles historian Thomas Allsen puts it."[14]

The Mongols' love of such luxuries may have been a reaction to their extremely humble beginnings. At one time, according to Juvaini, the possession of iron rather than wooden stirrups signified a rich and important man among the Mongols, and they were much more likely to be dressed in dog and mice furs and hides than in silks and satins.[15] The fact that a man was dressed in clothes made from fine fabrics marked him as someone special. The *Secret History* notes that when the Mongols finally defeated the tribe known as the Tatars (c. 1195), they captured a small boy who was adorned with gold earrings and dressed in a robe of gold-stitched satin or damask lined with sable fur. Presented to Chingis himself as a prize-of-war, Chingis in turn gifted him to his mother who, on the basis of his clothing and jewelry, concluded, "He must be the son of a noble man. The man's family probably had good origins." She adopted him as her own son and gave him the name of Shigikhutug. This is the same Shigikhutug who, as we have seen, gained Chingis's favor by turning down gifts from the vice-regent of Zhongdu and informing on his two colleagues. (Some have suggested that Shigikhutug was the author, or at least one of the authors, of the *Secret History of the Mongols;* this assertion has its detractors.[16])

As implied by this incident, the Mongols, who themselves had no tradition of weaving, were deeply impressed by luxurious fabrics, and as their status on the Mongolian Plateau rose, such materials very quickly became synonymous with wealth and prestige. According to the Persian scribbler Rashid al-Din, Chingis himself, while camping with his retinue in the Altai Mountains, once observed:

> "As my quiver bearers are black like a thick forest and my wives, spouses and daughters glitter and sparkle like a red hot fire, my desire and intention for all is such: to delight their mouths with the sweetness of the sugar of benevolence, to adorn them front to back, top to bottom, with garments of gold brocade, to sit them on fluid mounts, to give them pure and delicious water to drink, to provide verdant pastures for their needs..."[17]

On another occasion, peering into the future, he sounded a more somber note:

> "After us, our posterity will wear garments of sewn gold, partake of fatty and sweet delicacies, sit on well-formed horses, and embrace beauteous wives. [But] they will not say, '[all] these things our fathers and elder brothers collected,' and they will forget us in this great day."[18]

As Thomas Allsen points out, most of the commodities Chingis cherished—fatty delicacies, well-formed horses, beauteous wives, etc.—could be found in the steppe. Only luxury fabrics like gold brocade needed to be imported. They were the epitome of luxury goods. "In many ways," intones Allsen, "gold brocade came to symbolize the glorious future of the Mongolian people and perhaps became the benchmark to measure their success in the quest for empire."[19]

Gold brocade was used not only for clothing. It was also extensively used to line the interiors of gers. These were not the humble abodes of herdsmen, but rather the huge pavilions favored by the rulers. According to Juvaini, Chingis's son Ögedei had one such seasonal structure erected for his use near the Mongol capital of Kharkhorum (in current-day Övörkhangai Aimag): "And...in the summer he would go into the mountains, where there would be erected for him a Khitayan pavilion, whose walls were made of latticed wood, and its ceiling was gold-embroidered cloth, and it was covered all over with white felt; this place is called Shira-

Ordu." Rashid al-Din and the Christian monks and missionaries, John of Plano Carpini (Giovanni da Pian del Carpineca [1180–1252]) and Benedict the Pole, also described this structure at Shira-Ordu. Carpini noted that the "'roof above and the sides on the interior were of brocade.'"[20]

Ögedei, it would appear, favored fabrics from the Islamic world. In one notorious incident, he was being entertained by some Chinese actors who had the gall to ridicule Islam in their act. The greatly perturbed Ögedei promptly halted the performance and ordered that fabrics from both China and the Muslim countries be brought in from a warehouse for comparison. The "gold brocades [nasif-na] and garments" from Khorasan and Iraq were found to be much superior to those from China, much to the chagrin of the Chinese actors.

These incidences involving Ögedei occurred long after 1215, indeed after Chingis's death in 1227, but they underscore the importance fine fabrics would assume in the Mongol Empire and help to explain why back in 1215 Chingis was so keen on establishing trade relations with the Islamic Khwarezmian Empire to the west, the source of so many of these luxurious textiles.

Having already received an embassy from the Khwarezmshah and having met with traders from the Khwarezmian Empire, Chingis decided to respond in kind by sending his own emissaries to the Khwarezmshah's realm. He took a two-pronged approach. A diplomatic mission would make contact with the Khwarezmshah himself in hopes of establishing the peaceful relations necessary for further trade, and an officially sanctioned trading mission would demonstrate to the Khwarezmshah and his subjects just how lucrative trading with the Mongols could be. According to Juvaini, the three merchants who had earlier visited Chingis would accompany the Mongol-sponsored caravan of traders back to the Khwarezmshah's realm and presumably act as intermediaries. According to Juzjani, Baha al-Din Razi and his embassy would also return to Mawarannahr with the Mongol missions. If this is the case, Baha al-Din Razi's embassy and the traders must have remained in Chingis's domains for a couple of years, since the Mongol embassy did not reach Mawarannahr until the spring of 1218. Apparently the Mongol embassy and trade mission left for Mawarannahr at the same time, accompanied by Baha al-Din Razi and the three traders, but then at some point en route the embassy hurried on ahead for a meeting with the Khwarezmshah himself.[21]

The leaders of the diplomatic embassy were three Muslim traders who were themselves from the domains of the Khwarezmshah: Mahmud, from somewhere in the Khwarezmian Empire; Ali Khwajah, from the city of Bukhara; and Yusuf Kanka, from the city of Otrar. It is significant that these three men were nominal subjects of the Khwarezmshah but had now engaged themselves as agents of Chingis Khan. That Muslim traders like themselves would work for Chingis demonstrates the ever-widening gap between the ambitions of the Khwarezmshah and the interests of the mercantile class of his own empire. As Silk Road traders, they might well have considered their services available to the highest bidder, and it would seem that they were not hesitant about throwing in their lot with Chingis Khan, the rising power in the East. For Chingis's part, he was no doubt eager to use their knowledge of trade networks, their language skills, and their familiarity with the social conventions of Inner Asian Muslims for his own purposes. The fact that they were Muslims obviously did not bother him at all. He had long dealt with Muslim traders—Jafar, one his long-time supporters, was one of the most notable—and apparently interacted well with them (except of course with those who tried to cheat him).

The three emissaries reached the court of the Khwarezmshah sometime in the spring of 1218. Some sources suggest that his court was in Bukhara at the time.[22] The embassy, which did not involve itself in actual trading, did bring numerous gifts from Chingis Khan to the Khwarezmshah. These included "a nugget of pure gold as big as a camel's neck," which was so heavy it had to be carried in its own cart; ingots of various precious metals; walrus ivory from the northern shores of Asia and rhinoceros horns which had somehow fallen into the hands of the Mongols; fine fabrics, including a material known as *targhu*, made from the wool of white camels, each length of which was worth fifty or more *dinars*; and musk.[23] The Khwarezmshah deigned to accept the gifts and granted the three ambassadors a public audience where they relayed the messages sent by Chingis Khan. According to Nasavi, the ambassadors proclaimed:

> The Great Khan sends you felicitations and entrusted us with the following words, "I do not overlook neither the elevation of your rank nor the extent of your power. I am familiar with the magnificence of your empire, and I know that your authority is recognized in the majority of countries in the world. Therefore, I consider my duty to strike up friendly relations with you, whom I consider the dearest and most beloved of my sons. On your part, you know equally well that I have

seized the kingdom of China as well as the neighboring Turk countries, and that all the tribes of these lands submit to me; and you know better than anyone that my provinces are nurseries for soldiers, of mines and silver, and that may produce an abundance of things. If you agree that we open up, each from our own side, an easy access for negotiations between our countries, this will be an advantage for us all and we would both benefit."[24]

That night or the next day the Khwarezmshah called Mahmud of Khwarezm onto the carpet for a private interview. First, the Khwarezmshah pointed out that Mahmud was a native of Khwarezmia and thus nominally one of the his subjects. He then demanded that Mahmud henceforth work as his spy in the court of Chingis Khan. As payment in advance for the ambassador's subordination, the Khwarezmshah took a huge pearl from his bracelet and handed it to Mahmud, sealing the deal. Then said the Khwarezmshah, "'Answer me frankly. Chinggis Khan claims that he is master of China, and that he has seized the city of Tomgach [the Chin capital, Zhongdu]. Is it true or is it a deception?'"[25] Mahmud allowed that "'It was the very truth. Such an important event cannot remain secret ...'" The now angry Khwarezmshah thundered, "'You know the grandeur of my country and you also know how numerous are my armies. How then does this accursed dare call me his son in this speech?'" Chingis's message that he considered him "'the dearest and most beloved of my sons'" was what really irked the Khwarezmshah. Even if he had conquered North China, the Khwarezmshah protested, this did not give Chingis Khan— who was after all an infidel whose true religious convictions were hazy at best—any right whatsoever to call him, the mighty Khwarezmshah, the ruler of a great Islamic empire, his son. In the Khwarezmshah's eyes, "son" was synonymous with "vassal", and the use of the word implied that Chingis Khan considered himself the Khwarezmshah's superior. Such an assumption was an outrage, and the Khwarezmshah was infuriated.

Frightened by the Khwarezmshah's anger over this issue, the ambassador quickly backtracked. While it was true Chingis Khan had conquered much of northern China, his armies, no more than "'a trickle of smoke through the night's shadows,'"[26] according to Mahmud, were vastly outnumbered by those of the Khwarezmshah, and he in no way posed a threat to the Khwarezmian Empire. Mollified by this flattery, the Khwarezmshah relented and seemed to agree at least in principle to a peace treaty with Chingis Khan and apparently signed some sort of accord to that effect, although the status of actual trade relations remained hazy at best.

Meanwhile, the trade mission that Chingis had authorized was still on its way to the Khwarezmshah's territories. As mentioned, the embassy and the trade mission may have left together and the three emissaries had then hurried on ahead of the slower-moving trade caravan.[27] In any case, the caravan continued on to Otrar, one of the first major entrepôts in the Khwarezmshah's empire. The members of the mission may not have been aware of the outcome of the diplomatic mission.[28] If they were, they might well have assumed that the peace treaty proposal also sanctioned trade, or at least guaranteed their safe conduct. This would lead to a fatal misunderstanding. The Khwarezmshah had no interest in either peace or trade.

Chingis himself believed that trade in itself promoted peace, and that the trade mission would contribute to a mutually beneficial relationship between the Mongols and the Khwarezmshah. In a personal message for the Khwarezmshah which he sent with the traders he affirmed these beliefs:

> "Merchants from your country have come among us, and we have sent them back in a manner that you shall hear. And we have likewise dispatched to your country in their company a group of merchants in order that they may acquire the wondrous wares of those regions; and that henceforth the abscess of evil thoughts may be lanced by the improvement of relations and agreement between us, and the pus of sedition and rebellion removed."[29]

The trade mission was a sizable undertaking. As an indication of how much importance Chingis placed on it, he ordered his sons and his top army commanders to each provide two or three men from their retinues to make up the party and to provide each of them with a *balish* of gold or silver as capital for trading ventures.[30] According to Juvaini, a total of about 450 merchants were thus selected, all of them Muslims, since Muslims were much more experienced in the Silk Road trade than the Mongols, and it was thought they would be better able to deal with their co-religionists in Mawarannahr.[31] From this it would appear that Chingis's sons and army commanders already had sizable contingents of Muslims in their ranks, some of them from Islamic areas that Chingis had already conquered and others from Khwarezmia who had already thrown in their lot with the Mongols. The *Secret History of the Mongols* and some Chinese sources mention that a delegation of one hundred Mongols led by a man named Ukhuna ("Billy Goat") was in charge of the trade mission. Interestingly enough, Juvaini does not mention the Mongol delegation, and the *Secret History* is silent about the Muslim merchants.[32] Some commentators have suggested that Juvaini's account is incorrect and that the trade mission consisted of only the one hundred Mongols.[33] Whether the Mongols were entrusted with capital for trading ventures is unclear. More importantly, Ukhuna and perhaps other members of the Mongol delegation were apparently considered official envoys of Chingis Khan and thus enjoyed—at least from the Mongol point of view—what we would now call diplomatic immunity.[34] Al-Athir asserts that the mission was comprised of both "merchants and Turks [by which he meant Mongols]," and it may be that the mission included both 450 Muslim traders and a one hundred-man Mongolian contingent.[35] Juzjani would seem to concur; he mentions "the traders and travellers, and the emissaries (from the Chingiz Khan)."[36]

Along with Juvaini's 450 merchants and/or the one hundred Mongols, all of whom who were presumably riding camels, the caravan had 500 pack camels laden with trade goods, including gold, silver, Chinese silk, *targhu* (as mentioned a fabric made from the wool of white camels), and various furs, including sable and beaver.[37] Throw in camel men, servants, cooks, and the usual assortment of hangers-on (religious pilgrims had a way of attaching themselves leech-like to such caravans) and we are probably looking at a string of well over a thousand camels.

According to Juvaini, the caravan was led by four men: Umar Khoja al-Otrari (his name implies that he was from Otrar); al-Hammal al-Maraghi; Fakhr al-Din Danzaki al-Bukhari (presumably from Bukhara); and Amin al-Din al-Haravi. At least two of these men were thus from Khwarezmia itself, demonstrating yet again that the Khwarezmian mercantile class favored trade with the Mongols and vice-versa. As the Russian Orientalist Barthold points out, "the interests of [Chingis Khan] fully coincided with those of the Muslim capitalists." He adds, however, "There was not the same harmony between Muhammad's [the Khwarezmshah] political ambitions and the interests of the merchants of his kingdom."[38] This became painfully apparent when the caravan finally reached Otrar.

Today there is no city known as Otrar, and very few people have even heard of the Otrar that flourished back at the beginning of the thirteenth century. The scattered ruins of this once-sizable metropolis which still do exist turn up on the itineraries of only the most determined tourists who venture into what is now southern Kazakhstan. Yet when the Mongol-sponsored caravan of merchants and envoys turned up at its gates in 1218 it was famous as one of the most important trade centers in Inner Asia and renowned for its arts and crafts and intellectual accomplishments of its citizens. The caravan men were no doubt looking forward to resting in the city's well-appointed caravansaries and refreshing themselves in its famous bathhouses. The events that soon overwhelmed them would, in the words of nineteenth-century Orientalist E. G. Browne, trigger:

> a catastrophe which, though probably quite unforeseen, even on the very eve of its incidence, changed the face of the world, set in motion forces which are still effective, and inflicted more suffering on the human race than any other event in the world's history of which records are preserved to us; I mean the Mongol Invasion.[39]

Browne, who translated into English many of the thirteenth-century documents that recorded the Mongol irruption, may from the vantage point of the twenty-first century sound overwrought here, but his appraisal did contain a kernel of truth. The events that followed in the wake of the calamity at Otrar did rock all of Inner Asia, led to the fall of at least two empires, and inflicted on the entire Islamic geosphere a blow from which some might argue it has never fully recovered.

Otrar was located on the north bank of the middle stretches of the Syr Darya River (the Jaxartes of classical antiquity) near its confluence with the Arys River, about 105 miles northwest of the current-day city of Shymkent in Kazakhstan. It was situated just west of the so-called *Zhetysu*, or Seven Rivers, region, an area which included the watersheds of the Talas, Ili, Chu, and other rivers in current-day eastern Kazakhstan and western China (Xinjiang Province) which either flowed into Lake Alakol or Lake Balkash or petered out into the barren desert-steppes to the west. Much later this area would become known as *Semireche*, Russian for "Seven Rivers". As one geographer points out, "Semireche is an area where sedentaries and nomads have met at various points in history—co-existing, overlapping, or competing—because it lends itself to both ways of life . . ."[40]

Otrar's location on the boundaries of vast Kazakh Steppe to the north and the fertile valleys of Mawarannahr to the south made it the natural entrepôt for trade between these two divergent cultures. It was also at the nexus of several east-west trending Silk Road trading routes. One branch of the Silk Road went east along the Arys to Taraz and Balasag-hun (current-day Tolmak in Kyrgyzstan). From here a southern branch went on over the Tian Shan Mountains to Aksu (in current-day Xinjiang Province, China), on the Silk Road route that ran along the northern side of the vast Tarim Basin and on through the Gansu Corridor into north-ern China. From Balasaghun a northern branch proceeded up the valley of the Ili River and over the spurs of the Borohogo Shan Range to the Zungarian Basin on the north side of the Tian Shan. From there routes went to both Mongolia and China. Another route followed the Syr Darya to Shash (modern-day Tashkent) and then veered southwest to Merv in current-day Turkmenistan and Nishapur, in Khorasan, now eastern Iran. From here various routes continued on the Mediterranean. The road west from Otrar followed the Syr Darya to the Aral Sea before continuing on to the Caspian Steppe straddling the Volga River. From the old city of Xacitarxan on the Volga, just upstream from modern-day Astrakhan, branches led north up the Volga into Russia and west to the Black Sea, where land and water routes continued on to Istanbul, the main west-ern terminus of the Silk Road.[41] On this vast network of trade routes moved a wealth of various fabrics and textiles, leather, furs, porcelain, pot-tery, salt, spices, honey, jade and precious stones, musk, herbal medicines, weapons, slaves, and much else. By attempting to open trade with Otrar Chingis Khan hoped to gain access to the rest of the world.

The Silk Road trade had made Otrar a rich and influential city. It had its own mint, the coins of which now grace museums, was famous for its locally produced pottery, including beautifully decorated bowls, and boasted of one of the biggest libraries of Inner Asia, with a collection of over 33,000 items, including such exotica as Babylonian clay tablets and Egyptian papyrus scrolls which had somehow found their way thither. The library also contained the works of the city's most famous intellectu-al, Abu Nasr Mohammad Farabi (died c. 950), a polymathic philosopher, mathematician, linguist, poet, and composer who was called "the Second Teacher" by his students, meaning that he played second fiddle only to Aristotle. He is also credited with heavily influencing Al-Hasan ibn Ali ibn Sina, a.k.a. Avicenna (c. 980–1037), perhaps the greatest Medieval Is-lamic philosopher, who was born near Bukhara, also in the Khwarezm-shah's domains.

By the early thirteenth-century the city consisted of the triangular-shaped *Ark*, or citadel, located within the tightly packed *Shahristan* (walled inner city). The *Shahristan* itself was in the shape of a pentagon and covered about 200,000 square meters, or about fifty acres. The city was famous for its baths, and most homes were served by a city-wide sewage system. The big Friday mosque was also probably within the *Shahristan*. Surrounding the *Shahristan* was the *Rabad*, or trade quarter, which was also walled. Covering some 420 acres, it contained the extensive markets and caravanserais connected with Silk Road trade, local bazaars, craft shops, and lower-class residential areas. The medieval Arabic geographer Muqaddasi claimed the city had 70,000 inhabitants, but at least one modern historian has opined that this was a misprint and that he must have meant 7,000.[42] In any case, numerous small towns and villages in the immediate environs of the city contributed to a sizable conurbation.

The governor of Otrar was a man named Inalchuq, the nephew of the Khwarezmshah's mother, Terken Khatan.[43] Perhaps because of his close relations with the Shah's family he had been granted the lofty title of Gayer Khan. Although Juvaini maintains that all 450 of the traders sponsored by the Mongols were Muslims, a Hindu merchant from India had also managed to attach himself to the caravan.[44] This man had met Inalchuq previously, before he had become the Gayer Khan and the governor of Otrar, and apparently he had not been impressed. Now this Indian merchant, who was in Juvaini's words, "rendered proud by reason of the power and might of his own Khan [Chingis]," addressed his old acquaintance in a condescending manner, calling him by his common name of Inalchuq instead of by his title.[45] The proud governor was infuriated by the Indian's haughty, patronizing behavior, and Juvaini insinuates that he used this incident as a pretext to put the entire trade mission under house arrest and confiscate their merchandize. Other sources say nothing about the Indian merchant and say simply that Gayer Khan coveted their merchandize and soon concocted an excuse to seize it. Deciding that the merchants were in fact spies, he fired off a letter to the Khwarezmshah in which he accused them of engaging in espionage:

> "These men come to Otrar under the guise of negotiators whereas in fact they are spies who meddle in affairs that are none of their business. When they are alone with simple people, they threaten them saying, 'you shouldn't doubt that war is upon you. It will arrive soon, and you will face things you won't be able to fight.' Based on such testimony, and others of its kind, it would be best if the sultan authorized the seizure of these negotiators until he has made a decision in this case."[46]

Of course it might be said that all traders at that time were engaged in intelligence gathering. This may not have been limited to strictly commercial matters such as the price and supply of goods in the marketplace. They would have also gathered information about political events, gossip about rulers and court factions, the morale of the populace and any discontent with local rule, and other social factors which might have had an effect on trade and the markets and thus be of legitimate concern to merchants. Whether any members of the trading mission in Otrar crossed the line between this kind of information gathering and hard-core espionage is hard to say. As one historian points out, "Those sent by Genghis Khan would have spread stories about the power of the Mongol leader and the invincibility of his armies; they would have described the fearful fate which awaited those who resisted him; but also sung the praises of his generosity and his tolerance in religious matters."[47] Again, whether the merchants and envoys were actually engaging in this kind of propagandizing is unknown. In any case, Gayer Khan forwarded his suspicions about the trade mission to the Khwarezmshah.

The Khwarezmshah was predisposed to believe the accusations put forth by the governor of Otrar. He himself had dispatched an embassy to Chingis Khan shortly after the fall of the Chin capital in 1215 which gathered intelligence about the strengths and weaknesses of the Mongol conqueror. And he had just managed to suborn one of Chingis's ambassadors, turning him into a double agent. Thus the ever-suspicious Khwarezmshah might well have assumed that the trade mission then in Otrar had been sent to spy on him and foment discontent in his domains. And even its stated purpose, the pursuit of trade between the Khwarezmian Empire and the Mongol Realm, did not coincide with the interests of the Khwarezmshah, who clearly viewed Chingis Khan as his rival for power in Inner and East Asia. The Khwarezmshah decided to send a clear and unmistakable message about his views on peace and trade with the Mongols.

There are several versions of who was accountable for what happened next. Juvaini and Rashid al-Din imply that the Khwarezmshah himself gave the order to execute all the members of the mission and seize their property. According to Juvaini:

> Without pausing to think the Sultan sanctioned the shedding of their blood and deemed the seizure of their goods to be lawful, not knowing that his own life would become unlawful, nay a crime, and that the bird of his prosperity would be lopped off feather and wing ...[48]

Nasavi, on the other hand, implies that the Shah did not explicitly order the execution of the merchants but left the decision up to Gayer Khan, adding that the Otrar governor did claim all the stolen goods for himself. Other sources suggest that Khwarezmshah ordered that loot be divided between Gayer Khan and himself, and that he later sold his share of the loot to merchants in Bukhara, who then offered it for sale to the general public. As Barthold points out, "It is very likely that the sale of the merchandise to the merchants (with a profit to them) was partly due to the desire to compensate them for the cessation of trade with the nomads," which would have been the inevitable result of the Khwarezmshah's actions.[49]

One of the merchants, according to Juvaini (Juzjani maintains it was a camel driver), was in a bathhouse when the massacre occurred and thus managed to escape the slaughter.[50] "He set his face to road" and managed to return to Mongolia where he informed Chingis Khan of the trade mission's fate.[51] As noted, Ukhuna and perhaps other members of the one-hundred man Mongolian delegation were considered official envoys of Chingis Khan and thus supposedly enjoyed diplomatic immunity. Their murder was a grievous violation of accepted norms of behavior between states at the time, at least from the Mongol perspective. Chingis would have been fully justified to declare war against the Khwarezmshah at this point. Indeed, as we shall see, when he finally did decide to invade Khwarezmia he would cite as justification only the murder of Ukhuna and the other Mongols, making no mention of the Juvaini's Muslim merchants.

Instead of immediately declaring war, however, he decided to send a three-man embassy to the court of the Khwarezmshah to lodge a protest against the murder of the mission members and the confiscation of their goods. The leader of the embassy was one Ibn Kafaraj Bughra, whose father has once been an emir in the court Khwarezmshah Tekesh, the Khwarezmshah's own father. That this man, whose family previously had been aligned with the royal family of Khwarezm, and a fellow Muslim to boot, was now importuning him as an ambassador from the Mongols must have further irked the easily irritated Khwarezmshah. The ultimatum from Chingis presented to the Khwarezmshah by Ibn Kafaraj Bughra could not have improved the latter's mood:

> "You have, by signing our accord, pledged yourself to protect the merchants and not to harm them; but you have acted faithlessly and broken your word. Disloyalty is disgraceful, especially disgraceful in the case

of a sultan of Islam. If, however, you maintain that Inal-khan's [Gayer Khan] deed was not carried out at your behest, then hand Inal-khan over to me so that we may punish him for his crime, thus reassuring the masses and preventing the spilling of blood. Otherwise it is war. . ."[52]

If indeed the Shah had ordered the massacre of the merchants, he could not now claim that it was all Gayer Khan's fault, nor could he hand over Gayer Khan, his mother's nephew, without causing an uproar among his relatives, who commanded important segments of his army. And the accusation that his actions were disgraceful according to the tenets of Islam must have stung, coming as they did from someone he viewed as an idolator or worse. By this time the Khwarezmshah believed that Allah Himself had ordered him to fight the Mongols, who now were clearly vying with him for control of Islamic Inner Asia, and he was not about to accommodate the demands of an infidel like Chingis who he believed was guilty of *shirk* (polytheism).[53]

Instead, he ordered the execution of Ibn Kafaraj Bugra and had the beards shaved off of his two companions, a grievous insult according to the mores of the time and place. Perhaps Chingis knew all along the terms of his ultimatum would be unacceptable to the Khwarezmshah and that the embassy to be rebuffed. But as Juvaini pointed out, "'he who warneth hath an excuse.'"[54] Chingis had warned the Khwarezmshah, and war was now inevitable. "Alas," lamented Juzjani, "how much Muslim blood was spilled because of that murder! From all sides poured torrents of pure blood, and this movement of anger brought about the ruin and depopulation of the earth."[55]

When word got back to Mongolia about the fate of his envoys Chingis Khan was enraged. According to Juvaini:

> These tidings had such an effect upon the Khan's mind that the control of repose and tranquillity was removed, and the whirlwind of anger cast dust into the eyes of patience and clemency while the fire of wrath flared up with such a flame that it drove the water from his eyes and could be quenched only by the shedding of blood. In this fever Chingiz Khan went up alone to the summit of a hill, bared his head, turned his face towards the earth and for three days and nights offered up prayer, saying: "I was not the author of this trouble, grant me strength to exact revenge."[56]

It will be remembered that he had also retreated to a mountain and prayed for success before he rode south to attack the Chin Dynasty. Having descended from the mountain again, Chingis Khan was now determined to ride west.

Juvaini would live to see the sack of Baghdad and the destruction of the 508 year-old Abbasid Caliphate forty years later, in 1258, by Chingis's grandson Khülegü, the ultimate outcome of Chingis's decision to attack the Islamic world. Thus he had the advantage of hindsight when he made his pronouncement about the fatal consequences of the deaths of the traders at Otrar:

> Ghayir-Khan in executing his [the Khwarezmshah's] command deprived these men of their lives and possessions, nay rather he desolated and laid waste a whole world and rendered a whole creation without home, property or leaders. For every drop of their blood there flowed a whole Oxus [Amu Darya]; in retribution for every hair on their heads it seemed that a hundred thousand heads rolled in the dust at every crossroad; and in exchange for every dinar a thousand qintars were exacted.[57]

CHAPTER 3

The Flight of Khüchüleg
and
Jochi's Raid into the Kipchaq Steppe

WHILE EVENTS PLAYED OUT IN OTRAR another drama was unfolding high up in the hidden recesses of the Pamir Mountains on the southern edge of Inner Asia. Situated at the convergence of five other great mountains ranges—the Tian Shan, Kun Lun, Himalaya, Hindu Kush, and Karakoram—the range is often referred to as the Pamir Knot, the nexus which ties all the other ranges together. Although much of the range consists of high, grassy plateaus, it also lays claim to some of the world's highest summits, including 24,590-foot Ismoili Somoni Peak, 23,310-foot Evgenia Korjenevskaya Peak, and 23,406-foot Peak Lenin. Some geographers also include 24,757-foot Muztagh-Ata in the Pamirs, although most consider it part of the Kun Lun. Indeed, the exact boundaries of the range are unclear, but much of it would appear to be in current-day Tajikistan, and smaller portions in China (Xinjiang Province), Afghanistan, and Pakistan. An ancient southern extension of the Silk Road ran from Kashgar, at the western end of the Tarim Basin, over the Pamirs to India (now Pakistan). The modern Karakoram Highway, one of the highest roads in the world, now follows much the same route. Here, on what Tajiks call *Bom-i-Dunyo*, the Roof of the World, a confrontation that began in far-off north-central Mongolia fourteen years earlier finally reached its denouement. The main players in this drama were Jebe, one of Chingis Khan's most faithful and determined generals, and a Naiman chieftain by the name of Khüchüleg.

The Naiman were one of the most powerful tribes in Mongolia in the latter half of the twelfth century when Chingis Khan and his own tribe were on the ascendency, and they would prove to be one of his most formidable opponents. Their territories extended from the valley of the Orkhon River in central Mongolia south and west to the Altais and included much of central and western modern-day Mongolia. Their name *naiman* means "eight" in Mongolian, perhaps indicating the number of sub-tribes or clans which made up the tribe as a whole. Whether they were a Turkic or a Mongolian people is uncertain.[1] Until 1175 they were vassals of the Qara Khitai off to the west, but they later recognized the suzerainty of the Chin Emperor, who awarded their leader with the title of Tayang (*taiwang* = Great King) Khan.[2] They aspired to some level of culture and no doubt considered themselves superior to the Mongols of Chingis Khan. In a famous passage in the *Secret History*, the Tayang Khan's wife, Gürbesü, (she had started out as his mother-in-law but after the death of her husband married her son-in-law) spoke of the Mongols thus:

> "They stink and their clothes are filthy. They live at a great distance from us. Let them stay where they are. But perhaps we can bring their neat daughters-in-law and girls here. We will make them wash their hands and feet. Then they can milk our cows and sheep."[3]

These were words that she would live to regret.

At least some among the Naiman practiced Nestorian Christianity. This branch of the Christian faith, deemed heretical by the Council of Ephesus in 431 A.D., gravitated eastward to escape persecution and eventually become known as the Church of the East. Although little remembered now, it was once widespread throughout Inner and East Asia and exerted considerable influence. Following the great trade routes east, Nestorian Christianity reaching Xian, the main eastern terminus of Silk Road, no later than the 780s. It eventually seeped northward across the Gobi Desert and onto the Mongolian Plateau, where it found adherents among the Keraits, whose leader Tooril was Chingis's early patron, and their bitter enemies, the Naiman. Khüchüleg, son the Tayang Khan, would himself profess to Christianity, although there was little if anything in his tumultuously violent life to indicate that he ever practiced any of its tenets.

The events leading up to the showdown between the Naiman and Chingis Khan are beyond the scope of this narrative. Suffice it to say that by 1204 the long festering conflict had come to a head. Jamukha, the chieftain of the Jadirat and Chingis's bosom buddy from his younger days (according to the *Secret History* they had "swore their brotherhood and love for one another" and at night "slept under the same quilt"[4]) and now his bitter enemy, threw in his lot with the Naiman, as did Togtoga Beki of the Merkits. Chingis held a special animus for the Merkits since they had once kidnapped his wife Börte, and when Chingis finally managed to retrieve her she was pregnant. It was widely rumored that Chingis's oldest son Jochi had actually been sired by a Merkit. To say there was bad blood between Chingis and the Merkits would be an understatement.

The Mongols were highly outnumbered by the Naiman and their allies, but while camped on the Saar Steppe in current-day Arkhangai Province Chingis had each of his men build five campgrounds at some distance to each other. Naiman watchmen from the top of Azgart Khairkhan Mountain, overlooking the Saar Steppe, said to each other, "'Did we say the Mongols are few? . . . Daily they appear to grow in numbers. There are now more fires than stars.'"[5] Hearing this, Tayang Khan concluded that he was facing an immense army. A weak and indecisive man totally in the sway of his domineering ex-mother-in-law now-wife Gürbesü, Tayang Khan quickly lost all heart for confronting the Mongols directly. Instead he proposed a retreat south to the Altai Mountains where the Naiman army could then turn on the Mongols and engage them after they had exhausted themselves in the chase. He presented this as the tried and true tactic of the "feigned retreat", but his own son Khüchüleg and other army commanders interpreted it as cowardice. Upon hearing of his father's plans Khüchüleg exclaimed: "'Old Woman Tayang again! He must have lost his courage to utter such words . . . Tayang, who has never dared venture further afield than a pregnant woman would go to urinate, nor even a calf to graze.'"[6] A Naiman military commander chimed in: "'Had we expected that you were such a coward, we would have done better to send for Mother Gürbesü and, although she is only a woman, given her command of the army . . . You are stupid, Tayang. It is all over, you have failed.'"[7]

Overruled and held in contempt by his son and army commanders, Tayang Khan had no choice but to stand and confront the Mongols. "A dying life, a suffering body—they are common to all men. Given it is so, let us fight,'" he fatalistically concluded. The ever-vacillating Jamukha, perhaps still in his heart enamored of Chingis, the companion of his youth, deserted the Tayang Khan at the last moment, compounding the Naiman ruler's predicament. The by-then thoroughly demoralized Naiman sought the high ground of a mountain known as Tuleet Uul in current-day

Arkhangai Aimag, where they were quickly surrounded by the Mongol army. They tried a nighttime breakout, but according to the *Secret History*, "they rolled down from the summit, piling on top of one another. Their bones were smashed and fell to pieces, like rotten logs; thus they died."[8] The Naiman were thoroughly routed. Tayang was caught and executed without further ado. His wife Gürbesü was taken prisoner and brought before Chingis. "'Did you not say that we Mongols have a bad smell? So why have you come now?'" he chided her. He then made her one of his wives. History is silent about what pleasantries they exchanged on their wedding night. Tayang's son Khüchüleg and a band of his close follow-ers did manage to break out of the Mongol cordon and escape. It would be another fourteen years before the Chingis's general Jebe would finally track him down in the high Pamirs.

The final battle with the Naiman did have one unexpected consequence. Found wandering around the field of battle was a well-dressed man who appeared to be armed only with wooden pens. He also had in his pos-session the official seals of Tayang Khan. Taken before Chingis himself, he explained that he had been the Naiman ruler's personal scribe and seal bearer. His name was Tatatunga and he was a Uighur originally from Uighuristan. He had been hired by the Naiman as a scribe and court in-tellectual. He apparently spoke the Naiman language and presumably knew at least some Mongolian. Chingis was always quick to utilize tal-ented men captured in battle. Soon realizing how Tatatunga's particular skills might be used, he set him the task of developing a script for the Mongol language, which up until then did not have a writing system. This Tatatunga proceeded to do, adapting his own vertical Uighur script to the peculiarities of Mongolian. The Uighur script itself was based on that of the Sogdians, the merchants who for almost a thousand years had dominated trade on the Silk Road. The resulting Uighuro-Mongolian script—known in Mongolian as *Mongol Bichig*—would remain the stan-dard writing system among Mongols up until the twentieth century, when in Mongolia itself it was finally replaced with Cyrillic script.

Tatatunga was also tasked with teaching selected members of the Mongolian upper crust to read and write; the aforementioned Shigikhutag was reportedly one of his first students.[9] After the Uighurs recognized the suzerainty of the Mongols, still more Uighur intellectuals, teachers, and tutors came to Mongolia, creating the basis of a Mongol literate class that grew up amidst the court of Chingis Khan. Some member of this group (Shigikhutug has been cited, rightly or wrongly, as a candidate) went on to write the *Secret History of the Mongols* in 1228, just twenty-four years after Tatatunga had been captured, although some portions may have been written later. Thus this Uighur scribe who fell into Chingis's hands after the defeat of the Naiman would have an incalculable effect on Mongolian history.

His father dead and the Naiman army defeated, Khüchüleg and a band of his most devoted followers fled south across the Altai Mountain into the Zungarian Depression, in what now northern Xinjiang Province, China. As mentioned, Togtoga Beki and the Merkits had earlier aligned them- selves with the Naiman, but they too, like Jamukha, had apparently fled on the eve of the final battle. Chingis's soldiers pursued them and in the autumn of 1204 the Merkit army was almost totally annihilated. Only Togtoga Beki, some of his sons, including his youngest son Khutu, and a handful of his most devoted followers were able to escape the slaughter.

Khüchüleg and Togtoga Beki and their followers eventually joined up with Khüchüleg's uncle Buyirug, who had split with the main tribe earlier and had not taken part on the battle at Tuleet Uul. Now, refugees from Mongolia, they nomadizing in the upper valley of the Irtysh River, on the northern edge of the Zungarian Basin. But even here they were not safe from the long arm of Chingis Khan. In 1208 (the date differs in some accounts) his army crossed the Mongol Altai into the valley of the Irtysh and flushed out the escapees from Mongolia.[10] Togtoga Beki was killed, but Khüchüleg once again managed to slip out of the Mongol noose, as did Togtoga Beki's remaining sons (in an act of peculiar familial devotion, they reportedly cut off their father's head and took it with them).[11]

Khüchüleg and his ever-dwindling band hightailed it south across the Zungarian Basin to the Uighur Northern Capital of Beshbaliq. He was unwelcome among the Uighurs, who by that time may have already been aligned with Chingis Khan, and continued across the daunting Tian Shan to the Silk Road city of Kucha, at the foot of the mountains on the north- ern side of the Tarim Basin. Apparently the welcome here was no warmer, since, according to Juvaini, he then "wandered in the mountains without food or sustenance, while those of his tribe that had accompanied him were scattered far and wide."[12] This was clearly the low ebb in Khüchüleg's life. Yet he was nothing if not resourceful, and he would soon catapult from being a destitute wanderer in the Tian Shan to the nominal ruler of an Inner Asian empire who would vie with the Khwarezmshah himself for power.

Obviously at loose ends, Khüchüleg's and his few remaining followers fell in with the Gür Khan, ruler of the Qara Khitai Empire that then controlled much of Inner Asia between the Khwarezmshah's own domains and the Uighuristan to the east. The Qara Khitai were shards of the old Liao, or Khitan, Dynasty, which had come into power in 916 and ruled northern China until 1125 when it was unseated by the Jurchen, who founded the Chin Dynasty. Originally they were a nomadic people from the mixed forest and steppe east of the Khingan Mountains, in what is now the province of Inner Mongolia in China. At its height the Khitan Dynasty controlled, in addition to northern China, much of modern-day Mongolia, where the ruins of their formidable fortresses can still be seen. After their defeat by the Jurchens, the charismatic leader of the Khitans, Yelü Dashi, fled west with segments of the Khitan nobility and at least 100,000 followers. By 1234 he had established a capital at Balasaghun, near Tolmak in modern-day central Kyrgyzstan, and by 1137 had overran the fertile Fergana Valley in western Kyrgyzstan. On September 9, 1141, the Qara Khitai defeated the Saljuq Turks at the Battle of Qatwan, thus gaining control of much of Mawarannahr, the Land Beyond the River. From this point on, the domains of the Qara Khitai could legitimately be called an empire.

The Qara Khitai had brought with them the Buddhist faith they had practiced in China, and some Khitans also adhered to Nestorian Christianity. Thus it was not only territorial acquisition but also religion that put them on a collision course with the Islamic realms to the west. By the start of the thirteenth-century the Qara Khitai were locked in a fierce struggle with the Islamic empire of the Khwarezmshah. And in the east, tribes who had once submitted to them were now gravitating toward Chingis Khan and his Mongols, who were clearly on the ascendancy.[13] It was at this point in time, when the Gür Khan, ruler of the Qara Khitai, was fighting for the survival of his empire, that Khüchüleg providentially arrived in Balasaghun.

It is not clear if Khüchüleg had been captured by Qara Khitai patrols while wandering around in the Tian Shan or if he had turned up in the Qara Khitai capital of Balasaghun of his own volition.[14] In any case, he soon finagled a meeting with the Gür Khan. It will be remembered that the Naiman had once accepted the suzerainty of the Qara Khitai, and Khüchüleg may have played on this connection. Now the ever-resourceful Naiman made a bold proposal that conveniently addressed the Gür Khan's own needs at the moment. Scattered throughout Inner Asia, Khüchüleg pointed out, from the domains of the Uighurs north of the Tian Shan around Beshbaliq to the Seven Rivers region south of Lake Balkash, the broken shards of the tribes who had escaped from the domination of Chingis Khan on the Mongolian Plateau were now roaming leaderless. Khüchüleg, the son of a former khan in Mongolia and thus still a man of some standing among the peoples of the Mongolian Plateau, now offered to rally these diverse tribesmen, exiles in foreign and unfriendly lands, under his own command and then place them in the service of the Gür Khan. According to Juvaini:

> "If I receive permission, I will collect them together, and with the help of these people will assist and support the gür-khan. I shall not deviate from the path he prescribes and . . . I shall not twist my neck from the fulfillment of whatever he commands."[15]

The Qara Khitai leader readily acceded to this scheme and was apparently overjoyed with this seemingly powerful ally he had gained, showering him with robes of honor and other gifts and awarding him with a new title of Khan. And if we are to believe Rashid al-Din, the Gür Khan's daughter Qunqu was smitten with Khüchüleg almost at first sight, and three days after their initial meeting they were married.[16] In the thrall of his initial enthusiasm, the Gür Khan was unaware that he let a viper into his nest and that Khüchüleg's promises meant nothing. As Juvaini ruefully notes, "By such deceitful blandishments he cast the gür-khan into the well of vainglory."[17]

Khüchüleg, born the son of a khan in Mongolia, had no intention of playing second fiddle to the Gür Khan. He quickly set about assembling an army that was loyal to him alone. Juvaini:

> from all sides his tribesmen assembled around him. And he assaulted divers places and plundered them, striking one after another; and so he obtained a numerous army and his retinue and army was multiplied and reinforced.[18]

One reason Khüchüleg so quickly gained adherents was that he allowed his men to loot and plunder at will; the Gür Khan had kept a tight reign on his own troops and paid them a salary in lieu of the right to indiscriminately plunder, a policy almost unheard of at the time. Not only the exiled tribesmen from the Mongolian Plateau were attracted to Khüchüleg's free-booting ways; soon soldiers were deserting the Gür Khan's own army and joining up with the marauders of the Naiman adventurer. He was still fighting under the banner of the Qara Khitai, however, and in the autumn of 1209 the Gür Khan sent Khüchüleg east to deal with the rebellious Uighurs in Uighuristan, formerly clients of the Qara Khitai who had thrown in their lot with Chingis Khan earlier that year. The sortie east no doubt provided plentiful opportunities for looting the countryside, but the Uighurs would not to be budged from Chingis's camp. The Gür Khan, meanwhile, had ridden west to confront the Khwarezmshah. In 1210, personally leading an army of 30,000 men, he seized Samarkand from the Khwarezmshah, but in line with his polices he did not allow his men to plunder the city. Hearing that the Gür Khan was engaged in Mawarannahr, Khüchüleg now showed his true colors: " . . . turning on the gür-khan, he ravaged and plundered his territory, now attacking and now retreating," Juvaini states.[19] First he sacked the Qara Khitai imperial treasury at Özkend on the Syr Darya River, and then he occupied the Qara Khitai capital of Balasaghun.

Hearing of this treachery, the Gür Khan abandoned Samarkand and rode back east to confront the now overtly rebellious Naiman opportunist. Sensing the disarray among the Qara Khitai, the Khwarezmshah quickly sent an army eastward. In the early autumn 1210, this army collided with a Qara Khitai army led by Tayangu, the military commander of Taras (or Talas), a city on the Talas River in the Seven Rivers Region between the Syr Darya and Lake Balkash. Where this clash, which would prove to be the defining battle between the Khwarezmshah and the Gür Khan, took place is not exactly clear. At one point Juvaini says it occurred at the "steppe of Ilamish'" (apparently in the lower Ferghana Valley); elsewhere he implies it took place near Taras.[20] On the morning of battle the Khwarezmshah ordered his men to say their prayers, then, according to Juvaini:

> the whole army raised a shout and charged down upon those wretches [the Qara Khitai] . . . The greater part of that sect of sedition were destroyed beneath the sword, and Tayangu himself was wounded in the battle and had fallen on his face like the subjects of the Qara Khitai. A girl was standing over him and when someone tried to cut off his head she cried out: "It is Tayangu!" and the man at once bound him and carried him off to the Sultan.[21]

From this time on, Juvaini tells us, "dread of the Sultan was increased a thousandfold in the hearts of men."[22] One of the paid poets in the Khwarezmshah's court composed a lengthy paean to his recent exploits in which he termed the Khwarezmshah "the Second Alexander," referring of course to Alexander the Great. This epithet so pleased the Khwarezmshah that he had it added to his list of official titles. Tayangu, the Qara Khitai general who had recently been taken prisoner, fared less well. The Khwarezmshah had him beheaded and his body disposed of in a river.

The Khwarezmshah's forces moved on to the city of Otrar, in the Syr Darya basin, whose governor "refused to dislodge from his brain the arrogance of pride and vanity of riches" and had "turned aside from 'the straight path' by leaguing himself with the Khitai," according to Juvaini. The traders of Otrar, pointing out to the governor that he had "ignominiously cast thyself and us into the jaws of a leviathan," urged him to surrender the city to the Khwarezmshah, which he did. The Khwarezmshah give him and his family safe passage out of town on condition that he not return, then, as we have seen, appointed his mother's nephew Inalchuq as military governor and gave him the title of Gayer Khan.[23]

The Khwarezmshah's armies proceeded up the Fergana Valley and soon took the city of Özkend. The Gür Khan was now trapped between the ever-advancing Khwarezmshah in the west and Khüchüleg in the east. Khüchüleg was by now in clandestine contact with the Khwarezmshah, and the two soon hatched a plot to defeat the Gür Khan and divide his empire among themselves.[24] But the Qara Khitai emperor was not yet ready to throw in the towel. In 1211 he confronted his rebellious son-in-law near Balasaghun and in the ensuing battle took many of Khüchüleg's men prisoner and even managed to recover some of the imperial treasury that Khüchüleg had looted earlier. Khüchüleg escaped, fleeing eastward, and began gathering his scattered troops and reorganizing his army.

Meanwhile, the citizens of Balasaghun, by now fed up with the Gür Khan and hearing that the Khwarezmshah's army was approaching, decided to take their chances with the Khwarezmshah, whose star it seemed was on the rise. They barricaded themselves within the city walls and for sixteen days held off the Qara Khitai. Finally, with the aid of war elephants they had earlier captured from the Khwarezmshah (who had apparently obtained them on one of his forays into India), the Qara Khitai broke down the gates and entered the city. The Qara Khitai army, now an unruly mob no longer obeying the Gür Khan's strictures against plundering, allegedly killed 47,000 townspeople and thoroughly looted the city.[25]

By then the Qara Khitai Empire was in shreds. The Khwarezmshah was advancing from the west and somewhere in the east Khüchüleg was biding his time, waiting for the right moment to once again spring upon the Gür Khan. The time would soon come. In the autumn of 2011 the Gür Khan retired to the western end of the Tarim Basin, near Kashgar, for a spot of hunting. Given the predicament he was in, it seemed a peculiar way to spend his time, but maybe he needed to rest his shattered nerves by indulging in one of his favorite pastimes. Maybe he was enjoying himself so much that his guard was down. In any event, Khüchüleg and 8,000 men swooped down on the unsuspecting Gür Khan and captured him.[26] He choose not to kill the emperor of the Qara Khitai. Instead, he assumed the Gür Khan's titles and married one of his sons to a Khitan princess in an attempt to link himself with the Khitan nobility. He tried to ingratiate himself further by adopting Khitan customs, clothes, and religion.[27] According to Rashid al-Din, his Khitan wife Qunqu at this point managed to convert him from Christianity to Buddhism, the prominent religion among the nobility. (Juvaini claims he married one of the Gür Khan's wives who had caught his eye and implies that it was she who converted him to Buddhism.)[28] Clearly the upstart adventurer from the Mongolian Plateau wanted to be seen as the new Gür Khan, ruler of the Qara Khitai Empire. But the real Gür Khan finally died in 1213, and most commentators, including Juvaini, concluded that the Qara Khitai Empire died with him.[29]

The fall of the Qara Khitai, even though they not were Muslims themselves, was not viewed with universal favor by all Muslims in Inner Asia. After the huge defeat suffered by the Tayangu-led Qara Khitai army in 1210 there was much rejoicing among some elements in the Khwarezmshah's realm. Juvaini:

> The order of ascetics offered thanks to God; the great men and notables feasted and revelled at the sound of timbal and flute; the common people rejoiced and made merry; the young men frolicked noisily in gardens; and old men engaged in talk one with one another.[30]

But the more reflective graybeards had reservations. Some held the belief that the Qara Khitai had served as a useful wall or dam between themselves and the Mongols. They remembered that according to the Quran (Sura Al-Kahf, "The Cave", 18:83–9), a mysterious individual called Zul Qairain ("The Two-horned One") had journeyed to a distant northern land where he found a people who were suffering from the mischief of mysterious entities known as Gog and Magog. Zul Qairain then erected an iron wall to keep out Gog and Magog, but he warned that the wall would be removed as the Day of Judgement drew near. By the thirteenth century the Mongols had become identified with Gog and Magog. Juvaini goes on to tell of a Muslim scholar named Sayyid Murtaza who did not join in the general rejoicing after the Khwarezmshah had decisively defeated the Qara Khitai in 1210. When asked by Juvaini's cousin, from whom Juvaini claims to have heard this story, why he sat brooding in a corner with a sad look on this face, the scholar replied:

> "'Beyond these [the Qara Khitai] are a people [Mongols] stubborn in their vengeance and fury and exceeding Gog and Magog. And the people of Khitai were in truth the wall of Zul Qairain between us and them. And it is unlikely, when that wall is gone, that there will be any peace within the realm or that any man will recline in comfort and enjoyment. Today I am mourning for Islam.'"[31]

For the moment Khüchüleg held the broken remnants of the Qara Khitai Empire in his hands. But in far-off Mongolia Chingis Khan had never forgotten about the Naiman prince who had somehow slipped out of his grasp back in 1204. Khüchüleg's days were numbered, and once he was gone nothing would stand between the Islamic Khwarezmian Empire and the spawn of Gog and Magog.

Chingis Khan had also not forgotten about the Merkits who had escaped from Mongolia back in 1204. He had never forgiven them for kidnapping his wife and he still longed for revenge. As mentioned, the Merkit chieftain Togtoga Beki, his sons, including the youngest, Khutu, and close followers had evaded the annihilation of the Merkit tribe and, fleeing south, had linked up with Khüchüleg in the upper valley of the Irtysh River, on the northern edge of the Zungarian Basin. Later, perhaps in 1208, a Mongol force had crossed the Mongol Altai Mountains and routed the remnants of the Naiman and the Merkits on the Irtysh, killing Togtoga Beki in the process. Khüchüleg split with the remaining Merkits at this point and rode eastward to pursue his own destiny. Togtoga Beki's youngest son Khutu and his followers fled eastward on their own. At this point Chingis Khan, apparently more concerned with the Merkits than the Naiman, dispatched Sübedei, one of his most promising young commanders, in pursuit of Khutu and his cohorts. Sübedei was one of Chingis Khan's "Four Hounds", about whom he said:

"You, Khubilai, Jelme, Jebe, and Sübedei—these 'four hounds' of
mine—when I sent you off, directing you to the place I had in mind,
When I said, 'Reach there!'
You crushed the stones to be there;
When I said, 'Attack!'
You split up the rocks
You shattered the shining stones,
You cleft the deep waters."[32]

The details of this campaign are hazy, but apparently Sübedei caught up
with the Merkit escapees somewhere around the river Chu in what is now
northern Kyrgyzstan or southern Kazakhstan. Two of Khutu's brothers
were killed in the ensuing melee, but he and his dwindling band of followers escaped, apparently fleeing back eastward into Uighuristan. As we
have seen, however, it was just at this time—around 1209— that the Uighur *Idikut* Barchuk was cementing his allegiance with Chingis Khan and
the Mongols. Chingis's bitter enemies, the Merkits, were not welcome in
Uighuristan and were forced to flee back to the west. Eventually Khutu
and his men hooked up with Khüchüleg, who was at the time deep into
his machinations to seize control of the Qara Khitai, and the Merkits
were among the 8000 troops under the command of Khüchüleg when he
finally defeated the Gür Khan and declared himself the new ruler of the
Qara Khitai.[33]

While not adverse to helping Khüchüleg overthrow the previous Gür
Khan, Khutu may have bridled against serving under the Naiman prince
now that he was the ruler of the Qara Khitai. He may have even envisioned returning to the Lake Baikal region and reclaiming the lands of
his forefathers that had been seized by Chingis Khan. In any case, he
soon moved north beyond Khüchüleg's sphere of influence, eventually
reaching the upper Yenisei Valley in Siberia (now the Autonomous Re-
public of Tuva, part of the Russian Federation). From here, just north of
Uvs Aimag in current-day Mongolia, he launched a series of raids into
the western territories already conquered by Chingis Khan. The various tribes inhabiting the upper Yenisei River Valley and the forests and
steppes west of Lake Baikal, and who had earlier submitted to Chingis
Khan, took heart from these challenges to Mongol power in the region
and themselves rebelled against their overlords.

The much-hated Merkits under Togtoga Beki had not only escaped Chingis's grasp in Mongolia and later, when led by his son Khutu, evaded an
army under the command of Sübedei sent to bring him to bay, they were

now, in Chingis's view, instigating a full-scale insurrection against his rule in the northwest of his empire. In response, Chingis decided to send his oldest son Jochi and an army of 20,000 men to deal with the obstreperous Merkits once and for all. Jochi was the titular head of the expeditionary force, but accompanying him were three generals who acted as advisors and field commanders: Sübedei, who already had one campaign against the Merkits under his belt; the up-and-coming Tokhuchar, apparently Chingis's son-in-law; and a Khitan prince who was now serving in the Mongol army. This force was much larger than that needed to deal with Khutu's band of renegades, but Chingis may have anticipated that while chasing after Khutu the Mongol army would also collide with the Qara Khitai under Khüchüleg. By this time, however, Khutu and Khüchüleg had fallen out for good, and the Merkit adventurer was no longer welcome in the realm of the Qara Khitai. Hearing of the approach of the Jochi and his army, Khutu fled not south but west to the territories of the Qangli Turks, the vast Kipchaq Steppes north of the Syr Darya River in what is now Kazakhstan. Jochi and his men were not far behind. Perhaps in the spring of 1216—the actual year is the subject of much dispute—Jochi finally managed to corner Khutu and his followers north of the Aral Sea, somewhere near the Irghiz River. Over two thousand miles west of the Mongol heartland in Mongolia, this may have been the farthest westward advance of Mongol armies to date. Greatly outnumbered, most of the Merkits were slain, although a few did manage to escape and eventually sought refuge with the Qangli who lived west of the Volga River. Khutu himself was taken prisoner. The saga which had begun twelve years earlier in Mongolia when Togtoga Beki and his sons had fled from the Mongols was finally drawing to a close. Chingis Khan would soon have his revenge.

The Khwarezmshah's mother Terken Khatan was herself a Qangli, and through her some of the Qangli were at least nominally subjects of the Khwarezmian Empire. The Qangli territories straddling the lower Syr Darya was already a part of the Khwarezmshah's domains, and two sons of the local ruler were held hostage in Gurganj to ensure his obedience. But north of here on the vast Kipchaq Steppes many of the notoriously contentious Qanglis refused to submit to the Khwarezmshah. In the spring of 1216 the Khwarezmshah was in the city of Jand on the Syr Darya preparing to lead an expedition against the unruly and disobedient Qanglis when he heard that a band of Merkits with a larger army of Mongols in pursuit of them were crossing the Kipchaq Steppe to the north.[34] These interlopers into the domains claimed by the Khwarezmshah could not be countenanced, and, in the words of Juvaini, he decided to "kill two hares with one stone" by attacking them both.[35]

Leading an army of 60,000 men, the Khwarezmshah rode from Jand to the Irghiz River, north of the Aral Sea. By now it was early spring, and the ice was just breaking up. Waiting until the river was free of ice, the Khwarezmshah and his army crossed over and rode on to confront the Merkits and their Mongol pursuers. The Khwarezmshah and his men arrived on the battlefield on the very day the Mongols had decimated the Merkits. The Mongols had already left, but after ascertaining details of the battle from a wounded Merkit the Khwarezmshah and his army set out in pursuit. They caught up with the Mongols the next day at dawn. A parley ensued, in which Jochi explained that he and his Mongol army had been sent by Chingis Khan to track down the Merkits, and that neither he nor his father had any quarrel with the Khwarezmshah and that there was not need for hostilities. The Khwarezmshah, who commanded an army of 60,000 and apparently felt he held the upper hand against the Jochi and his 20,000 Mongols, rejected Jochi's entreaties and declared that all infidels—Jochi and his Mongols were obviously not Muslims—his enemies. Although the Mongols, according to Juvaini:

> refrained from giving battle, the Sultan could not withhold himself but set his face toward the wilderness of error and hallucination. As he was not rebuffed by admonishments they prepared for action. Both sides attacked, and the right wing of both armies routed its opponents. The rest of the Mongol army was emboldened by this success; they attacked the centre where the Sultan was stationed in person, and he was nearly taken prisoner, and Jalal-ad-Din repelled the attackers and bore him out of that strait.

Juvaini could not resist praising the Khwarezmshah's son Jalal-ad-Din (this would become a recurring theme his work):

> *What is finer than a furious male lion, his loins*
> *gird before his father?*

The battle went on all day until the evening prayer; as it grew dark the combatants "sheathed the sword of combat, and each army rested in its own quarters. The Mongol army then withdrew."[36]

Apparently the Khwarezmshah, despite his near defeat on the first day of battle, intended to fight again the next day. He had, after all, a three-to-one numerical superiority. Jochi, however, had been given a very specific brief by Chingis Khan: defeat the Merkits and if possible capture their leaders. Nothing had been said about confronting the Khwarezmshah, whose embassy Chingis had peacefully received several months before. That evening the Mongols built innumerable campfires, giving the impression that a huge host was resting and preparing for the next day's battle. Later that night they quietly broke camp and rode off en masse to the east. When the sun rose the next day the Mongols were already long gone, and the Khwarezmshah made no attempt to pursue them.

Despite the refusal of the Mongols to continue the battle, the Khwarezmshah, who had almost been captured during the first day's melee, was stunned by their performance against his much larger army. "A fear of these infidels was planted in the heart of the Sultan," according to Nasavi, "and an estimation of their courage; if any one spoke of them before him, he said that he had never seen men as daring nor as steadfast in the throes of battle, or as skilled on giving blows with the point and edge of the sword."[37] Indeed, much of the Khwarezmshah's subsequent pusillanimity and indecision when confronted with the full brunt of the Mongol invasion when it finally came may have been a result of the fear that had been instilled in his heart during this initial encounter with a Mongol army. The Khwarezmshah would lose his entire empire to the Mongols, but only once again, near the very end of his life, would he himself face them on the field battle. He would leave almost the entire war against the Mongols to his subordinates, and in the end none of them were up to the task.

When the Mongols rode back east from their confrontation with the Khwarezmshah they had with them the captive Khutu, former leader of the Merkits. At some point Jochi asked his father, Chingis Khan, what he should do with the errant Merkit. Khutu was renowned for his skills as an archer, and supposedly for this reason Jochi, an archer of some note himself ("'If you beat me in long-distance arrow shooting, I will cut off my thumb and cast it away,'" he had once taunted his brother Chagaadai), begged Chingis to spare his life. Whether Jochi harbored some sympathy for Merkits, since he was alleged to be half-Merkit himself, is unknown. Chingis was having none of it. He felt no sympathy whatsoever for the tribe that had kidnapped his wife, one of whom may have actually been the father of Jochi:

"There is no tribe more wicked than the Merkit. How often have we fought them? They have caused us much vexation and sorrow. How can we spare his life? He will only instigate another rebellion. I have conquered these lands for you, my sons. Of what use is he? There is no better place for an enemy of our nation than in the grave!"[38]

Khutu was duly executed, and the Chingis's final revenge against the Merkits was complete. That left Khüchüleg of the Naiman as the only remaining loose thread that had slipped out of Chingis Khan's grasp back in 1204.

The Gür Khan of the Qara Khitai, whatever his personal failings, had enjoyed during most of his reign the popular acclaim of many of the people in his realm. Not until his army under Tayangu was defeated in the autumn of 1210, after which many of his disheartened troops went on a looting spree, did the Gür Khan's subjects turn on him. Khüchüleg, who had usurped the position of the Gür Khan, was cut from different cloth. Although he entertained pretensions of ruling the old Qara Khitai Empire, he was basically a freebooter who was more interested in loot and plunder than the day-to-day administration of a functioning society. A nomad from the steppes of Mongolia, he was particularly insensitive to the needs of the sedentary peoples whom he now at least nominally ruled. And not of all the local chieftains who were loyal to the Gür Khan were ready to bow down to the Naiman marauder.

Trouble started first at Almaliq, near the current-day city of Ili in the valley of the Ili River, the easternmost of the rivers in the Seven Rivers Region. Separated by formidable mountains from the basins and depressions to the east, it was oriented more westward, towards the vast steppes and deserts that stretch off to the shores of Caspian Sea. Until 1211 much of the Seven Rivers Region, including the upper Ili Basin, had been ruled by Arslan Khan, nominally a subject of the Gür Khan.[39] After the defeat of Tayangu's army, Arslan Khan had held his finger to the wind and decided that it was time to align himself with Chingis Khan, who was already the suzerain of the Uighurs across the mountains to the east. He went personally to the court of Chingis Khan to declare his loyalty. While he was gone an adventurer by the name of Ozar seized control of the upper Ili Basin and the steppes along the western edge of the Zungarian Basin, including the Bor Steppe and the area around Lake Sayram. According to Juvaini, he:

used to steal people's horses from the herds and commit other criminal actions, such as highway robbery, etc. He was joined by all the ruffians of that region and so became very powerful. Then he used to enter villages, and if the people refused to yield to him obedience he would seize that place by war and violence.[40]

Khüchüleg marched against Ozar Khan, as he now styled himself, several times, but to the Naiman's fury he was unable to bring the highwayman to heel. Then Ozar Khan, like Arslan Khan, decided to declare his loyalty to Chingis. Khan. He also traveled to the Mongol court, where he was royally received. Chingis, eager to gain his services and cement his loyalty, offered him one of his granddaughters, the daughter of his oldest son Jochi, in marriage. But before Ozar left to go back to the Ili Basin Chingis had some advice for him. Ozar was an avid huntsmen, but Chingis warned him not to go on hunting parties lest he himself fall prey to other hunters. Chingis was so adamant on this subject that he gave Ozar a thousand sheep so he would not have to hunt game for food. Perhaps Chingis had a premonition about Ozar's death. In any case, when Ozar returned to the Ili Basin, he failed to heed Chingis's advice. While out hunting he was ambushed by troops loyal to Khüchüleg and captured alive. He was taken in chains to Almaliq, where his captors apparently hoped to ransom him. Instead the residents of Almaliq closed the gates of the city and took up arms against Khüchüleg's men. At this point, rumors arrived that a Mongol army under the command of Chingis's famous general Jebe was on the way to Almaliq. Khüchüleg's men retreated south with their prisoner, and since he was now worthless they slew him somewhere along the road. At least this is the story told by Juvaini. Other sources suggest that Arslan Khan, eager to recover his hereditary fiefdom, had Ozar Khan killed.[41]

Juvaini paints him as a highwayman and ruffian but adds that Ozar, "although rash and foolhardy, was a pious, God-fearing man and gazed with the glance of reverence upon ascetics." One day a Sufi approached Ozar and announced: "I am on an embassy to thee from the Court of Power and Glory; and the message is thus, that our treasures are become somewhat depleted. Now therefore let Ozar give aid by means of a loan and not hold it lawful to refuse.'" Ozar bowed to the Sufi and "while tears rained down from his eyes" offered him a *balish* of gold (about seventy-five *dinars*). Mission accomplished, the Sufi departed.[42]

ɕɔ

Having lost the Ili Basin, Khüchüleg turned his attention south to the
Tarim Basin. The people of Kashgar, at the western end of the basin,
had revolted against the Qara Khitai back in 1204. In retaliation the Gür
Khan had seized the son of one the local rulers as a hostage and kept
him under house arrest in Balagasun. Khüchüleg now sent this princeling
back to Kashgar in hopes that he would smooth the way for his own arrival. The local nobles, whose loyalties in the meantime had wavered, had
him killed at the city gates before he even set foot in town. Outraged,
Khüchüleg descended on Kashgar. He made the local people quarter his
troops and for three or four years running had ravished the countryside
at harvest time. "And oppression, and injustice, and depravity were made
manifest; and the pagan idolators accomplished whatever was their will
and in their power, and none was able to prevent them," Juvaini laments.[43]

Religion quickly became an issue. The lapsed Christian Khüchüleg,
who under the influence of his wife had come to profess Buddhism, now
declared that people of the western Tarim Basin must accept "the Christian or idolatrous creed [Buddhism]," Juvaini relates, or "don the garb of
Khitayans." The details of Khitayan accouterments are not known, so it is
not clear exactly what this entailed. In any case, the locals considered con-
version an anathema: "And since it was impossible to go over to another
religion, by reason of hard necessity they clad themselves in the dress of
Khitayans."[44] Khüchüleg also prohibited the call-to-prayer from the min-
arets of Kashgar and Khotan and closed all Islamic schools and colleges.
In Khotan, the venerable Silk Road city famous for carpets, silk, and jade,
Khüchüleg called all the local imams out into the countryside and engaged them in debate about the merits of their respective religions. Not
liking what he heard from an imam named Ala-al-Din Muhammad, he
had the Muslim scholar crucified on the door of his own college. Juvaini:

> Thus was the Moslem cause brought to a sorry pass, nay rather it was
> wiped out, and endless oppression and wickedness were extended over
> the slaves of Divinity, who set up prayers that were blessed with fulfill-
> ment..."[45]

The fulfillment of their prayer soon arrived in the person of Jebe, one of
Chingis Khan's "Four Hounds".

Juvaini believed that the arrival of the Jebe and his Mongols in the realm
of the Qara Khitai was an act of Divine Providence:

God Almighty, in order to remove the evilness of Küchlüg [Khüchü-leg], in a short space dispatched the Mongol army against him; and already in this world he tasted the punishment of his foul and wicked deeds and his ill-omened life; and in the hereafter the torments of hell-fire. Ill be his rest![46]

Chingis Khan may have been acting out of more down-to-earth considerations. Khüchüleg had earlier escaped from the Mongols at both the battles at Tuleet Uul and on the Upper Irtysh, and this must have rankled. Then he had gathered under his own banner all the disaffected tribesmen who had fled the Mongolian Plateau, thus posing a threat to the Uighurs and others at the western end of Chingis's own domains. Perhaps the Naiman adventurer even had his sights set on some day leading his assembled forces back to Mongolia and challenging Chingis Khan on his home turf. And by 1216 Chingis, as we have seen, was already making overtures to the Khwarezmshah about trade relations between the Mongols and Khwarezmia. Now Khüchüleg, essentially a freebooting marauder, sat astride the great trade routes linking the two realms, ready to swoop down on any trade caravans that might pass through the territories over which he now ruled rough-shod. There is also the school of thought, promoted by various modern historians, that Chingis, even at this stage of his career, entertained some overarching vision of world conquest and considered Khüchüleg simply as one more obstacle that had to be overcome on the inevitable march west, perhaps even to the Atlantic Ocean.[47]

Whatever his motivations, in the summer of 1218 Chingis sent his now-seasoned general Jebe west to finally deal with the Naiman upstart Khüchüleg.[48] Jebe was a member of the Taichuud tribe, once one of Chingis Khan's many enemies.[49] As a young man Temüjin, the future Chingis Khan, had been captured by the Taichuud and held prisoner. He later made a daring escape with the help of a man named Sorkhon, who had divined a great future for the young Temüjin and who would eventually become one of his followers. The Taichuud were just one of the many tribes Chingis would defeat in his rise to power. In the decisive battle against the Taichuud, someone shot an arrow which according to the Secret History hit Chingis's yellow war horse in the neck. It may have been Chingis himself who was wounded in the neck, but apparently he did not want to reveal this. Anyhow, after the battle the Taichuud who were taken prisoner were interrogated to find out who had shot the arrow at Chingis. "'Who shot that arrow from the mountaintop," Chingis demanded. A man named Zurgadai replied:

"I shot that arrow from the mountain top. If I am put to death by the
Qahan (Chingis), then I shall be left to rot on a piece of ground the size
of the palm of a hand. But if I am granted mercy, then shall I go ahead
on behalf of the Qahan.
I will attack for you:
I will slash the deep waters
and erode the shining stone.
At your word, I will go forward
and smash the blue stones.
If you order me to attack,
I will slash the black stones.
I will attack for you."[50]

Chingis Khan was impressed that the man had admitting to shooting
at him, even though there was a good chance he would be put to death
for such an act, and had not attempted to lie his way out of it. A man
like this, Chingis concluded, would make a good addition to his armies.
Chingis gave Zurgadai the new name of Zebe, which means "arrow" in
Mongolian, and proclaimed that "'I shall use him as an arrow.'"[51] Zebe (or
Jebe, as it is more commonly rendered in English) would become the arrow that would unflinchingly fly at any target to which Chingis aimed it.
The target now was Khüchüleg.

Jebe and an army of some 20,000 men rode westward through Mongolia, then turned south and crossed the Mongolian Altai, perhaps via the
9715-foot Ikh Ulaan Davaa, the traditional pass across the mountains, in
what is now Khovd Aimag of Mongolia.[52] According to the biography of
a Chinese army officer who was serving under Jebe in this campaign, the
army then passed by Ulungur Lake in the Zungarian Depression and,
continuing south, skirted the eastern foothills of the Ukhashar Jair, Bar-
lik, and Ala Tau mountains to Ebi Nuur, a lake at the western end of
the Bor Tal (Brown Steppe).[53] At some point on this route a contingent
of Uighur troops from Uighuristan to the east joined up with Jebe. The
army then veered west past Sayram Lake and over the Borohogo Range
via the Ak-Tasi Pass into the valley of the Ili River. At Almaliq, in the
upper basin of Ili, they linked up with more tribesmen who had already
declared their allegiance to Chingis. With these reinforcements Jebe proceeded to the old Qara Khitai capital of Balagasun, where he defeated
an army of some 30,000 men who had earlier obeyed the Gür Khan but
who now were now nominally aligned with Khüchüleg. Now reading the
prevailing winds, other local rulers threw in their lot with Jebe and the

Mongols, including Yisimaili, a prominent Qara Khitai commander from the city of Kasan in the Ferghana Valley. With Yisimaili, who was apparently familiar with the country, leading Jebe's vanguard, the Mongol army headed south toward Kashgar, where Khüchüleg was reputed to be holed up. They probably crossed the Tian Shan at the Bedel Pass (12,600 feet) south of Issyk Kul, and then passed by the towns of Uch-Turpan and Aksu on the northern side of the Tarim Depression before proceeding on to Kashgar. Khüchüleg, hearing of the imminent arrival of the Mongols, fled from Kashgar south toward the Pamirs, perhaps hoping to eventually reach the dubious safety of India.

Jebe and his army of 20,000 Mongols and various auxiliaries were viewed as liberators by the Muslim population of Kashgar. According to Juvaini, the local people said:

> "each group of Mongols, arriving one after another, sought nothing from us save Khüchüg, and permitted the recitation of the *takbir* and *azan* [call to prayer], and caused a herald to proclaim in the town that each should abide by their religion and follow their own creed. Then we knew the existence of this people to be one of the mercies of the Lord and one of the bounties of divine grace."[54]

After rounding up and executing all of Khüchüleg's soldiers who had remained in the city, Jebe and his men set out on the scent of the Naiman runaway. They probably followed the ancient caravan road (and now the route of the Karakoram Highway) up the valley and canyon of the Gez River, past Khökh Nuur (Blue Lake) and the immense massif of 24,757-foot Muztagh-Ata (later Marco Polo may have used this same route). Somewhere near the border of Badakhshan and the Wakhan region, deep in the Pamir Knot (perhaps in modern-day Tajikistan), Khüchüleg took the wrong road (Juvaini cannot help opining that "it was right that he should do so") and ended up in a dead-end valley.[55] Jebe, coming up behind, met some local hunters and made them a deal: if they would bring him Khüchüleg no harm would come to them; if they did not, they would to be aiding and abetting Khüchüleg's escape and would have to face the consequences. The hunters captured the errant Naiman and brought him to Jebe, who rewarded them with much of the loot—jewels and money—that they had seized from Khüchüleg's traveling party. The Naiman adventurer had led a wild and tumultuous life after fleeing Mongolia in 1204, throwing a good portion of Inner Asia into turmoil, but it all ended here in a desolate valley in the high Pamirs. He was executed and beheaded. One source maintains that Jebe took his head back with him and displayed it in Kashgar and Khotan to prove that the oppressor of the local Muslim populations was finally, at long last, dead.[56]

With the death of Khüchüleg, Jebe was now the *de facto* ruler of a huge swath of land from Khotan north to the Seven Rivers region. Did the thought cross his mind that he could have declared himself the new Gür Khan and founded an empire of his own? Apparently back in Mongolia even Chingis Khan began to worry that Jebe "in the pride of victory would mutiny," as Barthold puts it.[57] But Jebe was made of different stuff. He had sworn his loyalty to Chingis Khan back when his life had been spared after the defeat of the Taichuud, and he was not about to turn on his sworn lord and master. As a sign of his fealty, he gave his commander-in-chief a gift of 1,000 yellow horses like the one Chingis had ridden at the final battle with the Taichuud, the horse that he, Jebe, had supposedly hit in the neck with an arrow. Tracking down Khüchüleg and seizing his territories was certainly a feather in his cap, but his greatest exploits as a general in the Mongol army were yet to come. He would remain loyal to Chingis until his death in 1225.

Khüchüleg died sometime in 1218. Around this time the merchants of the Mongol caravan to Otrar had been killed, along with the emissary Chingis had sent to demand compensation for the massacre. War with the Khwarezmshah was now inevitable, and the last obstacle between the Mongols and the Khwarezmian Empire—the Naiman adventurer Khüchüleg—had been removed. Chingis Khan was now ready to ride west.

Chapter 4

Advance on Khwarezmia, The Khwarezmshah, and the Attack on Otrar

Chingis Khan was now resolved to invade Khwarezmia. According to the *Secret History*, he announced:

> "I shall set out against the Sartuul people [Khwarezmians],
> To take revenge
> To requite the wrong
> for the slaying of my hundred envoys with Ukhuna at their head . . ."[1]

His anger over the murder of his envoys to the Khwarezmshah may have cooled, but his resolution to exact retribution had stiffened. His intelligence networks would have informed him that while the Khwarezmshah was inflicted by infighting among his family and court, and by rising discontent among the populace of his empire, he was still capable of putting half as million or more soldiers into the field. It would not do to ride off half-cocked against such an enemy. Chingis organized the invasion of Khwarezmia in the same step-by-step methodical way that he had attacked and finally defeated the Chin in northern China.

As the final preparation were being made to depart from Mongolia, one of his wives, Yesüi Khatan, decided that it was time to speak up. Yesüi Khatan seemed to hold a special place in Chingis Khan's heart. She was a member of the Tatar tribe, whom the Mongols had earlier defeated. He had first married her younger sister, but the latter soon intimated that her older sister Yesüi might be a better wife for Chingis. In the confusion following the defeat of the Tatars the older sister Yesüi had somehow disappeared. Chingis sent men to track her down, and they eventually found her in the company of a man to whom she had been betrothed. Confronted by Chingis's men, this swain quickly vamoosed. Yesüi was taken back to Chingis and he fell for her forthwith, making her one of his principal wives. Sometime later the man to whom she had been betrothed sneaked into Chingis's camp, apparently just to get a look at the woman he had once hoped to marry and perhaps still loved. Yesüi inadvertently betrayed his presence by heaving a deep sigh when she saw him. The sharp-eyed Chingis Khan, noticing her reaction, ordered that he be seized and later had him executed.[2] Despite this momentary lapse in her decorum, Chingis Khan still had a high regard for Yesüi and valued her counsel. According to the *Secret History*, she offered the following advice to Chingis Khan:

> "The Khan has thought of
> Establishing order over his many people,
> Climbing high passes,
> Crossing wide rivers
> And waging a long campaign.
> Still, living beings who are but born to this world are not eternal:
> When your body, like a great tree,
> Will fall down,
> To whom will you bequeath your people
> Which is like tangled hemp?
> When your body, like the stone base of a pillar,
> Will collapse,
> To whom will you bequeath your people
> Which is like a flock of birds?
> Of your four sons, the heroes you have begotten, which one will you
> designate as your successor? . . . Your order shall decide!"[3]

Chingis thanked Yesüi Khatan for bringing up a subject that none of his other advisors had dared to broach. "Even though she is only a woman," Chingis Khan declared, Yesüi Khatan's "words are more right than wrong." He then asked Jochi, as his oldest son, to offer his opinion. Before Jochi could get a word in edgewise, Chingis's second son Chagaadai blurted out, "When you say 'Jochi, speak up!', do you mean by that that you will appoint Jochi as your successor? How can we let ourselves be ruled by this bastard offspring of a Merkit?" Here Chagaadai gave voice to, perhaps for the first time in Chingis's presence, what many in the Mongol camp already believed: that Jochi was not actually Chingis Khan's biological son.

As mentioned earlier, after their marriage Chingis's wife Börte had been kidnapped by the Merkits, a tribe that dwelled around Lake Baikal to the north of the Mongolian Plateau, and when Chingis finally rescued her, she was pregnant with Jochi. Despite the doubts about Jochi's paternity, which must have been known to most of the Mongol ruling class, Chingis had always accepted him as his son. Indeed, he had sent Jochi on an important expedition to track down and bring to heel the Merkits, and Jochi had not only accomplished that task but also had acquitted himself well when confronted by the much larger force of the Khwarezmshah. Jochi now felt compelled to defend his place among his brothers. Grabbing Chagaadai by the collar, he declared:

> "I have never been told by my father the Qan that I was different from my brothers. How can you discriminate against me? In what skill are you better than I? Only in your obstinacy you are, perhaps, better. If we shoot arrows at a long distance and I am outdone by you, I shall cut off my thumb and throw it away ... Let the order of my father decide which of us is better!"

At this point, two of Chingis's most trusted advisers had to intervene and pull the two quarreling brothers apart. Another one of Chingis's advisers chastised Chagaadai:

> "At such time your mother was abducted
> It was not her wish ...
> She was not running away from her home ...
> She was not in love with someone else ...
> You speak so as to harden the butter of your mother's affection, so as to sour the milk of that august lady's heart.
> From the warm womb, coming forth,
> Suddenly, were you two
> Not born of the same belly?"

The advisor went on in this vein at length, emphasizing that Börte had gone to great effort to bring up her sons as equals and that Chingis himself had made many sacrifices for his family, including Jochi, without ever questioning his paternity.

Chingis Khan finally broke his silence: "How can you speak thus about Jochi?" he admonished Chagaadai, "Isn't Jochi the oldest of my sons? In future do not talk like that!"

Chagaadai did not dare mouth back to his father, but he could not resist getting in a jab at Jochi, implying that his older brother was all talk and no action:

"Game that has been killed only with one's mouth
Cannot be loaded on one's mount;
Game that one has slain only with one's words
Cannot be skinned."[4]

After firing off this Parthian shot, Chagaadai relented and promised
that in the future he would cooperate with his older brother. He then
proposed that Chingis bypass both him and Jochi as the future Khan of
the Mongols and appoint his third son Ögedei as his successor. Chagaadai may well have been aware that Chingis considered him too hotheaded
and stubborn to be a good ruler, and since he was out of the running, it
would be better to have his younger brother, whom he could to some
extant control, as the head of the Mongols, rather than his older brother
Jochi, who he clearly hated. Chingis then asked Jochi whether he agreed
with this proposal. He concurred that he and Chagaadai would cooperate
in the future and that Ögedei should be named Chingis Khan's successor
as ruler of the Mongols. Ögedei and Tolui, the youngest of Chingis's four
sons, were themselves questioned and they too agreed to the proposed
arrangement. Thus it was decided that Ögedei should succeed Chingis as
the Great Khan of the Mongols. Chingis Khan, however, no doubt knew
his boys very well, and he was not convinced by the promises of Jochi and
Chagaadai to cooperate in the future. "'Why should you two go so far as
to cooperate with each other? Mother Earth is wide: its rivers and waters
are many. Extending the camps that can be easily divided, We shall make
each of you a ruler over a domain and We shall separate you."[5]
     For the moment, on the eve of the departure of the Mongol army from
Mongolia, the feud between Jochi and Chagaadai had been papered over,
but in the upcoming war against the Khwarezmshah the rift would once
again become palpable, and it would have incalculable effects on the subsequent history of the Mongol Empire.

In the spring of 1219 Chingis Khan assembled his armies on the Saari
Steppe, located in the valleys of the upper Kherlen or upper Tuul rivers,
or somewhere in between.[6] At the end of May or beginning of June, the
Mongol army departed on what would turn into a monumental multi-
year campaign into the Islamic lands of Inner Asia, Iran, and India. Accompanying Chingis Khan was another one of his wives, Khulan Khatan.
Yesüi Khatan had given Chingis exemplary advice, but apparently he
considered Khulan Khatan a better bed mate on a long campaign.[7] In

the front ranks the army were all four of his sons, for the moment reconciled with each other; his adopted son Shigikhutug, whose career we have already mentioned; various favored nephews; his best generals not already engaged in the continuing struggle with the Chin in China; and a contingent of Chinese or perhaps Khitan officers who had sided with the Mongols.

The amassed Mongols advanced along the north side of the Khangai Mountains and arrived in the upper valley of the Ider River, which combines with the Moron River to form the Selenge, the major river flowing north from Mongolia into Lake Baikal, around the end of June or beginning of July. Near the headwaters of the Ider the army crossed the nearly 10,000-foot Jigestei Pass and moved down the valley of the Bogd Gol in what is now Zavkhan Aimag. Proceeding southwest through what is now northern Gov-Altai Aimag and southern Khovd Aimag, the army then crossed the Mongol Altai, probably through the 9715-foot Ikh Ulaan Davaa (Big Red Pass), then as now one of the main passes across the mountains. Around the beginning of August they had reached the basin of the Irtysh River, on the northern side of the Zungarian Depression.[8] On the rich grassland straddling the Irtysh Chingis Khan and his men spent what remained of the summer fattening their horses. They no doubt also took time to engage in huge hunts for wild game, which not only provided food but also served as training exercises for the troops.

At this time, while camped on the Irtysh, Chingis Khan may have dispatched envoys to the various rulers who recognized him as suzerain, including the *Idikut* of the Uighurs; Burqan, the ruler of the Tanguts; Arslan Khan in the Seven Rivers Region; and others, telling them that he was expecting their armies to fight by his side in the upcoming war against the Khwarezmshah. Except for Burqan, the others apparently agreed to honor their obligations to Chingis Khan. As we have seen, back in 1210 the Tanguts of the Xi Xia realm had accepted the Mongols as their overlords, and in Chingis Khan's view this meant that they were obligated to provide auxiliary troops whenever he required them. Even back then, however, the Xi Xia ruler had pointed out that "We are a nation of town-dwellers. We would not be in a state to fight as auxiliaries in the event of a long march followed by a heated battle." Now, on the eve of the invasion of Khwarezm, Chingis sent envoys to Burqan, demanding that he provide Xi Xia troops for the upcoming campaign. The envoys delivered the message to Burqan, but before he had a chance to reply, one of his army commanders, a man known as Asa Gambu, piped up, insolently wondering how Chingis had ever become the Khan of the Mongols if he needed help from others to defeat his enemies. Asa Gambu, apparently speaking on behalf of Burqan, thereupon refused to provide auxiliary troops and instead, according to the *Secret History*, "sent back the envoys with haughty words."[9]

Chingis Khan was infuriated by the report brought back to him about the Tangut's behavior.

> "How can we bear being spoken to in this manner by Asa Gambu?" And he said, "The best plan would be for us to send troops against them at once by detouring in their direction. What difficulty would there be in that? But now, when we are indeed moving in the direction of other people, let that pass. If I am protected by Eternal Heaven, when I come back pulling strongly on my golden reins, then surely this matter shall be dealt with."

Thus, he declared that if he lived through the upcoming campaign against the Khwarezmshah, he would return and deal with the defiant and recalcitrant kingdom of Xi Xia. Later on, in 1227, he would indeed exact a terrible revenge on the Tanguts for their refusal to provide troops during the Khwarezmia campaign. Unfortunately for him, he would die in the process.

By the early autumn, when the grass began to yellow, commanders and men were familiarized with each other and their horses were fattened and well-rested. The march west continued. Most accounts imply, even if they do not state outright, that his entire army proceeded en masse from the Irtysh to the western end of the Zungarian Basin. Leaving the bottom of the basin, they rode through the Bor Steppe and by Lake Sayram, areas which as we have seen were in the domains of Ozar Khan and now claimed by his son Siqnaq Tegin, and then crossed over the Borohogo Range via the Ak-Tasi Pass. Then, via switch-backed trails, they dropped down the imposing ramparts on the western side of the Borohogo Range into the Ili Valley.[10] (The importance of this route as a gateway from the Zungarian Basin, in current-day Xinjiang Province, China, into the vast Kazakh Steppes beyond, has been underlined by the recent construction of a railway line from Urumqi, the capital of Xinjiang, to the city of Korgas, on the Chinese-Kazakhstan border, following this route, with a lengthy tunnel under the Ak-Tasi Pass.)

Following the Ili River past the last spurs of the mountains they soon emerged out onto the vast steppes of the Seven Rivers Region. Here Chingis Khan rendezvoused with his various allies: the *Idikut* of the Uighurs from Beshbaliq in Uighuristan, who had sworn allegiance to Chingis back in 1209; Siqnaq Tegin, the son of the now-deceased Ozar Khan, from the upper Ili Basin; and Arslan Khan, from the Seven Rivers Region (with 6,000 men, according to Juzjani).[11] Juzjani numbered the assembled multitude at 600,000 men or more, but this was clearly an exaggeration. Barthold, after thoroughly examining all the various and conflicting accounts, concluded that Chingis's army, including auxiliaries, numbered about 150,000.[12] Juvaini could barely restrain himself when praising the Mongol troops:

> They were archers who by the shooting of an arrow would bring down a hawk from the hollow of the ether, and on dark nights with a thrust of their spear-heads would cast out a fish from the bottom of the sea; who thought the day of battle the marriage-night and considered the pricks of lances the kisses of fair maidens.[13]

This multitude was now ready to descend on the realm of the Khwarezmshah.

Ala al-Din Mohammad, the Khwarezmshah who had ordered or acquiesced to the murder of the Muslim traders and Mongol envoys in Otrar, was the fifth of the Khwarezmshahs to rule Khwarezm in the twelfth and thirteenth centuries. His line began when the Saljuq Turks conquered the province of Khwarezm, the area encompassing the lower reaches of the Amu Darya River and its delta where it flows into the Aral Sea. Starting in the eleventh century, the Saljuq Turks, originally nomadic tribesmen from the steppes east and north of the Aral Sea, had created a vast empire encompassing much of current-day Turkey, Syria, Israel, Iran, Iraq, and Turkmenistan. In the early 1040s the Saljuqs invaded Khwarezm, and after taking control of the province, they appointed a succession of governors. In 1073 a Turkish *ghulam*, or slave-soldier, named Anustigin was appointed military commander of the region and given the title of *Tastdar*, or "Keeper of the Royal Washing Bowls". In 1097 his son Arslantigin inherited the position and assumed the title of Khwarezmshah (r. 1097–1127), thus initiating a line of rulers who would oversee the province of Khwarezm and subsequently the Khwarezmian Empire for over 130 years.[14]

Initially Arslantigin's son Atsiz remained loyal to his Saljuq overlords, but as their power began to wane he become increasingly independence. In 1141–42 he rebelled against Saljuq Sultan Sanjar (r. 1118–57), but he was twice defeated in battle.[15] He remained a vassal of the Sultan, while managing to retain nominal control of Khwarezm. Around this time the Qara Khitai, the non-Islamic invaders from the east whose incursion into the region we have already mentioned, impinged on Khwarezm and they, like the Saljuqs, demanded tribute from the Khwarezmshah. Atsiz's son Arslan became Khwarezmshah in 1156. A year later the great Saljuq Sultan Sanjar died and Saljuq power in the province of Khwarezm ebbed away. The Khwarezmshah Arslan still paid tribute to the Qara Khitai, but he had a much freer hand with the decline of the Saljuqs, and in 1158 he occupied Bukhara in Mawarannahr, then controlled by a Turkish dynasty know as the Qarakhanids.

The Qarakhanids were the first Muslim Turkic dynasty to rule in Inner Asia.[16] Their origins are obscure, but it appears that sometime in the ninth century a confederation of tribes coalesced around the Qarluq, who themselves were a shard thrown off from the disintegration of the Western Turkic Khaganate in the middle of the seventh century.[17] The Qarluq and other tribes of the confederation inhabited the steppes north of the Syr Darya, the foothills of the Tian Shan, and the western Tarim Basin in what is now Kazakhstan, Kyrgyzstan, and Xinjiang Province of China. Sometime in the middle of the tenth century Satuq Bughra (died c. 955), the son or perhaps nephew of the Qarakhanid khan at the time, was converted to Islam. Mass conversions followed, and the entire Qarakhanid confederation was soon Islamized. Their territorial ambitions fired by religious fervor, they expanded eastward, conquering the Buddhist city of Khotan, on the southern edge of the Tarim Basin, and westward into Mawarannahr. By 999 A.D. they had ousted the Samanids, the last Persian dynasty to rule north of the Amu Darya, and took undisputed control of Mawarannahr. The eastern Qarakhanids, based in Balasaghun near Tolmak in current-day Kyrgyzstan, and later in Kashgar, in current-day Xinjiang Province, China, were soon feuding with the western Qarakhanids, based in Samarkand, and in the 1140s two independent states emerged, the Eastern Qarakhanid Khanate and the Western Qarakhanid Khanate.

Both khanates were soon threatened by the rise of the Saljuqs to the south. Saljuq armies attacked Mawarannahr repeatedly in the 1170s and 1180s and in 1189 the Saljuq Sultan Malik Shah finally conquered the Western Qarakhanid Khanate, turning it into a vassal state. The Eastern Khanate fell to the Saljuqs not long afterwards. Both khanates retained nominal control of their territories but were now forced to recognize the Saljuqs as their suzerains and pay tribute to them. Then in the 1130s the infidel Qara Khitai from the East erupted onto the scene and quickly subdued the Eastern Qarakhanid Khanate, turning Balasaghun into their own capital and territorial base. In 1137 the Qara Khitai flooded westward into the territories of the Western Qarakhanid Khanate and seized Khujand on the upper Syr Darya River. Then they invaded Mawarannahr, and in 1141 they inflicted a crushing defeat on the forces of Sultan Sanjar at Qatwan near Samarkand This historic battle spelled the end of Saljuq suzerainty over the Qarakhanids, and for the next sixty odd years the Qarakhanids served as the vassals of the infidel Qara Khitai.

The Khwarezmshah Arslan, himself a vassal of Qara Khitai, made forays against the Qarakhanids of Mawarannahr, apparently with the acquiescence of the Qara Khitai, who presumably did not care who controlled the region as long whoever did continued to pay them tribute. Bukhara was captured by the Khwarezmshah in 1158 but he was soon forced to retreat. Mawarannahr remained in the hands of the Qarakhanids, with the Qara Khitai as their suzerains. Khwarezmshah Arslan's invasion of Khorasan, the former territory of the Saljuqs (modern-day Turkmenistan, northeastern Iran, and western Afghanistan), then controlled by the Ghurids, was also inconclusive. Despite these setbacks, it was clear that the Khwarezmshahs were becoming dominant players in Inner Asia during the latter half of the twelfth century.[18]

Arslan's successor, Tekesh (r. 1172-1200), continued the expansionist policies of his father while still recognizing the suzerainty of the Qara Khitai. In 1182 and perhaps again in 1198 he attacked Bukhara, hoping to replace the Qarakhanids there, but he too was apparently unable to hold the city for long.[19] He was more successful in the west. In 1192 Tekesh attacked Rayy (near current-day Tehran), one of the leading cities of Iraq-i Ajam (northwest Iran) and claimed much of the province for himself. In 1194 he defeated and killed one of the last great Saljuq sultans, Toghrul III (r. 1174–1194), cementing his hold on large portions of Iraq-i Ajam.

In western Khorasan (current-day eastern Iran and Turkmenistan), Tekesh was opposed by his renegade brother Soltan Shah, who had claimed the region as his own and may have intended to use it as a power base from which to attack Khwarezm. This scheme was forestalled in 1192, when the forces of Soltan Shah were defeated by the Ghurids, a then rising power in the region, in a battle near Merv, in current-day Turkmenistan. Soltan Shah himself was captured, and the Ghurids took control of western Khorasan.

The Ghurids were an Islamic dynasty, apparently of eastern Iranian origins, who were centered upon the province of Gur in the heartland of current-day Afghanistan. They liked to claim that they had received Islam directly from Ali, the Prophet's son-in-law, and that they had been given the province of Gur by the Abbasid Caliph Harun al-Rasid, he of *A Thousand and One Arabian Night* fame. These tales were no doubt apocryphal, concocted after the fact to burnish their credentials. Historical sources indicate that they were still pagans in the early eleventh century.[20] Their origins can be traced to a few charismatic chieftains who, in the great tradition of Inner Asian nomadic empires, were able to forge a coalition of tribes into a formidable if invariably short-lived military machine. Their rise to power outside of Gur itself was abetted by the power vacuum created in Inner Asia by the decline of the Saljuq Empire around the middle of the twelfth century. By the end of the twelfth century they had conquered a huge swath of territory from the Caspian Sea in the west to northern India in the east.

Caliph an-Nasir in Baghdad was initially alarmed by the incursions of these wild tribesmen from Gur into western Khorasan and central Iran, and he backed Tekesh's attempts at reining them in.[21] However, after Tekesh had established himself in Iraq-i Ajam in 1192, it was the Khwarezmians who appeared to pose the greater threat to the Caliphate. Meanwhile, the Ghurids were wooing the Caliph. Relatively recent converts to Islam—despite their claims to the contrary—they sought legitimacy by becoming stanch defenders of Sunnism, and they actively sought out the support and approval of the Caliphate in Baghdad.[22]

The Caliph an-Nasir now saw the Ghurids as a useful tool for halting the advances the Khwarezmshah Tekesh, who was already in Iraq-i Ajam, on the western edge of the Iranian Plateau, and after 1192 may have set his sights on the Abbasid Caliphate in Baghdad. Indeed, the Khwarezmshah Tekesh was poised to sweep off the Iranian Plateau and attack Baghdad when he died in 1200.[23]

To aid in his conquest of Iraq-i Ajam and the struggle in Khorasan, Tekesh had sought the aid of the Qangli and other tribesmen of the Kipchaq confederation, who nomadized around the Aral Sea to the north of the province of Khwarezm. To cement his relationship with these tribesmen he married a Qangli princess who was a member of the Bayaut clan and the daughter of a khan named Janski.[24] According to Juvaini, she was an "Ajami"—a barbarian or someone of non-Muslim birth.[25] As the

Khwarezmshah Tekesh's wife, she assumed the title of Terken Khatan. Although the addition of the Qangli to his realm strengthened the Khwarezmshah's hand militarily, they proved to be ambivalent allies. Their loyalty appeared to be to their kinsman Terken Khatan and not to her husband, the Khwarezmshah, a predilection that the ever-increasingly ambitious queen did little if anything to discourage.[26] Moreover, many of these nomads now nominally allied with the Khwarezmshah still adhered to the ancient shamanic beliefs of the steppe, and while they proved to be fierce and effective warriors, they soon found themselves at odds with the Islamic peoples of Khorasan and other areas that Tekesh invaded. "Mercy and compassion were far removed from their hearts," intones Juvaini, "Wherever they passed by, that country was laid in ruins and the people took refuge in their strongholds. And indeed it was their cruelty, violence, and wickedness that brought about the downfall of the Sultan's dynasty."[27] It was this behavior that had earned their nominal commander-in-chief, the Khwarezmshah Tekesh, the abiding hatred of the people of Khorasan and Iraq-i Ajam. Following his death, the people of Iraq-i Ajam revolted and expelled the despised Khwarezmians. It would eventually fall to Tekesh's son Ala al-Din Mohammad to retake Iraq-i Ajam.[28]

Ala al-Din Mohammad, the Khwarezmshah who would rule Khwarezmia at the time of the Mongol invasion, was the second son of Khwarezmshah Tekesh and his wife Terken Khatan.[29] The Khwarezmshah Mohammad spent the first years of his reign feuding with his nephew Hendu Khan, son of his older brother Malikshah, who had apparently died sometime before to 1200. Hendu Khan had allied himself with the Ghurids in Khorasan, perhaps in the belief that they could help him overthrow his uncle and put him on the throne of Khwarezmia with the Ghurids as suzerains.

In 1203 the Khwarezmshah went on the offensive and retook Merv and other cities in northern Khorasan from Hendu Khan and his Ghurid allies; however, a year later the Ghurid Sultan Moezz-al-din Muhammad invaded Khwarezmia and almost captured the Khwarezmian capital of Gurganj before being driven back. Ghurid power began to wane, and by 1206 they had ceded control of all of Khorasan except for the city of Herat to the Khwarezmshah. That same year Sultan Moezz-al-din Muhammad died, and the Ghurid empire, founded upon the charisma of its leaders, died with him. One of the few reminders of this dynasty, which once ruled from the Caspian Sea to northern India, is the 214-foot high Minaret of Jam, built in 1190 during the florescence of the Ghurids. It can still be seen today by intrepid travelers in current-day Gur Province, Afghanistan.

The Khwarezmshah now ruled Khwarezm and Khorasan, but he was still forced to accept the onerous overrule of the Qara Khitai. He was particular galled by the amount of tribute that he was forced to pay to the Qara Khitai in accordance with his predecessors' acceptance of them as suzerains. "Year after year," Juvaini moans, "the ambassadors of Khitai would come and he would pay that tribute, writhing with grief thereat and seeking a pretext for breaking the treaty." Finally fed up with the "contemptuous behaviour of Khitayan envoys and ambassadors," the Khwarezmshah had one of them "crushed to pieces" and his body disposed of in a river.[30] Clearly a showdown with Qara Khitai was in the offing.

The Qarakhanids in Mawarannahr had also grown weary of their Qara Khitai suzerains. They now looked to the Khwarezmshah for relief, hoping that he would unite with them against the infidels. Apparently they even offered to accept the suzerainty of the Khwarezmshah, who was after all a Muslim like themselves, provided that he could expel the infidel Qara Khitai from Mawarannahr. According to al-Athir, the Qarakhanid ruler Othman, vassal of the Qara Khitai in Bukhara and Samarkand, had "become recalcitrant and tired of infidels wielding authority over Muslims." Othman thereupon entreated the Khwarezmshah:

> "God (great and glorious is He), because of the extensive kingdom and numerous troops he has given you, has made it your duty to deliver the Muslims and their lands from the infidel hands and rescue them from the tyranny over their lands and possessions which they endure. We will cooperate with you to fight the Qarakhitay and will bring to you what we now bring to them."[31]

Juvaini sang a similar tune:

> the notables and chief men of Transoxiania [Mawarannahr] dispatched letter after letter to the Sultan [Khwarezmshah] calling upon him to turn in that direction and cleanse that region from the oppression of the Khitayan tyrants; for they were weary of yielding obedience to idol-worshippers . . .

Among the disgruntled notables of Mawarannahr Juvaini calls out "especially the people of Bukhara."[32]

It was on Bukhara that the Khwarezmshah moved first. Although Bukhara was nominally under the control of the Qarakhanids, who ultimately reported to the Qara Khitai, the city was actually ruled by the *sadrs* (religious leaders) belonging to the rich and powerful Borkan family. This old and distinguished clan traced its ancestry back to Arab settlers who had migrated to Merv, in Khorasan, back during the time of the fourth caliph Omar b. al-Khattab (r. 634–644). Apparently the first member of the family to live in Bukhara was Abd-al-Aziz b. Maza, a famous religious scholar who was known as "the second Abu Hanifa", Abu Hanifa being the founder of the Hanafite school of Sunni jurisprudence. In 1102 the Saljuq Sultan Sanjar, who had just imposed his suzerainty over the Qarakhanids, appointed Abd-al-Aziz b. Maza as the *sadr* of Bukhara. The Sultan also gave the imam one of his sisters as a wife. The powerful position of *sadr* was passed down through the family and eventually enabled the Borkans to extend their influence beyond the sphere of purely religious activities. They became owners of huge estates and other business interests, and they acted as more or less independent princes. By the beginning of the thirteenth century they were seen by many as oppressive and tyrannical overlords. The *sadr* in the early 1200s, Mohammad II b. Ahmad, also acted as a collector of tribute for the Qara Khitai and had managed to amass enormous wealth and political influence. It was said that he maintained at his own expense a school of 6,000 *faqihs* (experts in Islamic jurisprudence), and at least a hundred camels were required just to carry his personal baggage when he traveled. While on the way to Mecca on a pilgrimage he stopped in Baghdad, where he was received with great honor as the *de facto* ruler of Bukhara, but later on in Mecca his arrogant and ostentatious behavior earned him the nickname *Sadr-Jahannam* (Pillar of Hell), a play of words on his actual title, *Sadr-Jahan* (Pillar of the World).[33]

Othman now sought the Khwarezmshah's help in ousting the Borhans and their patrons, the Qara Khitai. The Khwarezmshah, however, did not entirely trust Othman—as events would show his doubts were more than justified—and he demanded that some of "the leading citizens of Bukhara and Samarqand" be sent to Khwarezm as hostages to ensure that the Qarakhanid ruler kept his end of the bargain.[34] This Othman agreed to. Before the Khwarezmshah himself could act against the Qara Khitai, however, the people of Bukhara, having grown tired of the more immediate impositions of the Borkan family *sadrs*, rose up against their perceived oppressors. The insurrection was led by a man named Sanjar, who was said to be the son of a shield-seller in the market. Although some sources paint Sanjar as a freedom fighter leading a populist uprising, Juvaini, perhaps not surprisingly siding with the *sadrs*, describes him as a ruffian who "had seen fit to treat with contempt and contumely those to whom respect and honour were due." He even claims that a Bukhara wit roasted Sanjar with this line:

> Kingship and a throne are not fitting for one whose
> father used to sell shields.[35]

In 1207 the Khwarezmshah crossed the Amu Darya and marched on Bukhara, determined to take it back from the Qara Khitai and the rabble under Sanjar who had raised the banner of insurrection. According to Juvaini the people of Bukhara welcomed the intervention of the Khwarezmshah: "the inhabitants were engulfed in the effects of his all-embracing justice and overflowing mercy and the whole area was made to blossom with the report of his copious equity . . ." He adds that Sanjar received a suitable punishment but does not say what it was. Other sources, painting a less benign picture, suggest that while overthrowing the Qara Khitai in the city the Khwarezmshah also crushed the Borkan family who had long dominated local society. The record is unclear, but their vast estates and other holdings may have been expropriated by Khwarezmians loyal to the Khwarezmshah. Sanjar was not executed, according to one account, but instead was sent, apparently unharmed, to Khwarezm, where he could not cause any more mischief. To consolidate his power in the city, the Khwarezmshah then rebuilt the Citadel, which had been destroyed in earlier fighting, and repaired the city walls.[36] These would be the fortifications that Chingis Khan and the Mongols would face when they arrived outside Bukhara in 1220.

The Khwarezmshah was now in control of Bukhara, one of the jewels of Mawarannahr, but he had accomplished this at the expense of the Borkan family and its *sadrs*. Thus he had alienated not only the rich landowners and local magnates but also the leading religious lights of the area. As usual, the ordinary people fatalistically accepted their new ruler; there is no record as to whether their lives actually changed in any way under the new regime. Likely life for them went on pretty much as before. But it is very doubtful that they felt any particular loyalty to the Khwarezmshah. He was, after all, just one of a long line of potentates stretching back over a thousand years who had ruled over them. Thirteen years later it would be the Mongols.

ↄ৲

The Khwarezmshah now turned his attention on Samarkand. Although Othman, the Qarakhanid ruler of the city, had asked for the aid of the Khwarezmshah in his struggle against the Qara Khitai, he still believed that he had the upper hand in the relationship. He retained the higher title of *Ulugh Sultan al-Saladin*, while the Khwarezmshah remained a mere *Sultan*. After taking Bukhara the Khwarezmshah had returned to Khwarezm, and from there he may have proceeded to Khorasan. In any case, he appointed governors to various of the recently conquered cities in the region and took care of various other administrative matters.[37] These details taken car of, he recrossed the Amu Darya and marched on Samarkand. His initial encounters with the Qara Khitai in the Samarkand region ended in a draw. "Many battles and skirmishes ensued between them," al-Athir tells us, "some of them the Khwarazm Shah won and some he lost."[38] Then the Khwarezmshah had to return to Khorasan to deal with revolts in Herat, Nishapur, and other cities. The chronology of events is extremely murky, but it would appear that Othman used the absence of the Khwarezmshah from Mawarannahr as an excuse to switched back his allegiance to the Gür Khan of the Qara Khitai. This is exactly what the Khwarezmshah had feared, and why he had taken hostages to ensure Othman's loyalty. What now happened to the hostages from Bukhara and Samarkand being held in Khwarezm is not recorded. Othman also had his eye on one of the Gür Khan's daughters, and this may have played a role in his defection. Othman was quite the lady's man, and according to al-Athir, he "was one of the most handsome of men and the people ... used to gather to look at him."[39] His request for the hand of the Gür Khan's daughter was rebuffed, however, and in a fit of pique the jilted Othman decided to return to the embrace of the Khwarezmshah. The chastised Othman was now forced to accept the Khwarezmshah as his suzerain, an admission of his lowered status.

In the summer of 1210 the Khwarezmshah finally confronted the Qara Khitai head-on. In August or September he led a huge army against the Qara Khitai general Tayangu, as related earlier. According to al-Athir, the Qara Khitai "suffered a terrible defeat and unknown numbers of them were killed or taken prisoner."[40] The Khwarezmshah then moved through Mawarannahr and "conquered it, city by city, region by region," according to al-Athir. With Mawarannahr added to his burgeoning empire the Khwarezmshah returned to Khwarezm. In his entourage was Othman, who while in Khwarezm took as a bride the Khwarezmshah's daughter Khan

Sultan, apparently a compensation prize for his loyalty. Presumably this also assuaged his bruised feelings after his rejection as the Gür Khan's son-in-law.

Othman then returned to Samarkand, but apparently the Khwarezm-shah still did not entirely trust him, because he appointed a prefect to oversee and rein in his notoriously see-sawing son-in-law. His suspicions were well-founded. The Khwarezmians occupying the city had quickly made themselves seriously unpopular by their domineering treatment of the local populace. Taking this as his cue, Othman yet again allied himself with the down but not yet out Gür Khan, who had sent an army to accept the surrender of the city. Othman then unleashed a vicious pogrom on the Khwarezmians in the city. "He ordered the killing of all the Khwarazmians in Samarqand", according to al-Athir, "both old and new residents, and seized Khwarazm Shah's men and would cut individuals into two pieces and hang them up in the markets just as a butcher hangs up meat."[41] According to some sources, at this time the Qarakhanid Lothario may have also married the daughter of the Gür Khan who had earlier spurned him.[42] Sultan Khan, the daughter of the Khwarezmshah whom he had recently married, had meanwhile holed up in the Citadel with the women in her retinue. Othman went to the Citadel intending to kill her, but he found the gates locked. Sultan Khan sent out a message: "'I am a woman. To kill such as me is wicked. I have done nothing to you that merits your acting so. Perhaps if you leave me alone, that will be better for you in the end. Fear God in what you do to me.'" He spared Sultan Khan's life but kept her locked up in the Citadel and surrounded by guards.

When the Khwarezmshah heard about the fall of Samarkand to the Qara Khitai and the massacre of his subjects, "all Hell broke loose," to use al-Athir's evocative phrase. Such was his anger that he ordered that all strangers in Khwarezm be arrested and killed. His mother put a stop to this, pointing out that there were people from all the regions of the earth in Khwarezm and they were hardly to be blamed for the actions of Othman and the Qara Khitai. Then the Khwarezmshah ordered that all the people from Samarkand be killed. His mother also countermanded this order.

Finally cooling off, the Khwarezmshah sent off separate detachments of troops to Samarkand, ordering them all to congregate before the city. After a huge army had been assembled, the Khwarezmshah himself appeared at the walls of the city. He dispatched a message to Othman stating:

"You have done what no Muslim has ever done. You have sanctioned the shedding of Muslim blood that no man of sense, either Muslim or infidel, would permit. God has forgiven what is over and done. Leave your lands and depart wherever you wish."

Despite all of Othman's betrayals, the Khwarezmshah was giving him one last chance to save his own life. The recalcitrant Qarakhanid ruler spurned this final offer, replying, "'I shall not leave and I shall do what I like.'"

The attack on the city began. "Ladders were set up against the walls", according to al-Athir, "and in no time at all they had taken the city." Acting on the advice of one of his generals, the Khwarezmshah ordered a detachment of troops to proceed straight to the foreign quarter where visiting merchants stayed and protect it against plunder, since these people had nothing to do with the previous slaughter of the Khwarezmians. According to al-Athir, not one foreigner died in the ensuing sack of the city. The rest of the city was looted and plundered for three days. Al-Athir claims 200,000 people were slaughtered.

That left the Citadel where Othman had taken refuge. Cornered in his lair, he now wanted to accept terms of surrender in exchange for his life. "'For you there are no terms from me,'" replied the out-of-patience Khwarezmshah. The Citadel was attacked and soon fell. Othman, taken prisoner, fell on his knees before the Khwarezmshah and begged for mercy, but his entreaties were ignored. He was summarily executed, ending at last his numerous oscillations. Many of his relatives and other high-ranking Qarakhanids in Samarkand met the same end. Sadly, al-Athir is silent about the fate of Sultan Khan, Othman's erstwhile wife and the Khwarezmshah's daughter.

With the fall of Othman and Samarkand other Qarakhanids princes quickly swore allegiance to the Khwarezmshah. The Qara Khitai themselves had still not been defeated, but most if not if not all of Mawarannahr and Khorasan now fell within his orbit. In official documents the Khwarezmshah now styled himself "The Second Iskandar" (the second Alexander the Great) and openly compared himself to the Saljuq Sultan Sanjar, another Inner Asian potentate who had acquired a vast empire. As an indication that he was no longer just the ruler of the province of Khwarezm, 1212 he moved the capital of his burgeoning empire from Gurganj in Khwarezm to Samarkand in Mawarannahr. He had gained control of the city in a bloodbath, however, and undoubtably there were many among the city's residents who had no love for the Khwarezmshah. Their ultimate loyalty to him would be severely tested when Chingis Khan and the Mongols arrived at the city's walls eight years later.

By moving the capital of his burgeoning empire from Gurganj in Khwarezm to Samarkand the Khwarezmshah was also able to get out from under the thumb of his domineering mother, Terken Khatan, who had her own power base in the former Khwarezmian capital. During the life of her husband, the Khwarezmshah Tekesh, she had carefully nurtured ties with her fellow Qangli tribesmen, who were a powerful contingent in the Khwarezmian army, and by the time he died she was powerful enough to assume the role of Queen Mother and rule alongside her son Ala al-Din Mohammed, the new Khwarezmshah.[43] Assuming the grandiose title of "The Inviolate One of the Present World and of Religion, Ulug Terken, Queen of the Women of the Worlds", she maintained her own court and administration, set up fiefdoms of her own, and issued orders in her own name. Her personal motto was "I Seek Refuge in God Alone". Later on she would even drop the Queen business and assume the gender-free title of "Lord of the World".[44] In the opinion of the historian Nasavi, who may have known her personally, Terken Khatan was a woman of sound judgment who could administer justice fairly, but when provoked she was capable of having people killed without the slightest remorse.[45]

She cultivated her power base by doling out large estates and governorships to Qangli military commanders, thus assuring their loyalty to her and not to her son, the Khwarezmshah. As we have, her nephew, the Inanch Khan, was the governor of Otrar, a post for which he was to end up paying dearly. Juvaini maintains that from her position of independence she was able to thoroughly dominate her son, controlling his finances and giving orders to officials he had appointed. Moreover, she allegedly indulged in "secret revelries," although the prim and proper Juvaini does not go into detail about this.[46] Nasavi concurs that the Khwarezmshah never contradicted her in any matter and sought her approval for any action that he planned to undertake. It would not take Chingis Khan's intelligence network long to sniff out the rifts in the royal family, and he would eventually attempt to exploit them for his own purposes.

As we have seen, by the early 1190s the Khwarezmshah Tekesh had occupied Khorasan, and he appeared to be the coming power in Inner Asia. Around this time, the Caliph an-Nasir in Baghdad was attempting to throw off the last vestiges of Saljuq domination of the Caliphate and once again become the uncontested religious and political leader of the Islamic geosphere. Since his ascension to Caliph in 1180 the Saljuqs had weakened considerably, and an-Nasir now saw the opportunity to get rid of them for good, creating instead a theocracy with him at the helm. With this in mind, the Caliph appealed to the Khwarezmshah for assistance in his struggle with the Saljuqs. In response, the Khwarezmshah invaded Iraq-i Ajam (northwest Iran) and captured the cities of Rayy (near current day Tehran) and Hamadan. In 1994 the Saljuq Sultan Toghrul III was taken prisoner and later on executed, thus the bringing to an end the Saljuq dynasty.[47]

With the Saljuqs gone a power vacuum was created, and Tekesh intended to fill it himself. He fired off a message to Baghdad demanding that the Caliph now recognize him as Sultan and political ruler of the Islamic geosphere. In effect, the Saljuqs were to be replaced by the Khwarezmshahs, with the Caliph once again the puppet of political and military leaders. This is not at all what the Caliph an-Nasir had in mind. His goal was to be both the religious and political leader of a newly revitalized Caliphate. Relations between the two potentates quickly cooled; the Khwarezmshah, once the Caliph's faithful defender against the Saljuqs, now became his sworn enemy. In the late 1190s the Khwarezmshah Tekesh demanded that the name of his son Muhammad—the future Khwarezmshah—be included in the sermon at the Friday Mosque in Baghdad.[48] By tradition, the mention of his name would have implied that the Caliph recognized the Khwarezmshahs as suzerains. Recognition of the Khwarezmshahs as the political rulers of the Caliphate was not forthcoming, and the Khwarezmshah Tekesh was planning a military assault on Baghdad to right the perceived wrong when he died in 1200.[49]

The newly installed Khwarezmshah Muhammad's attention was focused elsewhere during the early years of his reign, especially in fending off his nephew Soltan Shah and the Ghurids in Khorasan, and he did not have time for further advances on Baghdad. But he had certainly not forgotten his father's ambitions to rule the Caliphate, and the Caliph had certainly not forgotten about the Khwarezmshah. According to Juvaini, the Caliph sent a stream of messages to the Qara Khitai and the Ghurids imploring them to attack the Khwarezmshah, who he now saw as the biggest threat to the Caliphate.[50] After the capture of Ghurid-held cities in Khorasan some of these messages came to light and eventually fell into the Khwarezmshah's hands. Naturally he was appalled by the perfidy of the Caliph, who his own father had helped free from the domination of the Saljuqs. Moreover, the Caliph may have approached the Assassin sect based at Alamut in Persia with the goal having the Khwarezmshah assassinated.[51] The leader of the Assassins at the time, Jalal ad-Din (not to be confused with the Khwarezmshah's son Jalal ad-Din), had originally thrown in his lot with the Khwarezmshah, and even had prayers recited in the Khwarezmshah's name in the territories which he controlled. The ever vacillating Jalal ad-Din soon switched sides and backed an-Nasir, going so far as to arrange the assassination of an emir who had rebelled against the Caliph and aligned himself with the Khwarezmshah.[52] That a Sunni Caliph would conspire with the Assassins, an offshoot of the heretical Ismailis, to kill a Sunni potentate and his followers further stoked the feud between an-Nasir and the Khwarezmshah.

The Caliph an-Nasir may have been involved in even more nefarious schemes. Dark rumors were circulating that an-Nasir had initiated contact with Chingis Khan, beseeching him to attack the Khwarezmian Empire and overthrow the Khwarezmshah, thus eliminating the Caliph's main rival for power in the Islamic geosphere. Al-Athir refers to this when he says, "There is another report concerning the reason for their [the Mongols] irruption into the lands of Islam, such as is not to be mentioned within the covers of books."[53] Apparently he considered the idea of any kind of entente or cooperation between the Caliph and the infidel Mongols to be too scandalous to even mention directly. The Khwarezmshah's son Jalal-ad-Din would, much later, stoke this controversy by claiming that the Caliph "was the reason for the death of my father and the infidels coming to the lands and we have found his letters to the Khitay [he meant the Mongols] and orders to reward them with lands, horses, and robes of honour."

Admittedly, it is unclear when these alleged overtures were first made. As we have seen, Jochi had made a foray against the Khwarezmshah in 1216, and the Caliph may have decided to sound out the Mongols about further attacks on the Khwarezmshah's domains shortly after this. If not, word that the Mongol army was approaching Mawarannahr in 1218 may have motivated the Caliph to encourage the invasion and promise Chingis Khan unspecified rewards if it was successful. If these accusations against the Caliph were true (other sources question their accuracy), then presumably he did not consider the nomads from Mongolia a threat to the Abbasid Caliphate itself. If this was the case, then the Abbasid Caliph had made a miscalculation of inestimable proportions.[54] When the

Caliphate did eventually fall to the Mongols in 1258 there would be those who would view it as God's punishment for consorting with the Mongols in the first place.[55]

By the beginning of 1217 the Khwarezmshah was at the peak of his power. The Khwarezmian Empire stretched from the Tian Shan and the Pamirs in the east to the western edge of the Iranian Plateau, and from the Syr Darya in the north to the Persian Gulf in the south, an area encompassing current-day Uzbekistan, Kyrgyzstan, Tajikistan, Turkmenistan, western Afghanistan, southern Kazakhstan, and most of Iran. The only entity standing in the way of dominating the entire Islamic geosphere in Asia and the Near East was the Abbasid Caliph an-Nasir in Baghdad. Dusting off the plans of his father to invade Mesopotamia, the Khwarezmshah now decided that he would seize control of the Caliphate for himself. There were obstacles to this grandiose scheme. For one, the vast majority of the population of his empire were Sunnis, and they still felt at least a residual loyalty to the Caliph, the spiritual leader of the Sunni-Islamic geosphere. In contrast, the loyalty of many of his subjects to the Khwarezmshah was by no means a given. To counter the Caliph's influence the Khwarezm-shah now came up with a novel assertion. Acting out of what appeared to be purely self-serving motives, the Khwarezmshah, hitherto a Sunni, decided to adopt a pro-Shiite policy to counter the Sunni Caliph. He connived to have certain pliable religious authorities of his empire declare that the sitting Caliph, the Sunni an-Nasir, was not in fact the reigning Caliph because he was not a member of the House of Ali, the progenitor of the Shiite sect. In his stead, the Khwarezmshah nominated the *Sayyid* Ala al-Mulk Tirmidhi, a Shiite, as the Anti-Caliph.[56] He himself would install this new Caliph in Baghdad, and because Ala al-Mulk Tirmidh was his puppet, the Khwarezmshah would then become the effective leader of the Islamic geosphere. Many of the orthodox Sunni *ulema* in the Khwarezmshah's realm were no doubt outraged by this cynical and opportunistic scheme to overthrow the sitting Caliph. Despite this, the Khwarezmshah was finally able to garner enough support to mount an assault on Baghdad. Using Iraq-i Ajam as a springboard, the Khwarezm-shah marched toward Mesopotamia in the fall of 1217. Unprecedented snowfall in the Zagros Mountains on the western edge of the Iranian Plateau halted his advance, and his armies were forced to turn back. The invasion of Mesopotamia was a complete failure, and an-Nasir remained as the Caliph in Baghdad.

The chronology is uncertain, but somewhere around this time the Khwarezmshah had with the connivance of Gayer Khan instigated the murder of the envoys and Mongol-sponsored traders in Otrar. He also learned that a Mongol army of some 20,000 men led by a general named Jebe had suddenly appeared in Qara Khitai territories just east of his own realm. Jebe had tracked down and killed the faux-Gür Khan Khüchüleg and was now in control of the former Qara Khitai domains bordering his own. At some point the Khwarezmshah must have realized that war with the Mongols was inevitable. Out beyond the eastern horizon the Mongols were gathering, and it was only a matter of time until they flooded into Mawarannahr.

According to al-Athir, the Khwarezmshah had sought the advice of his military and political advisors about what to do in the case of war with Chingis Khan even before the arrival in Bukhara of the last Mongolian embassy led by Ibn Kafaraj Bughra to protest the murder of the traders and envoys in Otrar.[57] If this report was true, then he had probably concluded that the massacre in Otrar and Jebe's occupation of lands co-terminous with his own empire had made war inevitable. He summoned one of his chief advisors, Shihab ad-Din Khiwaqi, and asked for advice on how to counter the Mongol threat. According to al-Athir, Shihab ad-Din Khiwaqi was "a lawyer, a man of learning, who was held in great esteem by him [the Khwarezmshah], and whose advice he did not contradict." Shihab ad-Din Khiwaqi replied:

> "Your armies are numerous. We should write to the provinces and gather the troops. Let the call to arms be general, for it is the duty of all Muslims to aid you with money and with their persons. Then let us go with all the troops to the bank of the Jaxartes [Syr Darya] . . . We shall be there and when the enemy comes, having traveled a long distance, we shall meet him, having rested, while he and his troops will have been affected by exhaustion and fatigue."[58]

The Khwarezmshah had, of course, just attempted to unseat the Sunni Caliph in Baghdad, so it was uncertain just how willing the Sunni Muslims in the Khwarezmshah's realm were to offer up their money and persons to him. Also, all the Khwarezmshah's generals, many of whom belonged to the Qangli aristocracy loyal to his mother, would be gathered together in one place along with all their soldiers. It was not outside the realm of possibility that the assembled Qangli emirs would stage a coup d'etat and overthrow their nominal commander-and-chief.

With those doubts in mind, the Khwarezmshah convened a meeting of other councilors in his court and questioned them. They dismissed Shihab ad-Din Khiwaqi's proposal and offered one of their own. "'The best plan is to allow them [the Mongols] to cross the Jaxartes to us and journey through the mountains and narrow passes, for they are ignorant of our routes, while we know them. Then we shall overwhelm them and destroy them. None of them shall escape."'[59]

The Khwarezmshah dismissed both proposals. He finally decided not to confront the Mongols directly in Mawarannahr but to leave large garrisons in the major cities, essentially forfeiting the countryside. This way his generals would be separated, each in a city that they would have to defend if for no other reason than to save their own skins, and would not be able to unite against him. That they would also not be able to unite against the Mongols apparently escaped his notice.

According to al-Athir, he sent 20,000 troops to Bukhara and 50,000 to Samarkand with orders to prepare the cities against a siege. Nasavi claims that he sent 20,000 soldiers to Otrar, where it was expected that Chingis Khan would strike first; 30,000 to Bukhara; 40,000 to Samarkand; 10,000 to Shahrisabr, south of Samarkand, and smaller detachments to other important cities.[60] Al-Athir further avers that at this time the Khwarezmshah himself decided to retire south of the Amu Darya. "Hold the cities to enable me to return to Khwarezm and Khorasan and gather troops, call on the aid of Muslims and return to you," he told his generals. According to al-Athir he then left for Balkh in Khorasan, south of Amu Darya, and set up a base camp there. Apparently he hoped to tie down the Mongols in protracted sieges of the cites and then after they were exhausted return from Khorasan with a large army and flush them out of Mawarannahr. That was the plan, anyhow.

It did not take long for cynics to suggest that the Khwarezmshah was simply abandoning Mawarannahr to its fate, and that he had neither the will nor the means to defend his empire from the Mongols. Nasavi would later lament:

> It turned out that the sultan himself had fled the battle and escaped on the Jayhun [Amu Darya] river. Had he stayed in his position . . . the sultan would have been at the head of the most numerous army anyone had ever heard of, but nothing can resist the will of God, who . . . has the power to overturn or transform all things, and to move empires from the hands of one leader to another. . .[61]

Juvaini, as we shall see, implies that the Khwarezmshah himself did not leave Mawarannahr until after the fall of Bukhara. In either case, he would throw Mawarannahr and the great cities of Bukhara and Samarkand to the wolves in a vain attempt to save his own skin. What could have reduced a man who had already carved out a huge empire for himself to such pusillanimous behavior? Something about the Mongols had clearly spooked the Khwarezmshah. We might look back to his first face-to-face encounter with the Mongols in 1216 when he and his son fought Jochi and a Mongol detachment north of the Syr Darya. At that time, according to Nasavi:

> A fear of these infidels was planted in the heart of the Sultan, and an estimation of their courage; if any one spoke of them before him, he said that he had never seen men as daring nor as steadfast in the throes of battle, or as skilled at giving blows with the point and edge of the sword."[62]

The Khwarezmshah may have even believed that God Himself had turned against him. According to one story widely circulated in Sufi circles, "'at the time when Chingiz Khan came out upon the land' some of the saints of that era 'saw the holy Khvaja Khizr, ahead of that band of obstinate apostates and was helping them; he was saying, 'o tribe of infidels, kill these evildoers!'" Khizr was—and is—believed to be a righteous servant of God who since the beginning of time has appeared throughout history to carry out His handiwork. In the Quran he is depicted as the teacher of the prophet Moses, he of Ten Commandments fame. In his great wisdom, Khizr is able to see beyond mere temporal considerations and ascertain the true wishes of God. The implication here is that the Khwarezmshah, and the orthodox Islamic society of Khwarezmia in general, had strayed far from the path of righteousness, and that it was God's will that they should suffer a severe chastisement. In a continuation of this story, the Khwarezmshah's son, Jalal-ad-Din, asks his father:

> why, when the whole world knew of his [the Khwarezmshah's] valor and power, and when he had governed Iran for twenty years with unchallenged authority, he was now fleeing from before a band of infidels and allowing the Muslims to fall into their hands; the father first replied, "My son, you do not hear what I hear," and when pressed, explained further, "Every time I arrange my ranks for battle, I hear a group of the men of the unseen world saying 'O infidels, kill the evildoers!' . . . fear and terror and dread overcome me. Forgive me, my son."

The story goes on:

"And it is related by those to whom hidden realities are unveiled and by the saints of the faith that they saw the people of God and the prophet Khizr in front of the army of Chingiz Khan, guiding that army. The discernment of the intelligent is struck dumb by this phenomenon, and the wisdom of the wise is rendered weak by this fact; but 'God does what He wishes and commands what He wills.'"[63]

These tales may have been apocryphal, but even if they are not literally true they reveal an underlying sense of fatalism that seems to have inflicted many people in Khwarezmia.

Jochi had led a relatively small contingent of troops against the Khwarezmshah back in 1216. Now 150,000 or so of these Mongols and their Turkish auxiliaries were poised to sweep down on Mawarannahr and the cities of Bukhara and Samarkand. At this crucial juncture the Khwarezmshah may well have believed that even God Himself had deserted him.

CHAPTER 5

THE MARCH FROM OTRAR
AND THE
FALL OF BUKHARA

FROM THEIR RALLYING POINT in the Seven Rivers Region the armies of Chingis Khan descended upon the city of Otrar. As noted, Nasavi stated that the Khwarezmshah sent 20,000 horsemen to defend the city. On the other hand, Juvaini claimed that the Khwarezmshah sent a commander named Qaracha Khass-Hajib to Otrar with 10,000 regular soldiers and also sent 50,000 troops from his auxiliary armies.[1] In any case, the city appeared to be well-defended, at least at first glance. The Gayer Khan had strengthened and reinforced the walls of the *Rabad* (outer city), the *Shahristan* (inner city), and the *Ark*, or citadel, and had laid in a vast store of weapons. Despite all this, when he climbed to the top of the city wall to view the arrival of the Mongol army, he "bit the back of his hand in amazement" at the "tossing sea of countless hosts and splendid troops" arrayed before him, according to Juvaini.[2] As Barthold has opined, the entire multitude may have numbered 150,000 men.[3]

The siege of Otrar probably began sometime in September of 1219. Chingis Khan soon realized that his entire army was not needed to take the city, and he may not have wanted to give the other cities of Mawarannahr more time to prepare their defenses. At some point he decided to split up his army. It is not clear if this took place before the investment of Otrar or after the city was surrounded and no escape possible for its defenders.[4] In any case, several *tümen* (a division numbering 10,000 troops), including a *tümen* of Uighur auxiliaries, under the command of his two middle sons Chagaadai and Ögedei were ordered to stay and invest Otrar. His oldest son Jochi and several *tümen* were dispatched down the Syr Darya River toward Jand and other cities. According to one account, half a *tü-*

men proceeded up the valley of the Syr Darya to the cities of Banakat and Khujand.[5] Chingis himself and his youngest and perhaps favorite son To-lui would lead the main body of the army to Bukhara, the city that rivaled Samarkand as the most important in Mawarannahr.

While still in the Otrar region, Chingis Khan received a surprise visit from Badr al-Din al-Amid, the civilian governor of the Otrar region (Gay-er Khan was the military governor). Soon it became apparent that Badr al-Din al-Amid wanted to defect. It seems that after the Khwarezmshah had seized control of Otrar from the Qarakhanids in 1210 or early 2011 he had executed Badr al-Din al-Amid's father, uncle, and various brothers and cousins for unspecified acts of malfeasance. Despite the transgressions of his family members, Badr al-Din al-Amid had been allowed to remain on as the civil governor of the city. He nursed a grudge against the Khwarezmshah, however, and he was understandably eager to avenge the murder of his relatives by siding with the Mongols who now appeared at the city's walls. According to Nasavi,

> He said to the khan, "You know that the Sultan is the person I hate most in this world because he executed many of my ancestors. If I had to sacrifice my life in order to take revenge on him, to be sure I would do so voluntarily. In any case, I have to inform you that this is a very powerful sultan. Do not delude yourself as to the measures he had taken in disseminating his troops in every direction, because he still has with him a considerable number of troops who will give him the ability to abandon his other soldiers. If he so desires, he can still assemble an army twice as large in his vast empire and lands. I advise you then to de-vise a strategy of making him suspect his own military commanders."[6]

Badr al-Din al-Amid proceeded to pour into Chingis Khan's ears tales of the strained relations between the Khwarezmshah and his mother Ter-ken Khatan. Putting their two heads together, they soon came up with a scheme to sow further dissension between mother and son. Badr al-Din al-Amid forged a number of letters purporting to come from army com-manders whose ultimate loyalty was to Terken Khatan. These letters were addressed to Chingis Khan. According the Nasavi:

> The letters said the following: "We have come from the lands of the Turks ... to make ourselves available to the sultan, because we wish to render service to his mother. We have given him assistance against all the lords of the lands so that he would be able to conquer, thanks to us, the lands, vanquish the pride of the princes, and subject the people to his judgement. But today, when the feelings of the sultan toward his

mother have changed, when he is ungrateful and rebellious against her, she asks us to abandon her son. As a result, we await your arrival to tell us your instructions."[7]

Chingis Khan then arranged for one of his courtesans to travel to the court of the Khwarezmshah in the guise of a deserter and present him with the damning letters, which she claimed to have stolen from the Mongol camp. Faced with what appeared to be evidence that some of his most trusted commanders were ready to desert to the Mongols, the Khwarezmshah "saw the world crumble before his eyes," according to Nasavi. "His zeal had weakened that he would be betrayed by those he had trusted."

The Khwarezmshah's worst fears seemed to have been confirmed. The commanders of his army, it appeared, were not loyal to him and were even ready to desert to the Mongols. In a further twist of the knife, Chingis Khan dispatched an emissary to Terken Khatan with a message reading, "you know how much your son has shown ingratitude for the cares you had bestowed upon him. In accordance with that, I wish to march against him with a number of amirs [commanders loyal to Terken Khatan]. If you accept this arrangement send me someone in whom you have complete confidence."[8] Whatever hopes there had been that the Khwarezmshah and his mother would bury their difference and present a united front against the Mongols were dashed by this masterful Mongol exercise in misinformation. The Khwarezmshah was now more isolated than ever.

At this point Chingis Khan may have received another emissary from a totally unexpected quarter. As mentioned earlier, Jalal ad-Din Hasan III, leader of the Assassins, an offshoot of the Ismaili sect deemed heretical by many mainstream Sunni Muslims, had rather unexpectedly allied himself with Sunni Caliph an-Nasir in the latter's ongoing feud with the Khwarezmshah. Apparently he then went one step further. According to Juvaini:

> They [the Ismailis] said that when the World-Emperor Chingiz Khan set out from Turkestan, before he came to the countries of Islam, Jalal-ad-Din had in secret sent couriers to him and written letters tendering his submission and allegiance. This was alleged by the Heretics and the truth is not clear, but this much is evident, that when the armies of the World-Conquering Emperor Chingiz Khan entered the countries of Islam, the first ruler on this side of the Oxus to send ambassadors, and present his duty, and accept allegiance was Jalal ad-Din.[9]

Thus it may have been that Jalal ad-Din Hasan's emissaries first approached Chingis Khan in Otrar. It is not altogether clear what Jalal ad-Din Hasan's motives were for this attempted rapprochement between the Assassins and the Mongols. He may have wanted to be on what he perceived to be the winning side in the upcoming war in Mawarannahr, or he may have simply harbored a personal grudge against the Khwarezm-shah. In any case, he died shortly after the Mongols conquered Mawarannahr—probably poisoned by his wives and one of his sisters—and no more was heard of an Assassin–Mongol alliance. Several decades later the two parties would become mortal enemies, and it was the Mongols who would finally end the Assassins' 150 year-long reign of terror in the Islam geosphere.

Leaving Chagaadai and Ögedei to invest Otrar, Chingis Khan and his youngest and perhaps favorite son Tolui led the main Mongol army southwest to Bukhara, the city that rivaled Samarkand as the most important in Mawarannahr. With them were Turkish auxiliaries who by then had sided with Chingis. "These fearless Turks," marveled Juvaini, "knew not clean from unclean [i.e., were not Muslims], and considered the bowl of war to be a basin of rich soup, and held a mouthful of sword to be a beaker of wine."[10] No mention is made in any of the sources about crossing the Syr Darya, usually an intimidating operation, which leads Barthold to opine that the river was frozen over by the time the Mongol divisions reached it, allowing them to cross over on the ice.[11] This could have occurred no earlier than late November or early December, giving credence to the claim that Chingis Khan had only left Otrar after the siege of the city was well underway.

The first major town that the Mongols encountered south of the Syr Darya was Zarnuq. "When the king of planets raised his banner on the eastern horizon [at sunrise, to the more prosaic-minded]," Chingis Khan and his army appeared before the city walls, according to Juvaini.[12] The inhabitants retired into the Citadel, closed the gates, and at first were determined to resist the Mongol attack. A man named Danishmand, either a commander of one of the Turkish auxiliary units or a Khwarezmian trader who had attached himself to Chingis's army, was sent into the city to talk some sense into the local panjandrums. After they threatened him with bodily harm, he shouted at them:

"I am . . . a Moslem and a son of a Moslem. Seeking God's pleasure I am come on an embassy to you, at the inflexible command of Chingiz-Khan, to draw you out of the whirlpool of destruction and the trough of blood . . . If you are incited to resist in any way, in an hour's time your citadel will be level ground and the plain a sea of blood. But if you listen to advice and exhortation with the ear of intelligence and consideration and become submissive and obedient to his command, your lives and property will remain in the stronghold of security."[13]

After this verbal assault the local dignitaries thought it wise to surrender. But they insisted that Danishmand be held hostage while they negotiated terms with Chingis. If any of them were harmed it would mean Danishmand's head. First they sent forth a delegation of factotums with gifts for the Mongol potentate. Chingis did not appreciate this gesture. He dispatched a message to the city fathers telling them to quit wasting time and to appear before him in person immediately. Upon receiving this summons, "a tremor of horror appeared on the limbs of these people," and they presented themselves to Chingis forthwith.[14] Without further ado he accepted their surrender and then ordered all the inhabitants to vacate the city. During a headcount young men were singled out and drafted as levies for siege work in the anticipated attack against Bukhara. Then, while the people of Zarnuq were encamped on the plains outside the city, the Citadel was leveled. Juvaini does not specifically say the abandoned city was looted, but presumably it was. Still, the inhabitants had escaped with their lives and whatever personal possessions they had managed to keep out of the hands of the Mongols. After the invaders left, they were free to return to what remained of their city. The relatively benign fate of Zarnuq led Chingis's soldiers, perhaps Turkish auxiliaries, since the words are Turkish, to nickname the town Qutlugh-Baligh ("Fortunate" or "Blessed" Town).[15]

To reach Bukhara from Zarnuq the Mongols now had to cross a fearsome stretch of the mostly waterless Kyzyl Kum Desert. Normally this would have been a daunting if not impossible march for a large army, but a Turkish caravan man in Zarnuq, apparently with a grudge of his own against the Khwarezmshah or perhaps in return for coin of the realm, showed Chingis a secret road from Zarnuq to Nur, the first city south of the desert. After crossing 150 or so miles of desert the Mongol army skirted around the western end of 100-mile long Lake Aidarkul and proceeded another twenty-five miles to Nur. Henceforth, the route from Zarnuq to Nur directly across the desert became known as the Khan's Road (Juvaini tells us that he himself traveled this road years later, in 1251.[16]) The belief of the Khwarezmshah's advisors that his army would have an advantage over the Mongols because of their knowledge of local roads and terrain proved false in this instance. At least some elements of the local populace were more than willing to assist the invading Mongols.

The ancient city of Nur (now Nurata), 210 miles southwest of Otrar, had long served as a strategic outpost on the northern borders of Mawaran-nahr, a gateway between the nomad-dominated deserts and steppe to the north and the cultivated lands of the Zerafshan River Basin to the south. The armies of Alexander the Great had arrived here in 327 B.C. (it is un-clear if the Greek adventurer himself visited here), and they either built a citadel or enlarged and strengthened an already existing citadel on a hill-top on the edge of the city. His men also built a network of underground water pipes, parts of which remain in use down to the present today. One of Alexander's generals died here and was buried near the base of the citadel, where his tomb can still be seen. The town was also famous for its prodigious *chasma*, or spring, at the base of the citadel. According to legend the spring was created when the Prophet Muhammad's son-in-law Ali struck the ground with this staff and water gushed forth. There is no record of Ali ever visiting Mawarannahr, and this story is no doubt apocryphal, but the spring—apparently because of its alleged association with the family of the Prophet—would by the tenth century become an important pilgrimage site. Writing in the 940s, the Samanid historian al-Narshakhi noted:

> Nur is a large place with a grand mosque. It has many ribats [caravan-serais]. Every year the people of Bukhara and other places go there on pilgrimages. The person who goes on the pilgrimage to Nur has the same distinction as having performed the pilgrimage (to Mecca) . . . many of the followers of the Prophet are buried there (May God be pleased with them until the day of Judgement).[17]

A Mongol commander by the name of Dayir led the Mongol van-guard to Nur.[18] On the outskirts of town they halted in some groves of fruit trees—now barren, as it was January—and camped. That night they cut down trees and used the wood to fashion scaling ladders. The next morning they rode up to the city walls holding the scaling ladders in front of them. The sudden appearance of this Mongol vanguard via a route thought to be known only to merchants caused the watchmen on the walls to mistake it at first for a trading caravan. As the horsemen got closer the watchmen saw the ladders and realized that the mounted men

*Huge spring at Nur (now Nurata). Tales that it was created by the Prophet
Muhammad's son-in-law Ali are no doubt apocryphal.*

were invaders. The gates of the city wall were thrown shut and the city
fathers commenced debating among themselves what course of action to
take. After much argument it was decided that they had no choice but
to throw in the towel. In Juvaini's account of the city's fall no mention
is made of the citadel built or upgraded by the troops of Alexander the
Great. Either it was not longer an active fortification by the thirteenth
century or the local panjandrums decided that it could not be defended.

An envoy was sent to Chingis Khan, who was still advancing across the
desert with the bulk of his army. Accepting the city's surrender, he ordering the city fathers to submit to his general Sübedei, who had arrived at
Nur in the wake of the vanguard. Sübedei herded the inhabitants out of
town, allowing them to take along only "what was necessary for their live-
lihood and the pursuit of husbandry and agriculture, such as sheep and
cows . . ." He further ordered that "they should go out on to the plain leaving their houses exactly as they were so that they might be looted by the
army."[19] In return for this acquiescence the Mongols agreed not to inflict
bodily harm on anyone.

When Chingis Khan finally arrived in town he ordered the city's inhabitants to cough up 1500 dinars, the same amount that they paid in taxes to
the Khwarezmshah each year. Half of this sum, we are told, was paid in

Ruins of the fortress of Nur visible behind the spring.

Current-day city of Nurata from the ruins of the fortress.

women's earrings. The fact that the locals still had dinars to pay and women had earrings to hand over would seem to indicate that individuals had not been robbed at least of the possessions on their persons, even though the town itself had been sacked and looted. As usual, young men were dragooned as levies, although according to Juvaini only sixty were taken.[20] Compared with the devastation that the Mongols would later inflict on cities that resisted them, Nur, like Zarnuq, got off rather lightly, even if the women did bemoan the loss of their earrings. Both cities were essentially sideshows. The big prize was Bukhara, eighty-five miles to the southwest.

From Nur the Mongol army rode fifteen miles south-southwest through desert-steppe to a 2641-foot high pass, a thousand feet higher than Nur itself, through the Karatau Mountains, themselves part of the Aqtau Range, east-west trending mountains with peaks of up to 5,485 feet. To the northeast loomed the snow-covered flanks of the Nuratau Range, with peaks of up to 7116 feet. After crossing the pass they descended onto a strip of grassy steppe where the Mongol horses must have felt right at home. Even if the steppe was covered with snow in late January or early February the sturdy mounts would have had little trouble pawing down to the dry grass, which they must have craved after passing through the bleak Kyzyl Kum Desert.

Fifteen miles from the pass miles Chingis Khan and his army finally reached the cultivated lands along the fabled Zerafshan River. The valley of the river had hosted sedentary societies for more than 3,000 years, and it had always been the most populous region of Mawarannahr, with the two main cities of Bukhara and Samarkand alternating as the capitals of a long procession of fiefdoms, kingdoms, and empires.[21] The Greeks of the fourth century B.C. called the river Polytimetus.[22] Also known as the Sughd, or Sogd, River, its lower valley later became the heart of the old Sogdian realm. The name *Zerafshan* comes from the Persian *zar-afshan*, meaning "the sprayer of gold," a reference to the gold-bearing sands and gravels found in the upper reaches of the river.

The Zerafshan begins at the Zerafshan Glacier in the Koksu Mountains, themselves outliers of the Pamirs. From its source at an elevation of about 9,200 feet the river flows west for about 180 miles, flanked on either side by the Turkestan and Zerafshan mountain ranges.[23] Just below the ancient city of Panjikent the river debouches out onto the plains of Mawarannahr and twenty miles farther on passes by Samarkand. From here it flows about 115 miles west-northwest before turning to the south-southwest and flowing through the Bukhara Oasis. In pre-historic times the river may have drained into the Amu Darya River, but even by the time of Alexander the Great in the fourth century B.C. it was already petering out in the sands of the Kyzyl Kum Desert southwest of Bukhara.

Crossing the no doubt frozen river the Mongols emerged on the Royal Road, the main caravan thoroughfare between Bukhara and Samarkand.

The mausoleum of Mir Sayyid Barham in Karmana

Probably the first town they encountered was Karminiya (current-day Karmana), forty-five miles northeast of Bukhara. Known during Sogdian times as *Badiya-i-Khurdak* ("little pitcher"), the town got its new name from eighth-century Arab invaders who because of the water and soil in the area called it *ka-Arminiya*, or "similar to Armenia". Karminiya had been heavily damaged by the Khwarezmshah Arslan during his war against the Qara Khitai in the mid-twelfth century and apparently did not figure as an important city by the time Chingis Khan arrived on the scene.[24] The mausoleum of Mir Sayyid Barham, built in the late eleventh century during the rule of the Qarakhanids, is probably the only building in the town to have survived from the pre-Mongol days down to the present.[25]

About ten miles past the river, where the ancient caravan route swung back out into desert-steppe, they might well have passed the famous Rabat-i-Malik, an immense caravanserai built by the Qarakhanid Khan Shams-al-Mulk Nasr (r. 1068–1080). Its 40-foot high portal with elaborate brickwork decoration and its enormous walled courtyard signaled that the Mongols were now on the main trunk of the Silk Road, the ancient trade corridor between the Orient and the Occident. The surviving

Portal of Rabat-i-Malik

portal and ruins of the caravanserai can still be seen beside the modern highway between Bukhara and Samarkand. Nearby was a huge well of sweet water that would have slaked the thirst of the men and their horses (the brick dome that now covers the well was not added until the fourteenth century).

After riding another fifteen miles east-southeast the Mongol army finally reached the edge of the greater Bukhara Oasis, a forty-mile-wide and fifty-mile-long swath of cultivated land which in addition to Bukhara itself was home to dozens of small cities, towns, and villages. They probably saw the wall known as the *Kanpirak*, measuring over 150 miles in length, which had once surrounded the entire Bukhara Oasis.[26] *Kanpirak* is supposedly an archaic term for "old woman", which would at first glance seem an inappropriate term for a wall. One local historian points out, however, that the term "old virgin" might be a more accurate translation, in which case it might connote that the wall was thought to be impenetrable.[27] In any case, the wall was probably built in the fifth or sixth century A.D. Between the years 782 and 830 it was repaired and upgraded as a bulwark against the continuing incursions of nomadic peoples from the north. Maintaining the lengthy wall was an immensely expensive undertaking, however, and required enormous outlays of manpower. At the beginning of the Samanid era in the ninth century Amir Ismael famously declared, "While I live, I am the wall of the district of Bukhara," implying that he would guarantee the safety of the area by force of arms and that expensive walls were no longer needed.[28] The Kanpirak was henceforth abandoned, and by the time the Mongols arrived it may have been largely in ruins. In any case, neither Juvaini nor any other Persian historian mention the wall and it proved no obstacle whatsoever to the Mongol invaders.

The first settlement inside the wall was the town of Tawais. Formerly known as Arqud, in Persian, or Kut, in Turkish, meaning roughly "fortunate", Arab invaders renamed it Tawais (endowed with peacocks") in 710 because it was here that they saw their first peacocks—not a native bird of Arabia—in the gardens of the town's prominent citizens. The town had been well-fortified, but by the time Chingis arrived the local fortress had fallen to ruins, already destroyed in earlier fighting between the various contestants for the Bukhara conurbation. The town was formerly famous for its Zoroastrian temple, although presumably it had disappeared by the thirteenth century, by which time it boasted of a large Friday mosque. Tawais was also famous for its great trade fair, which was held every autumn and lasted for seven to ten days. Merchants from all of Mawarannahr and the Fergana Valley attended this fair, which operated under one unusual condition: no item bought could be returned, even if it was later proven that the seller had engaged in illegal trickery or deception.[29] Although probably in a hurry to get to Bukhara, presumably the Mongols took time to engage in at least a cursory looting of the town and to dragoon levies for the anticipated lengthy siege of Bukhara. Today Tawais remains as the small village of Tavois, next to the modern town of Kizil Tepe. Now, as in the thirteenth century, it marks the place where the cultivated land of the Bukhara Oasis abruptly ends and the desert steppe begins.

Fifteen miles east of Tawais was the town of Vabkent. The Mongols may have homed in on the town's minaret, which was visible for miles around on the flat Bukhara Oasis. Commissioned by *Sadr* Abd al-Aziz II, a member of the powerful Bukhara-based Borhan family mentioned above, the 127-foot high minaret was completed in 1198–1199, a year or two after the death of its sponsor.[30] It was probably the second highest minaret in Mawarannahr, after the Kalon Minaret in Bukhara itself, and served as a beacon for caravans and travelers approaching from the north and east. The Mongols left it unharmed, and it stands to this day, although the mosque to which it was once attached has long since disappeared.

The eighteen miles from Vabkent to Bukhara was an almost solid procession of towns, villages, gardens, and orchards. Among the more prominent towns were Shargh and Iskijkath (no longer existing under these names) on either side of one of the canals feeding off the Zerafshan River. In the twelfth century Arslan, the grandfather of the Khwarezmshah Mohammad, had built a substantial bridge made of burnt brick across the canal connecting the two towns. Both were important trading centers; Iskijkath had a trade fair every Thursday and Shargh every Sunday. An important local trader built a big Friday mosque in Iskijkath, but after imams in Bukhara complained that it was attracting their flocks only one service was ever held in it.[31] No mention is made in the various accounts of the plundering of the smaller cities and towns in the Bukhara Oasis, and perhaps the Mongols in their hurry to reach the city of Bukhara hurried on through them, but it is hard to imagine that sometime during their stay in the area these places were not subject to looting and pillage.

Not long after passing through these towns yet another minaret loomed on the horizon. This was the 155-foot high Kalon Minaret in the heart of Bukhara, the tallest in Mawarannahr.[32] Its appearance signaled to the Mongols that the long sought-after goal of Bukhara was now within their reach. By early February 1220, Chingis Khan, his son Tolui, and the Mongol army arrived on the outskirts of *Bukhoro-i-Sharif*—Holy Bukhara.[33]

Chingis Khan and his officers spent the first few day outside of Bukhara making a reconnaissance of the city's defenses. The extent of these is uncertain. Juvaini, our most detailed source for the Mongol assault on Bukhara, states only that the Mongols "encamped before the gates of the Citadel," making no mention of any city walls.[34] Yet in 1220 Bukhara, like most big cities of Inner Asia, almost certainly consisted of a *shahristan* (inner city) and a *rabad* (outer city, or suburbs), each surrounded by a wall, in addition to a citadel. When these walls were first built and their exact location is by no means clear from available accounts. We can say that whatever walls had existed earlier were repaired and strengthened in the 850s, during the time of the Tahirids, the predecessors of the Samanids; then again by the Qarakhanid Arslan Khan Mohammad (r. 1102–1129) in the first half of the twelfth century; again by Masud Tabghach Khan (r. 1161–1171) in 1165; and finally by the Khwarezmshah Muhammad in 1207.[35] The walls repaired or restored by the Khwarezmshah were the

Vabkent Minaret, built in 1198–1199.

ones encountered by Chingis Khan when he arrived at the city in 1220. The wall around the *Shahristan* apparently had seven gates and the wall around the *Rabad* eleven; other than that we know little about their configuration or how long and high they were.[36]

Outside the western edge of the *Shahristan* was the Citadel, or *Ark*. Some sort of fortress or citadel may have existed on the site as far back as the fourth century B.C. According to archeological evidence, by the third century B.C. this citadel had walls over twenty feet thick.[37] In the ensuing centuries the Citadel fell out of use and was in ruins by the end of the

Restored walls in current-day Bukhara. The walls that Chingis Khan and his army faced in 1220 may have been similar.

sixth century A.D. Around the middle of the seventh century the semi-legendary figure of Bukhar-Khudat-Biden, according to some accounts the king of all of Sogdiana, restored parts of the ruins and expanded the complex until it covered about 2.5 acres. Bukhar-Khudat-Biden also built (or perhaps restored) a palace within the citadel which served as his own residence. According to legend, this palace collapsed several times during construction. Upon the advice of local savants, a new palace was strengthened by seven stone pillars—the number of stars in the Big Dipper—and this version survived at least through the Samanid era.[38] In the upheavals following the collapse of the Samanid dynasty in 999 both palace and citadel were destroyed. The Qarakhanid ruler Arslan Khan Muhammad, who also built the Kalon Minaret, rebuilt the citadel and presumably the palace in the early twelfth century, but they were once again destroyed by the Khwarezmshah Atsiz in 1139–40. The next year the Qara Khitai arrived in town and their chieftain Alptegin rebuilt the complex, only to have it razed yet again by Turkish marauders in 1143–44. In 1165 materials from the ruins of the citadel where used in the upgrading of the *rabad* walls around the outer city. In 1207–08 the Khwarezmshah Muhammad once again restored the citadel. This was the version that stood when Chingis Khan arrived on the outskirts of the city in 1220.[39]

The number of defenders inside the city's walls is disputed: Juzjani says

there were 12,000 cavalry; Juvaini says 20,000 "auxiliary" troops from the
Khwarezmshah's army, apparently backing up a contingent of local fight-
ers; and Nasavi claims a total of 30,000.[40] Among those leading the forces
holed up in the city were Ikhtiyar al-Din Kushlu, the Grand Equerry of
the Khwarezmshah; Hamid Pür, a Qara Khitai taken prisoner by the
Khwarezmshah in 1210 and who later joined his army; a commander by
the name of Inanch Khan; and a certain Khökh Khan (Blue Khan), also
known as Gür Khan (not, of course the Gür Khan of the Qara Khitai,
who had died in 1213 or 1214). This Khökh Khan was a Mongol who had
earlier deserted to the cause of the Khwarezmshah and achieved a position of some prominence in Bukharan society. Historians would later
float the wild rumor that this Khökh Khan, or Gür Khan, was none other
than Jamukha, Chingis's close friend as a young man and later his arch-
nemesis, who had somehow escaped from Mongolia only to pop up again
here in Bukhara as the perennial thorn in Chingis's side.[41] Jamukha did
hold the title of Gür Khan (Universal Ruler), and this may have led some
to confuse him with this Mongol deserter who had assumed the same
moniker.[42] As the *Secret History* make perfectly clear, however, Jamukha
had been executed by Chingis's order back in 1205.[43] Whoever Khökh
Khan was, he was not Jamukha.

Surrounded by an army "more numerous than ants or locusts," it did
not take long for these commanders to conclude that they did not want
to stay and defend what now appeared to be a doomed city. Three days
after the arrival of the Mongols the commanders led their troops (20,000,
according to Juvaini, apparently the "auxiliary" troops referred to above)
out of the city gates.[44] Juvaini adds that numerous inhabitants of the city
decided to take their chances with the bolting soldiers. They finally managed to battle their way through the Mongol cordon and flee south. These
escapees from the city hoped to reach the Amu Darya River and cross
over to the supposed safety of Khorasan, where the Khwarezmshah was
thought to be gathering an army to finally confront the invaders. Mongol
detachments sent in pursuit harried them all the way to the Amu Darya.
Almost all of them were hounded down and massacred. Hamid Pür was
caught and killed before he reached the river. Only a handful of men led
by the Inanch Khan managed to cross the river and escape. Thus was the
ignominious end of the army that the Khwarezmshah had tasked with
the defense of Bukhara.

Only a few diehard troops holed up in the *Shahristan* and the Khökh
Khan and his 400 men in the Citadel remained to fight the Mongols. The

The Kalon Minaret (center) and the current-day Kalon Mosque (right) The Friday Mosque that Chingis Khan and his men entered was destroyed during or after the siege of Bukhara in 1220. The current Kalon Mosque was later built on the site of the mosque destroyed by the Mongols.

citizens of Bukhara having lost heart, their leaders had no choice but to forfeit the rest of the city. A local dignitary by the name of Badr a-Din Qadi Khan led a delegation out of the city to negotiate the surrender. On the 11th or 16th of February, depending on whose account we believe, Chingis Khan made a triumphal entry into the holy city of Bukhara.[45] He, his son Tolui, and their men headed first for the big Friday Mosque with its 155-foot high minaret, both built by order of Muhammad Arslan Khan in the 1120s.[46] They rode their horses into the mosque, where Tolui dismounted and ascended the *minbar*, or pulpit. According to Juvaini, Chingis then asked if this was the palace of the Khwarezmshah; he was informed by the imams in attendance that it was the House of God. He too then dismounted and climbed up onto the pulpit. Although it may have been the House of God, he had more earthly concerns. The Mongol horses were hungry and must be fed, he ordered. The city's granaries were opened and the grain was dispensed for horse feed. Chingis's men dragged the cases that were used to store Qurans out of the mosque, dumped out the sacred books, and used them as feeding troughs for their mounts. Their horses having been seen to, they ordered up wine and dancing girls for their own entertainment. Soon the mosque rang with the sound of

Mongol songs bellowed by the celebrating inebriates.[47]

Juvaini, although a scribe in the pay of one of Chingis's descendants, was a Sunni Muslim himself, and he could not keep out a note of disapproval in his account of these carryings-on.[48] Hitherto dignified imams, sheiks, and *sayyids*, he tells us, were made to look after the Mongol horses while their owners partied. When the bacchanalia was over the Mongols rode away, trampling under the feet of their horses the leaves of the Qurans that had been scattered around the courtyard of the mosque. At this point, an imam named Jalal-ad-Din Ali b. al-Hasan Zaidi, "chief and leader of the *sayyids* of Transoxiania . . . famous for his piety and asceticism," turned to an imam named Rukn-ad-Din Imamzada, "one of the most excellent savants in the world," and lamented, "'. . . what state is this? That which I see do I see it in wakefulness or in sleep, O Lord?'" Much of what he had just witnessed must have seemed like a nightmare. His companion replied, "'Be silent: it is the wind of God's omnipotence that bloweth, and we have no power to speak.'"[49] The wind was not about to abate, and for many in Khwarezmia the nightmare was just beginning.

According to al-Athir, the Mongols were at first lenient towards the inhabitants of Bukhara: "The infidels entered Bukhara and did not harm anyone. However, they said to the people, 'Everything that you have that belongs to the sultan [the Khwarezmshah], treasure and other things, bring out to us and help us to fight those in the citadel.' They made a show of justice and good conduct."[50] A few days later Chingis appeared at the Namazgah Mosque just south of the *rabad* walls. This mosque, like the big Friday mosque, had been built by Muhammad Arslan Khan in the 1120s (the partially restored ruins of this mosque can still be seen). From the *minbar* of the mosque he ordered that all the city's wealthiest people be brought before him. Two hundred and eighty people were produced, 190 from the city itself and ninety merchants from other cities who happened to be in Bukhara at the time. He then harangued these assembled worthies:

> "O People know that you have committed great sins, and the great ones among you have committed these sins. If you ask me what proof I have for these words, I say it is because I am the punishment of God. If you had not committed great sins, God would not have sent a punishment like me upon you."[51]

This is probably the source of the "I am the Scourge of God" declaration attributed to Chingis Khan that pops up in later accounts of the Mongol invasion of Mawarannahr. But did Chingis actually make this speech? Other contemporary sources, al-Athir for example, make no mention of it, although such a dramatic reproof of the citizens of Bukhara could hardly have escaped their notice. This leads later commentators to conclude that Juvaini inserted this speech simply to spice up his narrative. Barthold, after examining all the available sources, concludes that Juvaini's account of the speech "is quite beyond belief."[52]

Juvaini and al-Athir do agree, however, that Chingis ordered the assembled notables to cough up all of their accumulated wealth. "'There is no need to declare your property that is on the face of the earth; tell me of that which is in the belly of the earth,'" he told them, apparently meaning that he wanted them to reveal whatever possessions they hidden—perhaps buried—from him. To the most important merchants he assigned a Mongol or Turk overseer whose job it was to pry their wealth out of them. Juvaini claims, however, that as long as the merchants willingly handed over their possessions these heavies "did not torment them by excessive punishment or demanding what was beyond their power to pay."[53] Each morning more merchants were herded into an audience hall where Chingis harangued them, demanding that they turn over their riches to him. Of special interest to Chingis were the merchants who had dealt in the gold, silver, and goods plundered from the Mongol trade caravan at Otrar. As we have seen, the Khwarezmshah had sold of his share of the loot to Bukharan merchants, and they were now brought to account and made to produce their ill-gotten gains. Al-Athir confirms Juvaini's account, adding, "They [the merchants] came and he [Chingis Khan] said, 'I want from you the bullion Khwarazm Shah sold to you, for it is mine; it was taken from my followers and you have it.' Anyone who had any of it brought it before him."[54] The arm of Chingis Khan was long indeed.

Not everyone in Bukhara acquiesced to the Mongols' roughshod treatment of their city. The aforementioned Jalal-ad-Din Ali b. al-Hasan Zaidi, one of the leading imams of the city, and his son objected to the treatment meted out to prisoners and the rape of women by Mongol soldiers. A brawl ensued and both the imam and his son were killed. Others who protested, including the judge Sadr al-Din Khan and Majd al-Din Masud, brother of the Khwarezmshah's vizier Nizam al-Mulk, were also slain.[55] But these were exceptions. Most inhabitants of the occupied city had no choice but to simply submit to the Mongols. Except, of course, for Khökh Khan and his 400 men who remained holed up in the Citadel and

The heavily-restored Namazgah Mosque, located just outside the old city walls.

The minbar of the Namazgah Mosque. Although the current-day minbar is clearly a reproduction, presumably it stands on the same site as the minbar from which Chingis Khan addressed the citizens of Bukhara in 1220.

The 155-foot high Kalon Minaret, built by order of the Qarakhanid ruler Muhammad Arslan Khan in the 1120s. It is one of the few monuments in Bukhara that survived the Mongol attack on the city.

a few diehards in the *Shahristan*.

Twelve days after the Mongols had arrived in the city Chingis Khan decided to deal with these holdouts. Juvaini would have us believe that to flush out the remaining soldiers in the *Shahristan* Chingis ordered that the entire city be torched. Within days much of Bukhara had burned to the ground. It is not clear why the entire assembled Mongol army could not deal with what must have been a relatively small force holed up in the *Shahristan*, making such a drastic expedient necessary. Later commentators would suggest that the fire that consumed the city started accidentally while the city was being plundered and quickly spread through the

The Citadel that existed in 1220 was destroyed in the aftermath of the Mongol attack on Bukhara. The current-day Citadel, shown here, was built on roughly the same site.

districts made up mostly of wooden buildings.[56] The Friday Mosque was at some point destroyed, but the 155-foot high Kalon Minaret adjacent to it survived. No Persian historians mention it, but local legend maintains that Chingis Khan was so awed by this majestic structure that he ordered his soldiers to protect it. It stands to this day as one of the handful of pre-Mongol era monuments in the city.

In any case, the fire did not phase the defenders of the Citadel. The townspeople were now called upon to assist in the siege. According to al-Athir:

All [townspeople] presented themselves and were ordered to fill on the moat [around the Citadel]. They filled it with timbers and earth and other things. The infidels were even taking the minbars [pulpits] and Koran containers and throwing them into the moat. Verily we belong to God and to Him we do return. In truth did God call Himself patient and forbearing, otherwise the earth would have swallowed them up when they did such a thing.[57]

Then the Mongols set up mangonels and began heaving huge stones into the Citadel; the defenders responded by flinging out pots of burning naphtha. The Citadel was soon "like a red-hot furnace fed from without by hard sticks thrust into the recesses, while from the belly of the furnace sparks shoot into the air," claimed Juvaini. Using the local citizenry as human shields the Mongols stormed the walls. The fight went on for days. The Khökh Khan "who in bravery would have born the palm from male lions, engaged in many battles: in each attack he overthrew several persons and alone expelled a great army." All to no avail. Finally the last defenders of the Citadel were "drowned in the sea of annihilation."[58]

For reasons that commentators, including Juvaini, do not make entirely clear, Chingis Khan now decided upon a wholesale pogrom in the already defeated and burned city. Of the Qangli Turks within the city, "no male was spared who stood higher than the butt of a whip," and their womenfolk ("slender as the cypress") and children were sent into slavery. The remaining men and women (of the latter, both "ugly and beautiful," Juvaini dutifully notes) were driven out onto the surrounding plains, and the city walls were leveled. The healthy males, both adults and youths, were dragooned as levies for the upcoming siege of Samarkand. The remaining citizenry retired to surrounding villages, as nothing remained of their city.

One man who escaped from the carnage in Bukhara eventually ended up in Khorasan. Here he was questioned about the Mongols and the fate of Bukhara. His words, as recorded by Juvaini, have often been repeated: "'They came, they sapped, they burnt, they slew, they plundered and they departed.'" Juvaini, who knew his way around words, opined that "in the Persian language there could be nothing more concise than this speech."[59]

CHAPTER 6

THE MARCH ON SAMARKAND AND THE FALL OF THE CITY

BY THE BEGINNING OF MARCH Chingis Khan was ready to march on Samarkand. The two Jewels of Mawarannahr, Bukhara and Samarkand, were linked by the so-called Royal Road, an ancient thoroughfare that roughly followed the course of the Zerafshan River. Samarkand is 135 miles east of Bukhara as the crow flies, but upstream from Bukhara the Zerafshan River loops to the north before continuing on east, and the distance between the two cites via the Royal Road, which roughly follows the river, was between thirty-seven and thirty-nine *farsakhs* (148 to 156 miles).[1] This was a journey of six or seven stages, or days, by camel. Accompanied by the huge flock of levies who had been dragooned in Bukhara for the anticipated siege of Samarkand, the Mongol army proceed north on the Royal Road, probably passing once again through the towns of Shargh, Iskijkath, and Vabkent, and finally reaching the edge of the Bukhara Oasis at Tawais. After another eight miles they passed by the caravanserai of Rabat-i-Malik and continued on for twelve more miles to Karminiya.

At some point beyond of the Bukhara Oasis Chingis Khan may have divided his army into two parts, with one contingent crossing the Zerafshan River and proceeding east on the north bank, and the other riding east on the south bank.[2] According to a story told by the Chinese Daoist Chang Chunzi, who himself traveled along the north bank of the Zerafshan a year later in 1221, Chingis Khan himself led the army on the north bank. The Chinese holy man saw "on the road a well more than one hundred feet deep, where an old man, a Mohammadan, had a bullock which turned a drawbeam and raised water for thirsty people. The emperor Chinghiz, when passing here, had seen this man, and ordered that he should be exempted from taxes and duties."[3]

Beyond Karminiya the Royal Road veered to the south-southeast and passed through a region dotted with numerous cities and towns that had flourished for a thousand years in the rich oases lining the Zerafshan River. This was the very heart of old Sogdiana. Chingis Khan, in his haste to reach Samarkand, did not linger in this well-populated and prosperous region. According to Juvaini, "whenever the villages in his path submitted, he in no way molested them."[4] Al-Athir, however, asserts that Chingis Khan continued to seize able-bodied men in the towns he passed through, adding them to the already vast horde of levies that he had dragooned in Bukhara. Al-Athir further asserts that these men were forced to march on foot alongside the Mongol army and that any who fell from hunger or exhaustion were killed.[5]

We hear of only two cities that put up any real resistance. The first was Dabusiya, located twenty-four miles south-southeast miles east of the current-day town of Karmana on the south bank of the Zerafshan.[6] One of the half dozen or so major cities of ancient Sogdiana, Dabusiya had been a well-fortified city as early as 112 A.D., and in the early eighth century over 10,000 Sogdian and Turkish troops had unsuccessfully defended the city walls against Arab invaders. It was later on occupied by the Samanids, and was still a well-fortified city when it finally fell to the

Ruins of the walls of Dabusiya

The Zerafshan River upstream from the ramparts of Dabusiya

Qarakhanids during the reign of Ismail al-Muntasir, the last of the Samanid rulers.[7] With the defeat of the Qarakhanids it became part of the
Khwarezmshah's realm. Although still heavily fortified, with mammoth
walls facing the Zerafshan River, it did not provide much of an obstacle
to the Mongols. Chingis left a detachment of troops to besiege the city
while he and the bulk of his army hastened eastward to Samarkand. We
hear no more of Dabusiya from Juvaini or other historians, but eventually
the city fell to the Mongols and was at some point destroyed. It was never
rebuilt, and today there is no city or town of Dabusiya, although the ruins
of the old city walls still rear up from the south bank of the Zerafshan.
(Nowadays people come here to visit the tomb of Daliv Ismatulla Abriev-
ich Imam, a famous local saint, whose mausoleum now stands amidst the
ruins of the old city.)

   Only the city of Sar-i-Pul, about forty miles west-northwest of Samarkand (near current-day Kattakurgan, on the south bank of the Zerafshan
River), offered any further resistance.[8] Another detachment of troops was
left to invest Sar-i-Pul while the main army moved on to Samarkand.
Around mid-March the Mongols arrived on the outskirts of Samarkand.
The calvary approached the city walls first, followed by the foot soldiers
and prisoners. One man out of each ten prisoners was made to hold a
banner, giving the impression that they were fighting troops themselves.
According to al-Athir, "they advanced little by little, to be more terrify-

ing to the hearts of the Muslims. When the people saw the dense mass of them, they were terrified."[9] This was just a display of force, and no actual fighting took place during the first couple of days. Chingis himself encamped near the abandoned Khökh Serai palace in the western suburbs (not to be confused with the Khökh Serai later built by Amir Timur, a.k.a., Tamurlane; this earlier palace was apparently destroyed by Amir Timur's time.)[10]

At this point Chagaadai and Ögedei and the divisions under their command arrived in Samarkand. They had come straight from Otrar, which had finally fallen to the Mongols. After Chingis Khan and his son Tolui had left for Bukhara, Chagaadai and Ögedei had besieged Otrar for five months. As it become increasingly obvious that the city would never escape from the noose that the Mongols had thrown around it, the military commander Qaracha Khass-Hajib had advised surrender. Gayer Khan refused, knowing full well that given his role in the plundering of the trading caravan and the execution of Chingis's emissaries he could expect no quarter from the Mongols. To surrender was to die. Instead he argued: "'If we are unfaithful to our master [the Khwarezmshah], how shall we excuse our treachery, and under what pretext shall we escape from the reproaches of Moslems?'"[11] Juvaini's account of what happened next is muddled. Apparently one night Qaracha Khass-Hajib opened the Sufi-Khana Gate to the city and sent some of his forces outside the walls to do battle with the Mongols. That night the Mongols somehow entered by the same gate and managed to take Qaracha Khass-Hajib prisoner. Apparently now that he was in the hands of the Mongols he and some of his officers attempted to switch allegiance and throw in their lot with the besiegers. Unfortunately for Qaracha Khass-Hajib, the Mongols took a dim view of such self-serving expedients on the battlefield. "'Thou has been unfaithful to your own master in spite of his claims on thee on account of past favors. Therefore neither can we expect fidelity of thee.'"[12] Qaracha Khass-Hajib and his companions were then executed. Juvaini says that by their deaths they were able to "attain to a degree of martyrdom."[13]

Both the outer and inner sections of the city were finally overrun by the Mongols. The entire populace was herded outside the walls "like a flock of sheep" and the now-empty city looted by the victorious Mongols and their auxiliaries. If Gayer Khan had harbored any remaining doubts about fighting on against the Mongols the fate of Qaracha Khass-Hajib must have squelched them. He and 20,000 of his men retreated behind the walls of the *Ark* (citadel) and prepared to fight "as long as one of them had breath in his body."[14] They did not go down easily. "They set their hearts upon death and having bid themselves farewell sallied forth fifty at a time and spitted their bodies upon spears and swords." They got their wish for martyrdom but not before inflicting serious damage. Even Juvaini admits that "many from the Mongol army were slain."[15] After a month of vicious fighting only Gayer Khan, two of his bodyguards, and members of his harem remained alive.[16] They took final refuge on the roof of the Citadel. The Mongols had strict order to take Gayer Khan alive. They killed his bodyguards, and Gayer Khan finally shot the last of his arrows. His women then handed him bricks which he hurled down on his tormenters. Finally even these were exhausted. In light of his eventual fate he would have been well advised to commit suicide jump by off the Citadel. Instead, he allowed himself to be captured and bound in heavy chains. The Citadel was demolished and the walls of the city were completely razed. Many of the common people of the city were rounded up and made to serve as levies in upcoming battles. Artisans among the populace were ordered to practice their crafts for the benefit of their new Mongol overlords. Thus the deaths of the 450 merchants in the Mongol trade caravan and the execution of Chingis Khan's emissaries to Gayer Khan were avenged.

Chagaadai and Ögedei were now able to join their father in Samarkand. The additional divisions that they had brought with them resulted in an even greater stranglehold on city. The troops were accompanied by a throng of levies seized in Otrar and probably augmented by able-bodied men seized along the way. Samarkand is 225 miles south-southeast of Otrar as the crow flies. It is not known what route the Mongols took from Otrar to Samarkand, but they almost certainly would have had to pass through long stretches of waterless desert. The Mongols rode their horses, but the levies would have had to cover the entire distance on foot. There is no record of how many of the dragooned men died along the way.

Chagaadai and Ögedei also had a prize to present to Chingis Khan: Gayer Khan, the erstwhile commander of Otrar, who had been taken prisoner when the Citadel in the city had finally fallen. Chingis Khan would now take his revenge on this man who had earlier ordered the murders of the merchants and envoys at Otrar and the Mongol emissary who had been sent to protest the crime. Accounts differ as to how Gayer Khan died. Juvaini says only that he was forced to "drink the cup of annihilation and don the garb of eternity." According to Nasavi, the gold which Gayer Khan had earlier stolen from the Mongol trade caravan to Otrar was melted down and the molten liquid was poured into his eyes and ears.[17] As we have seen, Chingis had recovered some of this gold in Bukhara and now he may have put it to a fitting use. In any case, Gayer Khan, the nephew of the Khwarezmshah's mother, met a horrifying end. As Juvaini observes: "Such is the way of high heaven; in the one hand it holds a crown, in the other a noose."[18] Even Nasavi, a partisan of the Khwarezmshah's family, had no good words for Gayer Khan: "This cruel death was the just punishment for Inal [Gayer] Khan, whose ignoble behavior, barbarous acts, and former cruelties were worth the condemnation of all."[19]

Meanwhile, Chingis decided to deal with the Khwarezmshah. Perhaps remembering how Khüchüleg had escaped from his grasp and remained as a thorn in his side for years afterward, he now declared, "'It is necessary to make an end to him and be well rid of him before men gather around him and nobles join him from every side.'"[20] Juvaini implies that even before the assault on Samarkand began Chingis dispatched two of his Four Hounds, Jebe and Sübedei, and 30,000 troops in pursuit of the errant Khwarezmshah.[21] He also claims that two other generals, Khadag Noyon and Yasaur, were dispatched with attachments of troops to Vakhsh, probably located near the confluence of the Amu Darya and the Vakhsh River in what is now Tajikistan, and to Taliqan, south of the Amu Darya in what is now Afghanistan.[22] This was apparently a reconnaissance mission, an early indication that Chingis Khan intended not only to conquer all of Mawarannahr but also had Khorasan in his sights. Al-Athir avers that Chingis Khan did not sic his two Hounds, Jebe and Sübedei, on the Khwarezmshah until after Samarkand had fallen and that they had only 20,000 troops with them.[23] If this is the case, it means only that they departed a week or so later. The siege of Samarkand would be a very short-lived affair. As we shall see, they would dog the Khwarezmshah's trail like the very hounds of hell until he was finally brought to bay.

Since 1212, when the last revolts of the Qarakhanids had been put down, Samarkand had been the capital of the Khwarezmshah's dominion.[24] According to Juvaini it was the greatest city "in the Sultan's empire . . . the most pleasant of his lands in fertility and soil and, by common consent, the most delectable of the paradises of this world among the four Edens."

> If it is said that a paradise is to be seen in this
> world, then the paradise of this world is Samarqand."[25]

Not only was the city itself of paramount important; it also, as Nasavi pointed out, had strategic significance. By retaining control of Samarkand, the Khwarezmshah "would close before the enemy the path to other parts of his kingdom."[26] Thus he initially appeared determined to defend Samarkand at all costs. After concluding that the invasion of the Mongols was inevitable, he traveled to Samarkand and oversaw the fortification of the city himself. First he ordered the construction of a huge wall measuring twelve *farsakhs* (forty-eight miles) in circumference, encompassing both the center of the city and its environs. To pay for this grandiose edifice he ordered his tax collectors to demand from the entire populace triple the amount of taxes for the entire year.[27] Just how this huge project was to be completed before the arrival of the Mongols is unclear. At this point the Khwarezmshah may have thought that it would take several years for them to actually mount the invasion of Mawarannahr.

Like most cites in Mawarannahr, Samarkand no doubt already had a wall around the *rabad*, or outer city. The dimensions and course of this wall are not clear from the historical record and all traces of it have disappeared in the various upheavals that followed. Juvaini does tell us that the walls of the "citadel" within the city "were raised to the Pleiades" and a moat was dug around this inner fortress. Samarkand did have a citadel within the inner city (its ruins can still be seen today), but his description leads Barthold to conclude that by "citadel" Juvaini actually meant the *Shahristan*, or inner city. This ancient part of the city, known as Afriosab, measure about one mile east to west and 1.15 of a mile north to south, with a circumstance of around 3.4 miles.

Juvaini claims that while the Khwarezmshah was inspecting the defenses around this inner city area he gloomily remarked that the Mongols would only have to throw in their whip handles to fill up the moat and then ride over them. This supposedly demoralized the bystanders who overheard the remark. Barthold suggests that Juvaini made up this incident, since the Khwarezmshah would surely not have wanted to present such a depressing picture to the residents of the city. Then again, perhaps the Khwarezmshah was by this point already so demoralized that he was unable to resist spouting out the truth.

Leaving Samarkand to its fate, the Khwarezmshah he fled southwest some eighty miles to Nasaf (current-day Qarshi). It may have been here that he convened another meeting of his counselors and asked for their advice. Most believed that it would be futile for the Khwarezmshah to oppose the Mongols in Mawarannahr. Some proposed that the should cross the Amu Darya and concentrate on saving Khorasan and Iraq-i Ajam. To protect these portions of his empire the Amu Darya should be turned into a moat. Troops should be withdrawn from the cities of Mawarannahr, including Samarkand, and stationed in a long line of defense on the south bank of the Amu Darya, effectively cordoning off the Mongols north of the river in Mawarannahr. Chingis Khan, the advisors counseled "'must not be suffered to set foot across that river.'" The more pusillanimous advisers in the Khwarezmshah's retinue suggested that he abandon even Khorasan and Iraq-i Ajam and proceed directly to India, there to find final behind the bulwark of the Hindu Kush. At some point the Khwarezmshah astrologers chimed in, declaring that:

> the beneficent stars were cadent from the angles of the Ascendant and the Tenth House and the maleficent stars were in attendance; until the transmission (of power) to the Dark Houses had passed, it would be prudent to undertake no course of action which would involve an encounter with the enemy.[28]

The Khwarezmshah finally lost his nerve altogether:

> the Sultan withdrew from the conflict, the control of firmness having slipped from his hands and the attraction of constancy having been replaced by flight, while perplexity and doubt had taken abode in his nature; he deputized the protection of most of his lands and territories to his generals and allies.[29]

The Khwarezmshah, who was now "in a state of terror and bewilderment," cravenly decided to flee to India. All along the way from Nasaf to the city of Termez, on the north bank of Amu Darya, he warned people that he could not protect them against the coming Mongol invasion and they must now fend for themselves. To most of his subjects north of the Amu Darya it must have appeared that their Khwarezmshah had abandoned them altogether. He crossed the Amu Darya near Termez and proceeded first to Balkh in what is now Afghanistan.

While in Balkh the vizier of the Khwarezmshah's son Rukn-ad-Din arrived in Balkh from Iraq-i Ajam. Rukn-ad-Din had earlier been given control of Iraq-i Ajam and now ruled it as his personal fiefdom. The vizier, Imad-al-Mulk, first showered the Khwarezmshah with gifts and then offered counsel on behalf of Rukn-ad-Din. The Khwarezmshah should proceed west to Iraq-i Ajam and make a stand against the Mongols there: "'. . . we can gather together the army of that country and turn and do battle with open eyes and an abundance of equipment,'" he advised.[30] The Khwarezmshah's other son Jalal-ad-Din, who was also present in Balkh, took exception to this proposal. Perhaps he feared that if the Khwarezmshah fell back to Iraq-i Ajam and succeeded in saving the rump of his empire this would only increase the power of his brother, who was already the ruler of the area. Wary of his brother's ambitions, he rejected the counsel of Imad-al-Mulk and instead advised that all the scattered divisions of the Khwarezmshah should be united into one huge army which would then go on the offensive against the Mongols in Mawarannahr. If the Khwarezmshah himself did not have the stomach for this, then he should retire to the safety of Iraq-i Ajam and turn over the command of the united army to him, Jalal-ad-Din. The Khwarezmshah's son continued:

> "If fortune is kind we shall with the polo-stick of success have borne off the ball of our desire, and if our luck be unfavorable we shall at least not be the target of the reproaches of freeman and slave, nor will they lash us with the tongue of abuse and say, 'How many times did they exact tax and tribute from us! Yet in time of need they place us in the jaws of disappointment.'"[31]

Jalal-ad-Din stayed by his father's side night and day in an attempt to convince him that he, his son, should lead a united army against the Mongols, but the Khwarezmshah, "overcome with fear and dread," in the end refused to answer his supplications. At this point came the news of the fall of Bukhara.[32] (As mentioned earlier, Nasavi avers that the Khwarezmshah fled to Khorasan before the Mongols even arrived in Mawarannahr; Juvaini's account differs on this point). This was the final spur that the by-now pathologically indecisive Khwarezmshah needed. Abandoning his intention to flee to India, he decided to heed the counsel of Imad-al-Mulk, the vizier of his son Rukn-ad-Din, and proceed westward to Iraq-i Ajam, there hopefully to at long last find refuge from the Mongols.

Around this time the Khwarezmshah also sent word to his mother and family, including his young sons and harem, who were at that time still in Gurganj, the old Khwarezm capital on the lower Amu Darya, that they should leave Mawarannahr altogether seek refuge in the province of Mazandaran, just south of the Caspian Sea. Here they would be able to seek the protection of Rukn-ad-Din already in Iraq-i Ajam to the south. Thus by the summer of 1220 the entire royal family of the Khwarezmian Empire had fled Mawarannahr and left the citizens there to their fate.

❧

After setting up his headquarters at Khökh Serai, on the western edge of the city, Chingis Khan and his close advisors spent two days riding around the circumference of the city and inspecting the walls and gates.[33] The troops were allowed to rest and no fighting took place. No mention is made of the forty-eight mile-long wall that the Khwarezmshah had proposed during his last stay in the city. Apparently it had never been built, and the tax revenues meant for its construction, assuming they were ever actually collected, disappeared. Still, the city had a smaller outer wall and another wall, which had just recently been repaired and strengthened, around the *Shahristan*, called by Juvaini the Citadel. As befitting the capital of the Khwarezmian Empire, Samarkand was also the best garrisoned of all the cities in Mawarannahr. Juvaini claims that the defending troops numbered 110,000, 60,000 of whom were Turks commanded by "the Sultan's elite," and 50,000 Tajiks, by which he meant people of Persian ethnicity.[34] Each of the 50,000 Tajiks, he claimed, was the "Rustam of the age and the cream of the armies," Rustam being the hero of the Persian national epic known as the *Shahnama* and the paragon of military valor.

In addition the defenders had twenty war elephants, also the subject of a lengthy paean by Juvaini that need not be repeated here.[35] It should be noted that al-Athir claims there were only 50,000 troops in the city; Juzjani likewise says 50,000; and Nasavi says only 40,000.[36] The reason for these discrepancies is not clear, although Juvaini may have included in his number the townspeople who were not regular soldiers but who had taken up arms and formed a militia. Nasavi also claims that the governor of Samarkand was Tughay Khan, the brother of Terken Khatan, the Khwarezmshah's mother, and thus the Khwarezmshah's uncle.[37] To whom he owed his loyalty, his sister or his nephew, before the Mongols arrived is unclear; with the Mongols encircling the city it turned out that his ultimate loyalty was only to himself.

On the third day after the arrival of the Mongol army at Samarkand the battle for the city began in earnest. According to Juvaini, "when the flare of the sun's flame had risen from the darkness of the pitchy night's smoke and the nocturnal blackness had retired to the seclusion of a corner"— in other words, at dawn—the Mongol troops and attendant levies drew themselves up in a circle around the outer city walls. Accounts of what happened next vary. Juvaini claims that Alp-Er Khan, Shaikh Khan, Bala Khan, and some other khans along with the troops under their command emerged from the city gates and confronted the Mongols on the open battlefield. For most of the day the battle raged, and supposedly the Khwarezmshah's troops inflicted heavy losses on the Mongols and even captured some prisoners, who were then taken back into the city, while the defenders themselves suffered only a thousand casualties. But as Juvaini points out, "the light of the candle flares up a little before going out."[38]

Al-Athir and Juzjani paint an altogether different picture, both claiming that the Khwarezmshah's army took no part in the sortie outside the city walls. Al-Athir maintained that the defenders were made up entirely of "brave locals, men of steadfast strength," adding, "none of the Khwarezmian troops went out with them because of the fear of these accursed ones [Mongols] in their hearts."[39] He claims that the Mongols initially retreated, drawing the attackers away from the city, but then the Mongol flanks turned and cut off any routes of retreat to the city gates. The volunteer townspeople were completely surrounded. "Not one of them survived," says al-Athir, "They were killed to the last man as martyrs (may God be pleased with them). According to reports, they numbered 70,000."[40] This figure is almost certainly inflated. Juzjani claimed 30,000 died, and even this figure seems high, given the population of the city.

The next day Chingis ordered his troops to again surround the city and to guard the gates to prevent any defenders from making another sally out onto the open battlefield. By this time they had also set up mangonels and were hurtling huge rocks into the city. Unable to get their calvary out of the city gates the defenders—presumably now regular troops—tried to clear the way with their war elephants. Still the Mongols stood their ground, finally forcing the elephants to stampede back through the gates, crushing many of the defenders underfoot on their way. At dusk the defenders closed the city gates and hunkered down for the night.

Inside the city there was considerable dissension. Some factions "because of the aura diffused by Chingiz-Khan," wanted to concede defeat immediately, according to Juvaini, while others feared for their lives in the event of surrender and wanted to fight on.[41] On the morning of the fifth day of the siege the town fathers, attempting to save both their lives and property, decided to parley. The Islamic judge of the city and one of the leading sheiks led a delegation of "wearers of the turban" outside the city, and they offered to surrender Samarkand to Chingis Khan. Tughay Khan, the brother of Terken Khatan and the Khwarezmshah's uncle, not only surrendered but also offered the services of himself and the troops under him to Chingis. According to al-Athir, "The soldiers, who were Turks, said, 'We are of their race. They will not harm will us,' and so they

asked for terms, which were granted." There were of course Turk auxiliaries among the invading army, but it is not clear why the Turk defenders
of the city thought they had a racial affinity with the Mongols. In any case,
the soldiers, against the protests of the citizenry, opened the city gates and
let in the Mongol army. "'Hand over to us your weapons and mounts'", the
Mongols told the troops within the city, "'We shall convey you to a place
where you will be safe.'"[42] The Namazgah Gate on the northwestern side
of the city was thrown open and advance detachments of Mongol troops
entered without resistance. They immediately began to dismantle the city
walls and gates and continued their work through the night by torchlight.
The larger part of the city was now defenseless.

The factions who refused to surrender, knowing that they would probably be killed, remained holed up in what Juvaini calls the Citadel, the ancient part of the city also known as Afrosiab. The rest of the inhabitants
of the city were now driven out of the city by Mongol troops in groups
of one hundred each. Only the Islamic judge and other leading religious
lights of the city along with those under their protection were allowed
to remain. Juvaini claims that this group numbered 50,000, probably an
exaggeration. Whatever the actual number, this preferential treatment
would seem to indicate that Chingis Khan wanted to stay on the good
side of the Muslim elite in the city.[43] A proclamation was then issued
that anyone else who attempted conceal themselves and remain in the city
would be killed. The plunder and looting of the city began. Many who
had hidden in cellars and other places of concealment were flushed out
and killed. "They deflowered virgins and tortured people with varieties of
torture in search of money. Those not fit to be enslaved they slew."[44] At
this point the handlers of the war elephants that had survived the initial
battle rather impudently approached Chingis Khan and demanded forage
for their charges. Chingis ordered that the pachyderms be set free and allowed to graze for themselves, in the manner of Mongolian horses. All of
them eventually died of starvation.[45]

That left the Citadel, still held by the diehard Turk and Tajik troops.
The commander Alp Er Khan, realizing there was no way to withstand a
frontal assault by the Mongols, gathered together a thousand men and in
a show of "valour and intrepidity" rode out of the Citadel and managed to
cut a path right through the Mongol army, which at the time was engaged
in looting the city and apparently caught off guard. This desperate move
succeeded; Alp Er Khan and his men fought their way through the Mongolian lines and eventually managed to link up with the Khwarezmshah

Ruined walls of Afrosiab—what Juvaini calls the Citadel.

Ruined walls of Afrosiab.

in Khorasan. Disconcerted by the bold move on the part of Alp Er Khan, the Mongols completely surrounded the Citadel and set up mangonels, which were soon heaving huge rocks against the Citadel walls and gates. These were soon breached and Mongol troops entered the Citadel itself. But a thousand die-hard defenders who still refused to surrender fell back

Ruined walls of Afrosiab.

Ruins of the Friday Mosque, where the defenders of Samarkand made their last stand. The citadel of the city can be seen in the distance. This is the citadel within Afrosiab. Juvaini referred to Afrosiab itself as the citadel.

to the Friday Mosque for a final stand. Both sides flung blazing naphtha, a primitive form of napalm, at each other, and soon the mosque was ablaze. All of the defenders perished in the inferno. The various accounts differ slightly, but according to Juzjani the city fell on March 19, 1220.[46] The cap-

Ruins of the citadel within Afrosiab.

Ruins within Afrosiab.

ture of the city, which Chingis Khan had originally thought would take several years, was accomplished in about a week.

Now that the Mongols were in control, their attitude toward their captives changed. The 30,000 troops (according to Juvaini) who had earlier surrendered were now separated into two groups, Turk and Tajik, and

Afrosiab was never rebuilt after its destruction by the Mongols and remains uninhabitated to this day. The modern city of Samarkand surrounds the deserted area.

these parts were then divided into tens and hundreds. The front of their heads were shaved in the Mongol fashion, leading many to believe that they were going to be drafted into Chingis's army. Actually they were just being lulled into submission. At dusk the Mongols turned on their captives and slaughtered them to a man. Their commanders, Tughay Khan (Terken Khatan's brother), Barishmas (Turkish for "he who does not make peace") Khan, Taghai Khan, Sarsigh Khan, Ulagh Khan, and twenty other of the Khwarezmshah's emirs were also executed.

The last resistance crushed, the townspeople not under the protection of the Muslim leadership were dealt with. Thirty thousand craftsmen and artists were singled out and distributed to Chingis's sons and kinsmen as indentured workers. Another 30,000 or so young men was dragooned as levies. The remainder of the populace was allowed to return to the now thoroughly plundered city and take up their lives as best they could. But Chingis was not yet through squeezing them. The townspeople were forced to cough up some 200,000 dinars in indemnity, the collection of which was to be carried out by Siqat-al-Mulk and Amid Buzund, two Muslims who were the main pillars of the community. Chingis also appointed several local officials to rule the town. More levies were dragooned until most able-bodied men had been pressed into service. By 1222 the population of the city was only about one-fourth of what it had been before the Mongols arrived.[47] This left very few hands to rebuild the city and the local economy, "and for this reason," Juvaini tells us, "complete ruin overran the country."[48] Juvaini, although by necessity lauding the Mongol conquest of the city, was clearly saddened by the destruction of the once noble city of Samarkand. He tried to sound a philosophical note:

> O heart, lament not, for this world is only metaphorical;
> O soul, grieve not, for this abode is only transient.

If we are to believe al-Athir, the Khwarezmshah had not totally abandoned the people of Samarkand. From the safety of his camp near Balkh, south of the Amu Darya, he watched as events unfolded in Mawarannahr. He supposedly sent a relief army of 10,000 men to Samarkand, but they were unable to reach the city, and "they returned like defeated men, without having fought a battle." Another army of at least 20,000 men was also dispatched to Samarkand, but they also soon returned, apparently without having fired an arrow in anger. It now appeared that few among the Khwarezmshah's troops had the stomach for any battle with the Mongols. Al-Athir laments that it seemed like God Himself had forsaken the Khwarezmians: "We seek refuge in God from being so abandoned by Him."[49]

CHAPTER 7

JOCHI'S MARCH DOWN THE SYR DARYA
AND THE
FLIGHT OF TEMÜR MALIK

A S WE HAVE SEEN, WHEN CHINGIS KHAN first arrived at Otrar he had split up his army into three and possibly four parts. One contingent, commanded by Chagaadai and Ögedei, was tasked with investing the city of Otrar. Another, according to Juvaini, was dispatched up the Syr Darya River toward the cities of Banakat and Khujand. Chingis Khan and his son Tolui led the largest part of the army south to Bukhara. The final contingent, led by Chingis Khan's oldest son, Jochi, proceeded down the Syr Darya River toward the Aral Sea. Jochi may have been assigned the task of conquering this area, located north of Mawarannahr proper and on the southern edge of the Kipchaq Steppe, because it was a part of the territories that were to fall to him as part of his inheritance. Thus it was up to him to subdue the region.[1] We might also speculate that Jochi had been sent in a different direction from the bulk of the Mongol army to separate him from his brothers, especially Chagaadai, with whom he was not on the best of terms. Given the bad blood between Jochi and Chagaadai, it is hard to imagine them sharing the command of an army.

The first city that Jochi and his men approached was Suqnuq, on the north bank of the Syr Darya, about 110 miles northwest of Otrar. He sent on ahead to parley with the defenders of the city an envoy who Juvaini calls Hasan Hajji. This may have been the Muslim trader named Asan who, according to the *Secret History*, had offered his services to the Mongols perhaps as far back as 1202.[2] He had remained with the Mongols and was now assigned to Jochi's army. Hasan Hajji presented the town fathers of Suqnuq with the familiar Mongol ultimatum: surrender and submit and their lives and property would be spared, or oppose the advancing army and face plunder and slaughter. According to Juvaini, "the rogues, rascals, and ruffians" of the town, preferring "holy war," shouted "'Allah akhbar' and did him to death."[3] They may have been motivated at least in part by the fact that Hasan Hajji was a Muslim himself who had sided with Mongol idolators. The infuriated Jochi, "closing the door of forgiveness and mercy," surrounded Suqnaq and ordered his troops to attack in relays from morning to night for seven days. The city finally fell and almost the entire populace of the city was massacred. The city was handed over to the son of Hasan Hajji, who then tracked down and killed any survivors who had managed to hide themselves from the initial onslaught.

Between Suqnuq and Jand, perhaps the most important city on the lower Syr Darya, were three smaller cities: Özkend, Barchinlighkant, and Ashnas. Cities or towns by the name of Özkend and Barchinlighkant no longer exist and their exact locations in the thirteen century are unknown.[4] The city fathers of the two cities, no doubt cognizant of the fate of Suqnaq, quickly handed over their cities to the Mongols without a fight, avoiding a general slaughter. Ashnas, the ruins of which are reportedly located on the left, or south, bank of the Syr Darya, twenty miles from the current-day town of Berkazan, in Kazakhstan, was like Suqnaq inhabited by "rogues and ruffians," who according to Juvaini sought martyrdom; the greater part of them found it at the hands of Jochi and his men.[5]

The road to Jand was now clear. The exact location of this city is unclear, but it may have been located some twenty miles downstream from the current-day city of Qyzylorda.[6] Unlike some other cities of the Syr Darya Basin, notably Khujand, the origins of Jand did not date back to antiquity. Oghuz tribesmen from the steppes to the north may have built settlements and trading posts here at Jand and elsewhere on the lower Syr Darya earlier, but it was probably not until the tenth century that Muslim merchants established trading posts in the area. According to legend, it was here that Saljuq b. Duqaq, the semi-mythical founder of the Saljuq Empire, was converted to Islam. Under the Saljuqs and later the Khwarezmshahs the city enjoyed a brief florescence as both a trading post and a bulwark against the pagan tribes to the north. Jand's importance was underlined by the fact that the sons of Khwarezmshahs were by tradition appointed governor of the city and the surrounding district, and it was here, in this crucial border area, that they honed their military and administrative skills. As we have seen, in 1216 the Khwarezmshah himself led an expedition from Jand against Jochi, who had been hounding down fugitive Merkits on the Kipchaq Steppe to the north.

Word of the fates of Suqnaq, Ashnas, and other cities in the path of Mongols had reached Jand well before the Mongols arrived in the area. Frightened by what he had heard, Qutlugh Khan, the Khwarezmian general who had been charged with the defense of the city, and most of his troops abandoned the city without a fight, fleeing under cover of night across the Syr Darya and south to Khwarezm on the lower Amu Darya. His behavior prompted another yet pithy aphorism from the pen of Juvaini: "He that escapeth with his head has gained thereby."[7] The military presence having decamped, Jochi sent a man named Chin Temür into the city to parley with the civilian panjandrums. Chin Temür, who may have been a Qara Khitai who had sided with the Mongols, offered to spare the lives and property of the citizenry if they peacefully submitted to the Mongols. The city fathers had no clear spokesman or leader, however, and were unable to come up with a consensus on how to answer Chin-Temür's demands, as clear-cut as they might have been. Then the "common people," according to Juvaini, took matters in their own hand and in a replay of the events at Suqnaq apparently tried to poison Chin Temür. Even after this attempt on his life failed Chin Temür stuck to his conciliatory approach and finally managed to negotiate a treaty whereby the citizens of Jand would not be harmed if they agreed not to oppose the Mongols in any way.

Indeed, it appears that Jochi, who had apparently not even gone to Jand himself, had already decided not to sack the city at this time. Its military garrison had already fled, and its citizenry posed no real threat. Instead, he decided to retire to the Kipchaq Steppe to the north, an area that he was familiar with from his previous raid, and spend the spring and summer acquiring additional horses—his army was in need of fresh mounts—and fattening those that he already had. He could deal with Jand later, perhaps in the autumn. Then Chin Temür returned from Jand and Jochi heard straight from the lips of his envoy about the "weakness and impotence of the people and the divergence of their views and passions" and about the attempt on Chin Temür's life.[8] Perhaps it was the latter that tipped the scale. The Mongols considered envoys sacrosanct. Jochi abruptly changed his mind and decided to attack the city.

On April 21, 1220, the Mongol army appeared before the walls of Jand. The townspeople, who had no experience of warfare, mounted the walls of the city and watched "like spectators at a festival" as the Mongols pre-

pared catapults, battering rams, and scaling ladders. Apparently they at
first thought their city walls were impregnable, but the danger they faced
finally dawned on them and they made some half-hearted attempts at
defense. They set up a catapult to hurl stones back at the Mongols, but
it misfired, the stone falling back on the catapult itself and destroying it.
Facing very little resistance, the Mongols set up scaling ladders and soon
vaulted the city walls and opened the gates from inside. Jand fell with no
real fight. A few of the town fathers who had insulted Chin Temür earlier
and presumably the miscreants involved in the poisoning attempt were
put to death, but most of the inhabitants were driven out of the city and
forced to camp on the surrounded plains for nine days while the Mongols
looted the city. Thus Jochi got to claim a victory and garner the loot with
little if any loss of life among his own forces. Jochi then appointed Ali
Khoja, a native of Gizhduvan village near Bukhara, as the governor of
Jand and the surrounding district. Ali Khoja, it will be remembered, was
one of the three Muslim traders whom Chingis Khan had sent on his embassy to the Khwarezmshah in 1218. This governorship was presumably
the reward for his faithful service to the Mongols. "Held in high repute,"
Ali Khoja held the post until he transmigrated, or as Juvaini put it, "until
the Decree of Death for his dismissal went forth from the Palace of Fate."[9]

From Jand Jochi sent a commander with a detachment of troops downstream 160 miles to the town of Yanikent, located on the south bank of the
Syr Darya about fifteen miles from the current-day town of Kazalinsk.[10]
It was easily captured by the Mongols, thus completing their conquest
of the Syr Darya basin. Jochi himself and probably most of his troops
retired to the Kipchaq Steppe for the summer to rest and fatten their
horses. Jochi, operating on his own, apart from the rest of his family, had
acquitted himself well and was now in possession of an important part of
his future patrimony.

While Jochi was marching down the Syr Darya, a half-division of men
(5,000) under the command of Alaq Noyan, Sögetü, and Tughay was
moving up the river towards Banakat and Khujand, at least according
to Juvaini. Other sources suggest that this half-division and contingents
from the army of Chagaadai and Ögedei were sent to the upper Syr
Darya after the fall of Samarkand. Or, possibly, contingents from Samarkand linked up on the upper Syr Darya with the half-division sent
earlier from the Otrar area. In any case, Chagaadai and Ögedei do not
appear to have accompanied their men on this campaign.[11] Banakat was

located about 120 miles northeast of Samarkand on the north bank of the Syr Darya River.[12] The battle raged for three days, but on the fourth day the defenders "begged for quarter and came forth to surrender." The soldiers and townspeople were separated into two groups. All of the soldiers were executed, "some by the sword and others by a shower of arrows."[13] The civilians were separated into groups of hundreds and tens, and then the artisans and other skilled persons were assigned to work details. The young and unskilled were dragooned as levies for the upcoming siege on Khujand.

Khujand is located on the Syr Darya about sixty miles upstream from Banakat, near the mouth of the Fergana Valley, in what is now Tajikistan. An urban center existed on the site of Khujand at least as early as the fifth century B.C., and Alexander the Great appears to have founded a city named Alexandria either here or close by during his sojourn through the area in 329–327 B.C. In the 720s A.D. the city was seized by Islamic Arabs and the area eventually became part of the Baghdad-based Caliphate. During the Samanid era (c. 875–999) the city flourished as a trade entrepôt and became famous for its gardens, vineyards, and metals produced from ores in the nearby mountains. The tenth-century geographer Muqaddasi (c. 945–1000) allowed that Khujand was a "city of joy" and deserved the praise by poets and wise men alike. In the eleventh and twelfth centuries the city was ruled by the Qarakhanids, and after their defeat at the hands of the Khwarezmshah it had become at least nominally a part of the Khwarezmian empire. By the time the Mongols arrived in 1220 the city consisted of a citadel, a walled inner fortress where the Friday mosque was located, and an outer artisan and trade quarter, also surrounded by a wall.[14]

By the time it reached Khujand the Mongol army numbered some 20,000 soldiers and 50,000 levies.[15] Obviously the original 5,000 man contingent, wherever it was sent from, had been heavily augmented by additional corps and levies. The military commander in charge of defending the city was one Temür Malik. This lion-hearted warrior would eventually achieve near-legendary status for his exploits in opposing the Mongols. Even Juvaini could not resist heaping him knee-deep in laurels: "Had Rustam lived in his age he [Rustam] would have been fit only to be his groom."[16] (Rustam, you will recall, was one of the main character in the Persian classic *Shahnama* and the exemplar of a military hero.) Temür Malik, having concluded that the city itself was indefensible, chose 1,000 of his best fighting men and retired to a high-walled and well-fortified stronghold on an island in the middle of the Syr Darya just north of the city. The city itself quickly surrendered, apparently without a battle, and the Mongols turned their attentions to Temür Malik and his holdouts on the island. They soon discovered that neither their arrows nor their mangonels could reach the fortress in the middle of the Syr Darya. Other measures were necessary. All of the young civilian men they had seized in the city together with the levies brought from Banakat and other cities were divided into detachments of tens and hundreds and made to carry rocks to the river in an attempt to build a bridge to the island fortress.[17] Meanwhile, Temür Malik constructed twelve covered barges. The barges were covered with felt which was then smeared with clay dampened by vinegar, which served as a fire retardant. The covered portions of the barges had peepholes from which his soldiers could fire their arrows and other weapons. Each morning Temür Malik dispatched these barges, six upstream (apparently rowed) and six downstream (apparently rowed back each day). The arrows of the Mongols were of no avail against the fortified barges, and the stones and burning naphtha that they flung at them had no effect. Instead, from these veritable dreadnoughts Temür Malik's men managed to inflict considerable damage on the Mongols lined up along the river. A stalemate soon ensued. Temür Malik had his own plan, however. According to Juvaini, "at the time when the loaf-like disk of the sun became food in the belly of the earth and the world from darkness was like a wretched hovel"—in other words, after the sun had gone down— Temür Malik loaded all of his soldiers, horses, and supplies in the barges and seventy boats and disembarked downstream on the Syr Darya.[18]

The Mongols followed this naval detachment downstream, but the bowmen on the barges continued to wreak havoc on the Mongol soldiers who followed their progress from both shores of the river. At Banakat the Mongols managed to stretch a huge chain across the river in hopes of stopping Temür Malik's convoy, but his big barges broke through and they proceeded farther downstream. Soon he reached the districts of Jand and Barjligh. By now Jochi had reached the lower Syr Darya, and he had been apprized the approach of Temür Malik and his flotilla. At Jand he stationed troops on both sides of the river and strung a line of boats across the river to impede Temür Malik's further progress. On shore catapults were hastily set up, ready to heave rocks at the passing barges. Temür Malik somehow got word of the trap waiting for him, however, and upstream from Jand, at Barjligh-Kent, he beached his boats and he and his men took off on horseback across the desert. The Mongols were soon in hot pursuit, but Temür Malik sent his baggage train on ahead and took rear-guard actions against his pursuers. This went on for several days and soon most of his men had been killed or wounded. Temür Malik himself had only three arrows left when three Mongol soldiers finally caught up with him, and one of these had no arrowhead. He fired the blank arrow and hit one Mongol in the eye, blinding him. Facing the two remaining Mongols, he declared, "'I have two arrows left. I begrudge using them when they are only enough for you two. It is in your best interest to retire and so save your lives."[19] According to Juvaini, they did in fact retire, and Temür Malik managed to escape across the desert, eventually turning up in Gurganj in Khwarezm.[20]

After rallying some troops in Gurganj he returned with them to the Syr Darya Valley and attacked the city of Yanikent, where he managed to kill the local Mongol governor. Then he retreated to Khwarezm. The situation there was quickly unraveling, however, and he soon fled to Khorasan where he finally managed to hook up with the Khwarezmshah. The chronology is unclear, but apparently by this time the Khwarezmshah was in frantic flight from Chingis Khan's two Hounds, Jebe and Sübedei. Temür Malik may have decided that the Khwarezmshah and his entourage were doomed, since he himself donned the "garb and character of a Sufi" and took off incognito for Syria.[21]

This was not the end of Temür Malik's adventures, which even up to now sound like some phantasmagorical tale from the *Shahnama*. Many years later, long after the Khwarezmian Empire had finally fallen to the Mongols, Temür Malik returned to the city of Osh, upstream on the Syr Darya from his old home town of Khujand, still in the disguise of a Sufi pilgrim. Here he became a familiar sight at the numerous Sufi pilgrim places. Eventually Temür Malik got word that his son was still alive in Khujand. Returning to Khujand, he soon discovered that he had long been thought to be dead and that his son had inherited all his former possessions. Approaching his son, he said: "'If you sawst thine own father, wouldst thou know him again?'" The young man replied, "'I was but a suckling when I was parted from him: I should not recognize him.'"[22] One of Temür Malik's servants when he previously had lived in Khujand was still alive, however, and when this man was produced he identified his old master from various marks on his body. Temür Malik then looked up people to whom he had previously lent money before the invasion of the Mongols and tried to collect the debts. Most denied that he was in fact Temür Malik and refused to pay back the loans. Not to be outdone in this, Temür Malik then boldly approached the local ruler, who by most accounts was Qadan, the sixth son of Chingis's third son Ögedei, and attempted to get redress. Not quite sure who he dealing with, Qadan slapped Temür Malik in irons and had him interrogated. According to the story retailed by Juvaini, in Qadan's court was the very man Temür Malik had blinded in one eye during his escape from the Mongols many years before. With his remaining good eye he recognized Temür Malik and denounced him to Qadan. The Mongol ruler confronted Temür Malik about his earlier actions against the Mongols and in replying the latter "neglected the ceremonies of respect that are incumbent on those that speak in the presence of royalty." According to Juvaini, "he was removed from this transient dust-heap to the Abode of Eternity" by the infuriated Qadan himself, who dispatched him with an arrow, his just reward for all the arrows he had shot at Mongols.[23]

As can be seen from this exegesis of his career, Temür Malik's actions displayed a near supra-natural combination of cunning, bravery, initiative, resourcefulness, and bravado. It was these very qualities that prompted Juvaini, even though he was the hired pen of the Mongols, to compare him favorably to the legendary character Rustam. Barthold took a different view; Temür Malik's exploits, he observed:

> . . . like the subsequent exploits of Jalal-ad-Din [the son of the Khwarezmshah] himself, are examples of personal heroism quite useless to the common cause. On the Muslim side we find heroes with a handful of people performing prodigies of valour (probably exaggerated, for the rest, by their own boastfulness, or that of others), but completely unable to organize larger forces, and for that reason constantly retreating before the main force of the Tartars [Mongols]. On the side of the Mongols we scarcely ever find examples of personal heroism in this war; the commanders are no more than obedient and skillful executants of the will of their sovereign, who detaches and unites separate corps of his army as occasion demands, and rapidly takes measures to evade the consequences of occasional failures. The strictly-disciplined Mongol soldiers sought no occasion to distinguish themselves from their companions, but carried out with precision the orders of their sovereign or the leaders appointed by him.[24]

Temür Malik was indeed a valiant hero, but in the end he lost his city, his cause, and his life.

CHAPTER 8

THE FLIGHT OF THE KHWAREZMSHAH

EITHER BEFORE OR IMMEDIATELY AFTER the fall of Samarkand Chingis Khan dispatched two of this best generals, Jebe and Sübedei, in pursuit of the Khwarezmshah, who by that time was believed to be at Balkh in Khorasan. "'It is necessary to make an end to him and be well rid of him before men gather around him and nobles join him from every side,'" Chingis explained.[1] It will be recalled that Jebe and Sübedei were two of Chingis's Four Hounds, commanders who could be expected to attain any target, no matter how distant or elusive. Jebe had of course already earned his stripes by hounding down and killing Khüchüleg in the High Pamirs. Sübetei was an up-and-coming commander who would eventually distinguish himself in campaigns in China, Hungary, and elsewhere and become one of Chingis Khan's most illustrious generals. Chingis told his two Hounds, "'Pursue Khwarazm Shah, wherever he may be, even if he has climbed to the sky, until you catch up with him and seize him.'"[2] Under their command were 30,000 troops, "each of whom was to a thousand men of the Sultan's army as a wolf to a flock of sheep," according to the ever-gushing Juvaini.[3]

From Samarkand the Mongol pursuit party rode south 190 miles to the Amu Darya and crossed the river at the well-known Mela Ford near the city of Termez.[4] Currently, the river here serves as the boundary between Uzbekistan and Afghanistan. Al-Athir described the manner of the crossing:

> Having arrived [at the ford], they found not a single boat there, so they made what resembled large troughs out of wood and covered them with cattle skins so that they would be impermeable to water. They placed their weapons and belongings in them and then urged their horses into

the water and held on to their tails with those wooden troughs tied to their own bodies. Thus each horse dragged a man and each man dragged a trough that was full of his weapons and other things. All of them crossed over at the same time and the first thing Khwarazm Shah knew of them they were with him on the same ground.[5]

Barthold questions this account, citing the scarcity of wood for making troughs along the Amu Darya, and suggests that the Mongols used the method of crossing rivers described by Plano Carpini in which gear was placed in tightly bound leather bags and not wooden troughs. The men sat on these bags, which served as rafts, and were pulled across the river by their swimming horses.[6]

From here it was about fifty miles ATCF southwest to Balkh. The Mongols arrived at city only to find that the Khwarezmshah had already fled westward even before they had crossed the river.[7] The city fathers, who at this point had no quarrel with the Mongols, sent out a deputation to parley with Jebe and Sübedei. The spokesmen, in hopes that Jebe and Sübedei would leave them in peace, offered provisions for the Mongol army and a local guide to assist them in their pursuit of the Khwarezmshah. With their eye on their main objective, the Mongol generals led their men onward. Thus Balkh escaped unscathed from this first encounter with the Mongols. According to al-Athir, they now "made no halts on their road, neither for plunder, or for murder, and only redoubled their pace in his pursuit, allowing him [the Khwarezmshah] no rest."[8]

They came next to the city of Zava, the current-day city of Torbat-i-Haidari in Iran, 480 miles south-southwest of Balkh, where Jebe and Sübedei demanded more provender for their troops. Here the city fathers were less cooperative. They closed the city gates and refused to give any assistance to the Mongols. At this point, apparently still under orders to track down and capture the Khwarezmshah and not to invest cities, Jebe and Sübedei decided to bypass the city. But after they had left word reached them that the citizens of the city were celebrating what they perceived to be a victory by beating on drums and pouring out streams of abuse at the Mongols who were apparently afraid to attack their city. This proved be to be too much for Jebe and Sübedei. The reputation of the Mongols as an invincible force was at stake. They wheeled their army around and returned to put the city under siege. On the third day, according to Juvaini, "they scaled the walls and left not alive whomsoever they saw; and being unable to stay they burnt and broke whatever was too heavy to carry."[9]

No sooner had they sacked the city than an enormous earthquake, the worst in living memory, hit eastern Khorasan (the area is notorious for earthquakes; huge temblors have rocked the area as late as 1986 and 1997). Juvaini could not resist the conclusion that these two events were somehow connected: "It was as though this fighting and slaying were the clue to the calamities of Fate and the disaster of cruel Destiny . . . an earthquake shook Khorasan, and from hearing that event, whereof they had never heard the like, the people were seized with terror."[10] Jebe and Sübedei, however, were not to be delayed by mere earthquakes. They and their men hurried on east to the city of Nishapur, sixty-five miles northwest of Torbat-i-Haidari where, according to the latest intelligence they had received, the Khwarezmshah was now holed up.

The Mongols who were now fastened on his trail were not the Khwarezmshah's only problem. While in route to Nishapur—or perhaps while still in Balkh (Juvaini is maddeningly imprecise in his chronology here)—he almost fell victim to an assassination plot. The perpetrators were Turkmen belonging to his mother's tribe who were in the detachments of troops accompanying the Khwarezmshah. Apparently the long-simmering dispute between the Khwarezmshah and his mother had not cooled down and some Terken Khatan loyalists decided to take matters into their own hands. It is possible that by this time they had decided that the only hope for saving the rapidly crumbling Khwarezmian Empire was to eliminate the ever-vacillating Khwarezmshah and replace him with someone capable of rallying the troops and taking the fight to the Mongols. Or perhaps they simply did not want their fates tied to a loser. In any case, someone in the Khwarezmshah entourage tipped him off to the plot and that night he secretly changed his sleeping quarters . The next morning the tent in which he was supposed to have stayed was riddled with arrows, but the Khwarezmshah, who had slept elsewhere, had survived. Already paralyzed by fear of the Mongols, now the Khwarezmshah had to watch his back lest his own soldiers kill him as they proceeded onward.

Somewhere in the area of current-day Meshed the Khwarezmshah and his party halted at the castle of Kalat. This fortress complex was surrounded by a long wall and appeared to be capable of withstanding long sieges. Some of his advisors suggested that the fortress be repaired and stocked with supplies and that the Khwarezmshah should take refuge here. Supposedly the Khwarezmshah was heading for Iraq-i Ajam with hopes of linking up with his son, but this advice suggests that his itinerary was by no means fixed and that at least some members of his entourage were looking for whatever safe haven they could find. Their advice was rejected by the Khwarezmshah. Perhaps the austere confines of a remote fortress held no appeal to him when Nishapur, one of the largest and most sophisticated cities of his realm, was probably no more than fifty miles away.

The Khwarezmshah arrived in Nishapur on April 18, 1220.[11] The city, located on a fertile plain at the base of the Binalud Mountains, served as an important entrepôt for trade between the Iranian Plateau and Mawarannahr to the northeast and as a strategic way-station on the Silk Road between China and the Mediterranean. Nishapur was famous for the turquoise mined nearby, which became an important trade item on the whole length of the Silk Road, and for the ceramics produced in the city itself. By the eleventh century it was probably one the ten largest cities in the world and was mentioned in the same breath as Baghdad and Cairo. The city was also home to numerous luminaries: the famous polymath and poet Omar Khayyam, he of "A loaf of bread, and jug of wine, and Thou" fame, was born here in 1048, as was Farid al-Attar (1145?–1221), the prolific Sufi poet who authored the famous allegory, *The Conference of the Birds*, and Haj Bektash Veli (1209–1271), founder of the Bektashi order of Sufis, which would eventually became enormously influential in the Ottoman Empire.

In this cosmopolitan environment the steadily unraveling Khwarezmshah gave himself over to bacchanalias:

> Here he turned his back on the affairs of his realm, amusing himself with songstresses and songs . . . He therefore constantly applied himself to the quaffing of cups of wine and had no fear of the arrows of reproach . . . Because of arranging the jewels on his women he could not concern himself with the training of his men, and whilst pulling down the garments of his wives he neglected to remove the confusion in important affairs.[12]

The Khwarezmshah was approached by numerous of the town fathers and other important personages of the area who petitioned him on various matters of state—he was in their eyes, after all, still the Sultan of the Khwarezmian Empire—but all came away "perplexed and bewildered" by his dissolute behavior.[13] Finally, having seen enough of their unwelcome guest, they assembled at the gate of the local vizier, Mujir-al-Mulk, and protested against the unseemly behavior of the Khwarezmshah. Mujir-al-Mulk, although a highly respected official, admitted that there was not much he could do:

> "What you say is perfectly true, and your complaints are fully justified
> . . . Because of my duties as a pander [*qavvadagi*, or pimp], I cannot
> attend to the business of leaders . . . and because I must see to the pro-
> vision of damsels I have no time to check the registers. Some days ago
> the Sultan commanded us to provide so and so many ornaments for
> the singing girls and to do nothing else. The Sultan's orders must be
> complied with . . ."[14]

It was just then, according to Juvaini, that news arrived in Nishapur
that Jebe and Sübedei and their army of 30,000 Mongols had crossed
the Amu Darya into Khorasan and were now baying on the trail of the
Khwarezmshah. The Khwarezmshah had indulged in the belief that re-
gardless of what happened to his realm in Mawarannahr he was safe here
in Khorasan. Now he was exposed to the harsh light of reality. "Having
drunk every drop in the goblet of pleasure he ought to have expected the
sting of the headache that followed," pontificated Juvaini, adding, "And for
every joy there was substituted a sorrow and for every rose was exchanged
a thorn."[15] Alerted to the imminent arrival of the Mongols in Nishapur,
the Khwarezmshah decamped from the city on May 12, 1220, according
to Juvaini.[16]

Although Juvaini's account of the Khwarezmshah's scandalous behavior
in Nishapur is certainly titillating, it must be mentioned that Nasavi, who
as the secretary of Jalal-ad-Din, the Khwarezmshah's son, should have
been well-informed on the Khwarezmshah's movements, tells a different
story. He implies that the Khwarezmshah in his haste to escape the Mongols passed right through Nishapur without even stopping for a day.[17] It is
possible, however, that Nasavi did not want to dwell on the reprehensible
behavior of the Khwarezmshah, the father of his patron, while in Nishapur, and chose instead to simply ignore this interlude.

Jebe and Sübedei arrived at the walls of Nishapur in early June.[18] They
immediately sent an envoy into the city to meet with the local officials
and demand food and other supplies. Three local envoys then came out to
meet Jebe and proffer gifts and provisions. They made an outward show
of submission, but Jebe was not satisfied. He harangued them about the
futility of any further resistance and to reinforce his point he presented to
the town fathers a copy of a decree in Uighur script from Chingis Khan,
apparently stamped with his own seal, which stated:

"Whosoever . . . shall submit, mercy will be shown to them and unto his wives and children and household; but whosoever shall not submit, shall perish together with all his wives and children and kinsmen."[19]

The import of this decree seemed to be that although Jebe and Sübedei might ride on, the city must immediately submit to any other Mongol armies that arrived in the future.[20] Chingis had probably already decided to invade Khorasan at this point, and was depending on Jebe and Sübedei—in addition to hounding down the Khwarezmshah—to demand in advance the submission of the region's cities. Indeed, according to one Chinese source, Jebe and Sübedei had been given specific orders by Chingis not to actually invest any cities until he himself arrived in Khorasan.[21] When sufficiently provoked, as at Zava, the two Mongol generals would overlook this order, but otherwise they were to keep their attention focused on the Khwarezmshah.

While in Nishapur, however, it became clear to Jebe and Sübedei that they had lost the scent of their quarry. The Khwarezmshah, in his desperation, was traveling fast and light, with only a small retinue and a few bodyguards, and was covering his tracks well. Even the historians al-Athir and Juzjani are unable to account for his movements at this point.[22] Jebe and Sübedei now decided to split up and head in different directions in hopes of coming across the Khwarezmshah's spoor. Jebe heading westward to the district of Juvain (home of our scribe, Juvaini) and the current-day city of Jagastai. Sübedei backtracked in case the Khwarezm had somehow slipped around behind his pursuers. First he headed southeast to Jam (current-day Torbat Jam in Iran), and finding no sign of the Khwarezmshah there, then looped around northward towards Tus, near modern-day Meshed.[23] Realizing that the scent here had long gone cold, he hurried on to Quchan and then to Isfarayin, on the great east-west Trunk Road through Khorasan. According to Juvaini, the Khwarezmshah had indeed passed through Isfarayin, and here Sübedei may have stumbled upon the traces of his trail. By now Sübedei's patience was apparently wearing thin, however, and he no longer felt bound by his orders to stay in hot pursuit of the Khwarezmshah and not attack cities. He offered Quchan and Isfarayin the same terms that he and Jebe had offered Nishapur, but they refused to submit and were subjected to savage assaults and massacres, according to Juvaini. He then moved on to Damghan, where he discovered that many of the town's most prominent citizens had fled the city and taken refuge in the Ismaili stronghold of Gerdkuh.

The fortress of Gerdkuh, built on a precipitous massif some ten miles west of Damghan, was considered so impregnable that the Ismaili Hassan Sabbah, founder of the Assassin sect, sent his own family here for safe-keeping when his own stronghold of Alamut—itself legendary as an impenetrable redoubt—was under attack. Overlooking the Khorasan Trunk Road—the main artery of the Silk Road through Khorasan—the occupants of the castle had grown rich by extorting fees from passing caravans. The living quarters of the fortress were extensive and a large number of people could live here for months or years, if necessary. Later on, in the 1250s, when Chingis Khan's grandson Khülegü attacked the Ismaili strongholds in what is now Iran, Gerdkuh held out the longest, withstanding a seventeen-year siege from 1253 to 1270.[24] Here the eminences of Damghan took refuge from Sübedei. Obviously he did not have time to invest and subdue such a formidable bastion as this. Instead he attacked the "ruffians"—Juvaini's term—who had remained behind in the city. These were soon routed by the Mongols. At this point Sübedei may have received intelligence that the Khwarezmshah was in Rayy, because he now headed straight for the city on the Great Trunk Road. Meanwhile Jebe, after rampaging through the Juvain district, had crossed the Elburz Mountains to the province of Mazandaran on the southern edge of the Caspian Sea and laid waste to Amol and other nearby cities and towns. He too, learning of the Khwarezmshah's whereabouts, immediately abandoned his raid on Mazandaran and headed south to Rayy.

According to Nasavi, while on his way to Rayy the Khwarezmshah had stopped briefly in the city of Bistam (Bastam, in current-day Iran), located almost exactly halfway between Nishapur and Rayy, on the southern edge of the Elburz Mountains. Here he met with the local governor Taj al-din Omar Bistami and handed over to him two chests filled with precious jewels with the instructions that the treasure should be taken for safe-keeping to the fortress of Ardahn, described by Nasavi as "one of the strongest fortresses in the world."[25] The fortress of Ardahn was located about a three-day journey (perhaps sixty miles) from Rayy, in the mountains between Damavand and Mazandaran.[26] Apparently the Khwarezmshah hoped that the jewels would be held there in safe-keeping in case he lost all his other financial resources in his precipitous flight from the Mongols. If so, he was sorely disappointed; the fortress itself eventually fell to the Mongols and the seized treasure was sent to Chingis Khan as war booty. Juvaini, it must be noted, does not mention the stop in Bistami nor this incident with the jewels. As we shall see, he does claim that after the Khwarezmshah's death his remains were eventually interred at Ardahn.[27] Thus while his earthly treasure stashed at Ardahn was lost, the Khwarezmshah's earthly coil will presumably remain here until the Final Resurrection.

Both Juvaini and Nasavi agree that the Khwarezmshah did not remain long in Rayy. According to Juvaini, patrols loyal to the Khwarezmshah soon turned up in the city with the alarming news that the Mongols were close at hand. The Khwarezmshah now fled toward the castle of Farrazin, located near modern-day Arak, about 150 miles southwest of Rayy on the Hamadan-Isfahan Highway. Here he linked up with his son Rukn al-Din, who had about 30,000 troops under his command. Up until now, Rukn-ad-Din had stayed out of the fray, apparently hoping to save the troops loyal to him for a final stand in Iraq-i Ajam.

With Rukh-ad-Din was the Khwarezmshah's mother Terken Khatan, members of his harem who were traveling with her, and another son Ghiyash-ad-Din. Earlier, right after he had crossed the Amu Darya in flight from Mawarannahr, the Khwarezmshah had sent word to his mother, who was then living in Gurganj, the original capital of Khwarezm on the lower Amu Darya, that she should seek refuge from the Mongols in the Mazandaran area south of the Caspian Sea.[28] Taking with her the vizier Nasir-ad-Din, the Khwarezmshah's own harem, her own younger sons and grandsons, assorted hangers-on, and a large cache of treasure, presumably gold, jewels, etc., she fled the city, leaving its defense to the local emirs. As we shall see, it was they who would have to deal with the Mongols under the command of Chagaadai, Ögedei, and Jochi who eventually invested the city.

Traveling by way of Delistan, in what is now southwestern Turkmenistan, Terken Khatan and her party reached Mazandaran. There they apparently heard that the Khwarezmshah was now somewhere between Hamadan and Isfahan. Proceeding south they finally linked up with him at the castle of Farrazin. The Khwarezmshah now sent her and her party for safekeeping to what Juvaini at one point calls the "castle of Qarun."[29] The location of this castle is unclear, but it may have been in the mountains south of Hamadan. In any case, with his family and women out of the way, the Khwarezmshah finally appeared ready to take some concrete action against the Mongols hounding his trail. First he summoned Nusrat-ad-Din, who ruled over the ancient kingdom of Luristan, centered around the Zagros Mountains on the western edge of the Iranian Plateau. While waiting for Nusrat-ad-Din to arrive he consulted with the local emirs on how best to deal with the Mongol incursion, which was now threatening them all. They advised that the best course of action would be to take refuge in the depths of Ushturan-Kuh ("Mountains of the Camel"), a chain of mountains in the High Zagros Range extending southward from the city of Borüjerd in the modern-day province of Lorestan (the current-day Iranian Nature Preserve of Oshtran Kuh, perhaps a modern-day spelling of Ushturan-Kuh, is located in this mountain range). The Khwarezmshah himself went off to inspect the proposed redoubt and was not impressed: "'This is no place for us to take refuge in nor can we withstand the Mongol army in such a fastness.'"[30] The emirs, Juvaini notes, "were much disheartened" by the Khwarezmshah's refusal to heed their advice.

By the time the Khwarezmshah had returned from his reconnaissance of the mountains the ruler of Luristan, Hazar-Alp, had arrived at his camp. Luristan was still nominally a part of the Khwarezmian Empire, and at his first audience Hazar-Alp honored the Khwarezmshah by kissing the ground in front of him seven times. The Khwarezmshah reciprocated the honor by allowing Nusrat-ad-Din to be seated in his presence. But apparently nothing of import was discussed at this first audience. Later the Khwarezmshah sent two of his advisors to Nusrat-ad-Din's tent to sound him out on how best to deal with the Mongol threat. Nusrat-ad-Din advised that the Khwarezmshah should pack up immediately and retreat to a mountain range between Fars and Luristan known as Tang-i-Balu. Within this mountain range was a rich and fertile valley that according to local lore was one of the Four Earthly Paradises. "'Let us go their and make our asylum,'" urged Hazar Asp, adding:

> "We shall muster a hundred thousand foot [soldiers] out of Luristan, Shuristan, and Fars and set men at all the approaches to the mountain. When the Mongol army arrives, we shall advance against them with a stout heart and fight a good fight. As for the Sultan's army, which has suddenly [been] overcome with fear and terror, if on that occasion we gain a victory, they will realize their own strength and might and the weakness and impotence of their enemies; they will take heart."[31]

The territory where Nusrat-ad-Din advised taking refuge was, however, apparently in the domains of the Atabeg of Fars, with whom the Luristan ruler had a quarrel. The suspicious Khwarezmshah surmised that Nusrat-ad-Din intended to somehow use him and his troops to seize the Atabeg's territory. Nusrat-ad-Din's counsel was rejected, and instead the now-chronically indecisive Khwarezmshah decided to remain where he was and await the turn of events.

He did not have long to wait. Patrols soon pounded into Farrazin with the news the Mongols under Jebe and Sübedei had reached Rayy. Juvaini appears uncertain of what happened at Rayy. At one point he says that the city had surrendered without a fight and the Mongols had rode on, leaving it unscathed; elsewhere he says that Jebe and Sübedei sacked the town and massacred its inhabitants.[32] According to al-Athir, the Mongols:

> came to Rayy in pursuit of Khwarazm Shah . . . They travelled with all speed on his tracks. Many troops, Muslims and infidels, had attached themselves to them, as also did those troublemakers who wanted to plunder and do mischief. They arrived at Rayy, taking the inhabitants by surprise. They had no inkling of them until they arrived. They took and sacked the city, captured the women and enslaved the children. They perpetrated acts unheard of, but did not stay and hurried away in the hunt for Khwarazm Shah. On the road they plundered every town and village they passed and in all of them did things much worse than what they had done at Rayy. They burned, destroyed and put men, women and children to the sword. They spared nothing.[33]

The Mongol commanders heard that the Khwarezmshah had fled in the direction of Hamadan. The two Mongol commanders now decided that the Khwarezmshah did not merit the attentions of both of them. Perhaps acting on rumors that the Khwarezmshah's family had fled north toward refuges in the Elborz Mountains, Sübedei rode northwest from Rayy to Qazwin in an attempt to cut off their escape route. Jebe and his men had hurried to Hamadan, where "the headman went out with money and clothes and with horses and other items to seek terms for the population."[34]

The Khwarezmshah's court was thrown into total disarray. Nusrat-ad-Din abandoned the Khwarezmshah altogether and headed home, the troops under him fleeing in all directions. The accounts of what happened next are even more muddled than usual, and Juvaini and Nasavi give widely varying versions. According to Juvaini, Jebe and his men encountered a large force loyal to the Khwarezmshah at Sujas, the location of which is unclear.[35] It will be remembered that when the Khwarezmshah had met up with his son Rukn al-Din southwest of Rayy on the Hamadan-Isfahan Highway, the latter had with him about 30,000 troops. Since this is the only large assemblage of troops in the area still loyal to the Khwarezmshah, it might be assumed that it was the remaining units of this army that Jebe confronted at Sujas. Apparently Rukn al-Din had fled with his grandmother, since the army was now under the command of Beg-Tegin Silahdar and Küch-Bugha Khan. According to Juvaini, their army was "utterly destroyed" by Jebe and his men.[36]

According to Nasavi, the Khwarezmshah, who up until then had been traveling with only his retinue, bodyguards, and perhaps a small contingent of troops, finally mustered some 20,000 troops and confronted the Mongols on the plain of Dawlatabad near Hamadan.[37] This may have been the battle of Sujas described by Juvaini, although again, given the muddled and conflicting accounts, it is difficult to say for sure. According to Nasavi, the 20,000 troops were surrounded by the Mongols under Jebe and most were killed. The Khwarezmshah himself just managed to escape. This battle, wherever it took place, would be the only time the Khwarezmshah actually engaged the Mongols in combat.

Fleeing the battlefield with a mere handful of survivors, the Khwarezmshah now beat a path for the castle of Qarun, where earlier he had sent his mother and harem for safekeeping. As mentioned, Juvaini's mysterious "castle of Qarun" was probably somewhere in the mountains south of Hamadan. Jebe had picked up his scent, however, and was soon yapping at his heels. The Mongols overtook the fleeing party but apparently did not realize that the Khwarezmshah himself was in the group. A skirmish ensued and the Khwarezmshah's own horse was badly wounded by arrows. He did manage to reach the castle of Qarun where he took refuge overnight and got fresh horses. The record is murky to say the least, but it would appear that his mother and his harem had already fled to the Elborz Mountains south of the Caspian Sea by this time. Juvaini, for one, makes no mention of them being at Qarun.

The next day the Khwarezmshah, aided by local guides, headed westward, with Baghdad apparently his ultimate destination. It is unclear what kind of reception he expected from the Caliph an-Nazir, who just a couple years earlier he had tried to overthrow. Perhaps he imagined that when he apprized the Caliph of the danger posed by the Mongols an-Nazir would join forces with him to combat this new and terrifying threat to the Islamic geosphere. Jebe arrived at the castle just an hour after the Khwarezmshah had decamped. Believing he was still inside, the Mongols invested the castle and began an assault. As soon as they learned that the Khwarezmshah had already escaped they abandoned the siege and set out on his trail. In his flight the Khwarezmshah had dismissed some of his local guides, and these men informed the Mongols that the Khwarezmshah was fleeing to Baghdad.

The Khwarezmshah, meanwhile, veered off the road to Baghdad and sought refuge in the castle of Sarchahan, located somewhere near the city of Zanjan. Perhaps he had never intended to reach Baghdad after all, and his flight in that direction may have been merely a feint to throw the Mongols off his trail. Jebe apparently did lose track of the Khwarezmshah at this point. Suspecting that he had been misled by the guides who had told him that the Khwarezmshah was en route to Baghdad, he had them killed. The Khwarezmshah stayed at the castle of Sarchahan for a week and then headed north towards the city of Gilan, at the southwest corner of the Caspian Sea, where one of the local emirs, Suluk, offered his assistance. But by then the Khwarezmshah appears to have become completely discombobulated. He spurned the emir's offer of protection and left the Gilan area after seven days. Juvaini claims that he now turned back eastward to Ustundar in the Mazandaran district south of the Caspian Sea. Here he lost the last of the treasure he had managed to carry with him. Around this time his mother and his harem turned up in Mazandaran—their whereabouts after leaving the castle of Qarun being uncertain—and he now dispatched them for safekeeping to the castles of Larijan and Ilal in the Elborz Mountains.

He then consulted the local emirs on where he himself should seek refuge. They suggested an island in the Caspian Sea. The Khwarezmshah, now accompanied by only a handful of servants and bodyguards, retired to this island, but after his presence here became widely known he moved to another nearby island. This was so close to shore that supplies were able to reach the Khwarezmshah on an almost daily basis. Barthold, after his usual meticulous study of the available sources, concluded that the island in question was near the mouth of Gorgen River, which runs through the plains to the north of the city of Gorgen. Nineteenth-century maps term this extreme southeast corner of the Caspian Sea the Bay of Astrabad. Satellite photos show several small islands just offshore near the mouth of the Gorgan River, and it may be on one of these that the Khwarezmshah found his final refuge.

At this point Jebe and Sübedei appeared to have lost interest in actually capturing the Khwarezmshah themselves. Perhaps they surmised that he was a totally beaten man who no longer posed any sort of threat to Mongol ambitions in Inner Asia. They now felt free to raid and plunder the cities of what is now western Iran. A detachment of troops had been left behind the Mazandaran region, and Jebe ordered them to track the Khwarezm-shah down to his final bolt hole.[38] Unable to locate the Khwarezmshah, they instead attacked the strongholds where he had deposited his harem and treasure. The Khwarezmshah's mother, Terken Khatan, was in the fortress of Ilal. This castle relied on the area's notoriously heavy rainfall for its needs and seldom suffered from a lack of water. No sooner had the Mongols invested the castle than the weather dried up. After fifteen days or so (according to Juvaini) or four months (according to Nasavi), all the water supplies were exhausted. The defenders of the castle had no choice but to surrender. As luck would have it, within hours after opening the gates of the castle a downpour ensued, a detail both chroniclers agree on.[39] By then, however, the Khwarezmshah's mother Terken Khatan, his daughters and younger sons, the vizier Nasir-ad-Din, and other members of their party had been taken prisoner. Of the sons, all but the youngest were killed immediately. The Mongol assault party would later hand the rest of the prisoners to Chingis Khan himself.

According to Juvaini, the Khwarezmshah was on his island refuge when he learned that "... his harem had been dishonored and his attendants disgraced; that his small sons had been put to the sword; that his veiled womenfolk were in the clutches of strangers; and that all of his wedded wives had fallen into the embrace of other men and had been crushed in the clasp of beggars ..."[40] Juvaini does not specifically mention her, but the Khwarezmshah's mother, the redoubtable Terken Khatan, had also been captured and would face a harrowing fate at the hands of the Mongols. The Persian penman waxes on for three or more pages about the Kh-warezmshah's sorry plight, his always florid prose reaching new heights of grandiloquence, before he finally concluded that the Khwarezmshah died of a broken heart: "... he preferred death to life and chose annihila-tion rather than survival ... He writhed with this anguish and bemoaned this calamity and disaster until he delivered up his soul to God. ..." The more prosaic Nasavi, who later personally interviewed members of the Khwarezmshah's retinue in his final days, reported that when he arrived at the island the Khwarezmshah was already suffering from a severe in-flammation of the lungs. It was this ailment—no doubt aggravated by the shock of losing his empire and the fate of his family—that finally brought about his death, according to Nasavi.

Two dates for the demise of the Khwarezmshah have been proposed: in

December of 1220 or January 11, 1121. The former is more likely.[41] Nasavi claims that in the end he was so destitute that he could not afford a proper burial shroud. He was finally buried in the shirt of one of his servants. Thus ended the life of the man who was once the most powerful potentate in Inner Asia; who had attempted to overthrow the Caliph in Baghdad and seize for himself the leadership of the entire Islamic geosphere; and who once referred to himself as the "Second Alexander" (the Great) and the "Shadow of God on Earth".

He was buried on the island where he died, but later, probably in 1230, his son Jalal-al-Din had his remains exhumed and brought to the fortress of Ardahan in the mountains between Damavand and Mazandaran mentioned earlier. Nasavi himself wrote the letter to the Khwarezmshah's paternal aunt, requesting that she have the coffin dug up and moved, and Jalal-al-Din may have acted on her instructions. Jalal-al-Din then ordered that a madrassa be built at or near Ardahin, and the Khwarezmshah's earthy coil supposedly came to rest here. There is no record of what eventually happened to the madrassa, and apparently no tombstone or other monument to the Khwarezmshah has survived.

Meanwhile, Jebe and Sübedei attacked Zanjan, Qazwin, and other cities in what is now western Iran. Zanjan sought terms and offered up money, clothes, horses, and other valuables to placate the Mongols, but at Qazwin, according to al-Athir:

> [the] population resisted them in their city. The Tatars [Mongols] engaged them fiercely and entered by force of arms. They and the citizens fought within the city, even fighting with daggers. On both sides untold numbers were slain. Eventually they left Qazwin. The dead from the people of Qazwin were counted and came to more than forty thousand.[42]

Jebe and Sübedei then turned north on a lightning raid along the western shore of the Caspian Sea, where in late autumn they sacked the city of Ardabil (in current-day Iran) and continued on into current-day Azerbaijan. With the onset of winter they retired to the Mughan Steppe, in the current-day Iranian province of Ardabil, where they took up winter quarters and rested from their nearly nine-month long pursuit of the Khwarezmshah and its aftermath. They were probably here when they received news that their elusive quarry, the Khwarezmshah, had died on an island in the Caspian Sea. In February they would interrupt their winter respite for a quick but devastating raid on Tiflis, the capital of current-day

Georgia, marking the farthest advance to date of Chingis Khan's march
to the west.

In the winter of 1121–22 Terken Khatan and her family and the vizier
Nasir-ad-Din were handed over to Chingis Khan, who by that time had
reached Talaqan in what is now Turkmenistan. Nasir-ad-Din was tortured and then killed. The remaining male child of the Khwarezmshah
was also killed. Two of the Khwarezmshah's daughters were given to
Chagaadai, Chingis's second-oldest son. One Chagaadai keep as his own
concubine; the other he gave to his vizier Qutb-ad-Din Habash Amid.
Other daughters were parceled out to various Chingis loyalists. One of
Terken Khatan's granddaughters, also named Terken, was only two years
old when she was captured. She was eventually given to someone in the
Mongol court at Kharkhorum, the Mongol capital in Mongolia (on the
site of Erdene Zuu Monastery on the outskirts of present-day Kharkhorin, in Övörkhangai Aimag). Over three decades later she would accompany Khülegü Khan, Chingis's grandson, when he invaded Mesopotamia
and overthrew the Caliphate. In 1258 Khülegü gave Terken to Malik Sa-
lih, the son of a Muslim commander who had sided the Mongols. She
was married to him according to Muslim rites, thus completing her long
circuitous journey from Islamic Khwarezm to Mongolia and back to Islamic Mesopotamia.

As for Terken Khatan, the Khwarezmshah's mother who had once
styled herself "Queen of the Women of the Worlds", she was also sent as
a prisoner to Kharakhorum in Mongolia, where she survived as virtually
a slave of her captors. She lived to see the death of her grandson Jalal-ad-
Din in 1131 and with his demise the final dissolution of the Khwarezmian
Empire over which her husband, son, and grandson had ruled. She finally
transmigrated, released at last from her sorry state, in 1132 or 1133.[43] There
is no record of what became of her earthly remains.

We'll allow al-Athir, who was dumbfounded by the great raid of Jebe and
Sübedei, to have the final say:

> Indeed, these Tatars had done something unheard of in ancient or
> modern times. A people emerges from the borders of China and before
> a year passes some of them reach the lands of Armenia in this direc-
> tion and go beyond Iraq [Iraq-i Ajam] in the direction of Hamadan.
> By God, there is no doubt that anyone who comes after us, when a long
> time has passed, and sees the record of this event will refuse to accept

it and think it most unlikely, although the truth is in his hands. When he deems it unlikely, let him consider that we and all who write history in these times have made our record at the time when everybody living knew of this disaster, both the learned and the ignorant, all equal in their understanding of it because of its notoriety. May God provide for the Muslims and Islam someone to preserve and guard them, [apart from] Muslim princes ... whose aspirations do not go beyond their bellies and their private parts. Since the coming of the Prophet (God bless him and give him peace) until this present time the Muslims have not suffered such hardship and misery as afflict them now.[44]

CHAPTER 9

THE FALL OF TERMEZ AND GURGANJ

WHEN SAMARKAND FINALLY FELL TO Chingis Khan in March of 1220 the death of the Khwarezmshah was still nine or ten months in the future. Having sent Jebe and Sübedei in pursuit of the Khwarezmshah, Chingis then ordered his two middle sons Chagaadai and Ögedei to proceed to the city of Gurganj in the province of Khwarezm on the lower Amu Darya. The chronology is unclear, but the formidable Terken Khatan, the mother of the Khwarezmshah and *de facto* ruler of Khwarezm province, may have already left the city at this time. Chingis Khan had earlier hinted about an alliance with Terken Khatan against her son the Khwarezmshah, but those offers, assuming they were ever serious to begin with, were now off the table. Gurganj was now squarely in Chingis Khan's sights.

After spending the rest of the spring in the Samarkand area, Chingis Khan himself and a contingent of troops proceed to the Nasaf region, centered upon the city of Nasaf (current-day Qarshi), about sixty miles southwest of Samarkand. This area, watered by the 230-mile long Kashka Darya River, which begins in the outliers of the Pamir Mountains to the east, was celebrated for its lush pasture lands. (Cultivated in Russian colonial and Soviet times, the region was and is a big producer of cotton and wheat and has become known as the breadbasket of Uzbekistan). Here Chingis Khan and his men spent the summer resting and fattening their horses.[1]

While relaxing in these rich grasslands Chingis Khan may have had occasion to meet with some Sufis who were living in the area. Throughout his career Chingis had always shown an interest in "holy men", be they Buddhists, Christians, Muslims, or Taoists, although he never actually

professed to any of their teachings. Now at leisure near Nasaf, he reportedly met with two young Sufis, the brothers Khazrati Qussam Sheikh
(1192-1238) and Djabbar Khoji, the grandsons of Akhmet Yassavi (1093–
1166). Yassavi, born in Sayram in what is now Kazakhstan, is believed to
have founded the first Turkic Sufi order, the Yassaviyya, and some credit
him with being the first Turkic poet to write poetry in a Turkic dialect.
One Sufi account even maintains that Chingis Khan himself met Yassavi,
apparently while staying in the Otrar region. Yassavi supposedly asked
Chingis Khan to kill Najm al-Din Kubra, a prominent Sufi who lived in
Gurganj, and Farid al-Din Attar, another celebrated Sufi from Nishapur
in Khorasan (the author of the famous fable *The Conference of the Birds*,
which is still in print today). Yassavi's disciples were shocked both by his
association with the infidel Mongols and his desire to have two fellow
Sufis killed, but he explained that both were guilty of grievous violations
of Sufi rules and thus deserved the penalty of death.[2] As we shall, Najm
al-Din Kubra was killed by the Mongols during their assault on Gurganj,
and later Farid al-Din Attar died during the Mongol siege of Nishapur.
This meeting between Chingis Khan and Yassavi was clearly apocryphal,
however, since Yassavi died in 1166, when Chingis Khan was four years
old.

There are many other stories about Sufis meeting with, influencing, and
guiding the Mongols as they proceeded through Mawarannahr. According to one, a detachment of troops was moving up the Syr Darya—this
was probably the 5,000 man contingent sent from Otrar to attack Banakat
and Khujand—when they encountered a disciple of Yassavi's named Baba
Machin. He was tending a flock of sheep at the time. The Mongols killed
several of his sheep and prepared a meal. After they were done, Baba
Machin gathered together the bones and commenced to pray over them.
The sheep were soon restored to life (a miraculous ability often associated
with Yassavi saints; curiously, this hagiographical motif also turns up in
the lives of Mongolian lamas). The Mongols were astonished by this, and
sent word back to Chingis Khan about the incident. Thereupon "'Chingiz
Khan ordered that Baba Machin should lead the [Mongol] army, proceed
to the realm of Mawarannahr, and seize that country,'" according to the
Sufi account. Baba Machin turned down the offer, claiming that there
was a Sufi much more powerful than he and thus better suited to guide
the Mongol army. This was "'the holy Qutb of the age, Shaykh Maslahat
Khujandi.'" Supposedly this man did join the Mongol army and was in-
strumental in their advance through Mawarannahr.[3]

The motif of a Sufi somehow guiding or actually commanding the Mongol army turns up again in the story about Qubt al-Din Haydar, a Sufi from Khorasan who was active during the first two decades of the thirteenth century. He was the eponym of the Haydariyya sect which became famous, notorious even, for the antinomian behavior of its members. According to this account,

> "When the emergence of Chingiz Khan was underway . . . Haydar one day turned to his companions and said, 'Flee from the Mongols . . . for they will prove to be overpowering . . . They are bringing a dervish along with them, and they are under the protection of that dervish. In my inmost being, I wrestled with that dervish; he threw me to the ground. Now the reality is that they will be victorious: you must flee!' After that he himself went into a cave and disappeared; and in the end it happened as he had said"[4]

These stories raise some intriguing questions. Why would Sufis, who were, after all, Muslims themselves, want themselves to seen as consorting with, encouraging, guiding, and perhaps even commanding the Mongol armies who were carrying out the wholesale destruction of the cities of Mawarannahr? Najm al-Din Razi (d. 1256), a student of Najm al-Din Kubra, addressed this issue in his writings. He portrayed the Mongols as an embodiment of God's wrath, sent to cleanse by fire a society seeped in sin, decadence, and corruption. The orthodox Muslims of the Khwarezmshah's time, he believed, had strayed away from the true teachings of Islam as the Sufis perceived them and instead had given themselves over to empty formalism. "'. . . the reality of Islam having disappeared,'" Najm al-Din Razi wrote, "'He [God] may also overturn the meaningless forms that remain.'"[5] Many Sufis believed that they were the purveyors of Islam's essential teachings, and thus it was only proper that they should play an active role in the destruction of the existing order—in this case the state led by the Khwarezmshah—and its replacement by some power sympathetic to its own beliefs.

That Sufis would condone the Mongol invasion of the Islamic realm of Khwarezmia may seem an extreme assertion. Yet as Sufi scholar Devin Deweese points out:

> Instead of Sufis decrying the destruction brought by the Mongols, or condemning their unbelief, or lamenting the short- or long-term effects of infidel domination, we find Sufis staking their claim to esoteric knowledge, of the real behind the hidden, in the assertion that the

Mausoleum of Khazrati Qussam Sheikh, located just west of Qarshi.

Mongols' destructiveness was in reality a good and necessary thing for the genuine values (as framed by Sufi communities) underlying Muslim society, whatever its impact may have been for the incidental interests and goals of particular Muslim rulers or institutions; that destructiveness was sufficiently good and necessary, moreover, to be envisioned not merely as the unavoidable and impersonal effect of "God's will", but as something actively helped along by the saints.[6]

It is possible that the many accounts of Sufis aiding and abetting the Mongols were all apocryphal. However, as for the dismantling of the Khwarezmian Empire and the ascendancy of the Mongols, we might want to look at the matter from the perspective of *cui bono*. According to Deweese, "It is clear that many Sufi communities proved particularly adept at exploiting the opportunities brought by Mongol rule [and] became significantly more prominent and influential, socially and politically, than they had been previously."[7] Indeed, the Sufi orders would play a leading role in the history of Inner Asia for the next seven centuries.

Presumably Khazrati Qussam Sheikh and Djabbar Khoji, the two Sufis that Chingis met while in the Nasaf area, were members of the Yassaviyya Sufi order founded by their grandfather. Just what these two worthies discussed with Chingis Khan is unrecorded. At some point, however, Djabbar Khoji must have done something to earn Chingis's ire. According to local legend, Chingis Khan ordered his execution. His mausoleum still exists in the Kyzyl Kum Desert sixty-five miles west of Qarshi. Although

Caretaker of the Khazrati Qussam Sheikh Mausoleum.

quite isolated, it is a very popular pilgrim destination. The imam in charge of the complex is quick to tell visitors, quite unbidden, that Djabbar Khoji was killed by order of the great Chingis Khan from Mongolia. The tombs of Khazrati Qussam Sheikh and numerous of his relatives can still be seen in his large mausoleum complex just west of Qarshi. There is even a legend that Ögedei Khan, son of Chingis Khan, is buried in this mausoleum, although there is no proof of this assertion. There are three very elaborate tombs in the mausoleum not belonging to Khazrati Qussam Sheikh's family. Even the otherwise very well-informed caretaker of the mausoleum does not know for sure who is entombed in them.

After the grass began to yellow in the early autumn of 1220 Chingis Khan and his army proceeded 135 miles southeast to the city of Termez, on the way passing through the famous Iron Gate, a narrow defile through the mountains that separate the drainages of the Kashka Darya and the Amu Darya (the modern-day road from Qarshi to Termez follows the same route). This was the ancient passageway between Sogdiana and Bactria. Alexander the Great probably came this way along with a host of other conquerors, ambassadors, and trade caravans. The name may not be just metaphorical; at one time, it appears, the defile was guarded by an actual iron gate.[8] The old city of Termez is located on the banks of the Amu

Tomb of Djabbar Khoji, who was allegedly killed by order of Chingis Khan.

Darya about four miles northeast of the outskirts of the modern city of Termez. According to local lore the city got its name from the ancient Sogdian word for "crossing" or "transition place". There was an important ford of Amu Darya here or nearby (the notorious "Friendship Bridge" linking Afghanistan and Uzbekistan is here now,) and the city did serve as a gateway between Mawarannahr and Khorasan to the south.

Termez celebrated the 2,500th anniversary of its founding in April of 2002. This date was chosen arbitrarily. In fact, the city may be much older. There was already a city here when armies of the Persian Acheamenid Dynasty occupied the area in the sixth century B.C. In 329 B.C. Alexan-

The tomb of Hakim al-Termedi, located next to the ruins of Old Termez.

der the Great conquered the city, and under Greek occupation it became known as Demetris, named after one of Alexander the Great's generals. In the first to third centuries A.D. the city was included in the Kushan Empire, and it became an important northern outpost of Buddhism (the numerous ruins of monasteries, temples, stupas, and caves can still be seen in the area today). Later on it became a part of the Persian Sassanid Empire. In 705 A.D. the city was captured by invading Arabs. Its population was Islamized, and under the Abbasid Caliphate the city became a focal point of Islam in the region. (The mausoleum of Hakim al-Termedi (c. 830 A.D.–c. 912 a.d), an influential early Sufi and theosophist, is located next to the ruins of old Termez and is to this day an extremely popular pilgrimage site for Muslims from throughout Inner Asia and beyond.) The city was subsequently ruled by Samanids, Ghaznavids, Saljuqs, and

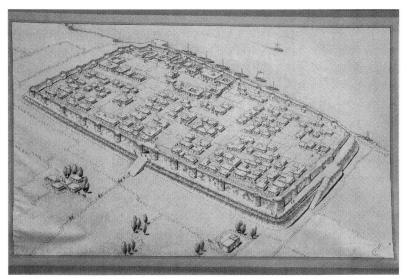

An artist's rendering of Old Termez.

Qarakhanids before becoming a part of the Khwarezmshah's empire in
1206.

As soon as Chingis Khan arrived in the area he sent, as usual, envoys
into the city to demand its immediate surrender. "But the inhabitants,
encouraged by the strength of the fortress, half of whose walls were raised
up in the middle of the Oxus [the Amu Darya River; he meant one side
of the city bordered on the river], and rendered proud by the multitude of
their troops, gear and equipment, would not accept submission but sallied
forth to do battle," according to Juvaini. The Mongols set up mangonels
and began a continuous day-and-night bombardment of the city. After
softening up the walls for ten days, on the eleventh day they stormed the
city and quickly seized it. As in Bukhara and Samarkand, all the inhabitants were driven out of the city so that it could be looted at will by Chingis's troops. The inhabitants were then "divided proportionately among
the soldiers in accordance with their custom; then they were all slain,
none being spared." One woman who did escape the initial slaughter approached some Mongol soldiers and said:

> "Spare my life and I will give you a great pearl that I have." But when
> they sought the pearl she said, "I have swallowed it." Whereupon they
> ripped open her belly and found several pearls. On this account Chin-
> giz Khan commanded that they should rip open the bellies of all the
> slain.[9]

The ruins of Old Termez.

From Termez the Mongol army rode upstream on the Amu Darya into the region of Badakhstan in what is now northeastern Afghanistan and southern Tajikistan. Little is known about this winter of 1220–21 campaign by Chingis Khan. The cities of Kangurt and Shuman (current locations unclear) were apparently sacked. Then, according to Juvaini's brief account, Chingis Khan "sent armies into the whole of Badakhstan and all that country, and conquered and subjugated the peoples, some by kindness, but most by severity; so that in all that region there was left no trace of their opponents."[10] Chingis Khan and his army spend the winter thus occupied, and March or April of 1221 returned to Termez.

As we have seen, Chingis Khan himself and portions of his army had retired to the famous pastures around Najaf on the lower Kashka Darya River for the summer. Here he and his troops would rest while their horses fattened themselves on the rich grasslands. It is not clear if Ögedei and Chagaadai and their divisions proceeded to Nasaf with Chingis and from there moved on to Bukhara, or if they proceeded instead directly to Bukhara via the Royal Road along the Zerafshan River. They did pass through Bukhara, however, and from there the army proceeded to Khwarezm.[11] Again it is not clear if they took the direct caravan route across the forbidding Kyzyl Kum Desert to Hazarasp, the first major town in

Khwarezm, or traveled south from Bukhara to the Amu Darya and then followed the river downstream to Hazarasp. Straight across the Kyzyl Kum from Bukhara to Hazarasp would have been a distance of about 200 miles ATCF; via the river route about 280 miles. The direct caravan trail from Bukhara to Hazarasp while shorter, (the modern road follows much the same route), suffered from a lack of water, making it a difficult trip using camels, let alone horses (the famous nineteenth century linguist and adventurer Arminius Vambéry nearly died of thirst and exposure on this route while trying to reach Bukhara in the 1860s). In either case, Chaagadai and Ögedei and their men soon found themselves in Hazarasp, at the southern edge of Khwarezm.

Khwarezm (also spelled Khwarizm, Khwarazm, Khorezm, Khoresm, Harezm, Chorezm, Chorasmia, etc.) was the core region of the Khwarezmian Empire and the home of the Khwarezmshahs. It is defined geographically as the land on either side of the lower Amu Darya River, including the broad delta estuary of the river on the southern edge of the Aral Sea. The region is bounded on the northeast by Kyzyl Kum Desert, to the northwest by the Ustyurt Plateau, and to the south by the Kara Kum Desert. To the east Khwarezm blends into Mawarannahr; geographically speaking, the boundary remains generally undefined. The existence of Khwarezm depended almost entirely on the Amu Darya River. Just as the Nile allowed for the birth of Egyptian civilization, the Amu Darya led to the development of a flourishing agricultural and town-dwelling culture in a region surrounded by deserts inhabitable by only the hardiest of nomads.

Khwarezm was inhabited at least as far back as the Neolithic period 6,000 years ago. Around the beginning of the sixth century B.C. a kingdom of Khwarezm was founded and the first large irrigation canals, each several miles long, were built. Khwarezm was conquered by the Persian Achaemenid Cyrus the Great (559-29 B.C.), and entered the historical record when it was mentioned in inscriptions dating to the reign of Darius I (c. 550–486 B.C.), the third king of the Achaemenid Empire. In the fourth century B.C. Aramaic script was introduced in Khwarezm, an innovation that would have immense consequences for Inner Asia. The Sogdians would adapt it into a Sogdian script; the Uighurs of East Turkestan would adapt the Sogdian script into the Uighur script; and the Mongols, as we have seen, would adopt the Uighur Script into traditional

Mongolian script, or *Mongol Bichig*.

In the fourth and third centuries B.C. Khwarezm flourished. Irrigation canals of up to 180 miles long were dug and dozens of *qalas*, or fortresses, were built throughout the region. Around the first century A.D. a capital of Khwarezm was founded at Toprak Qala, north of the Amu Darya (the extensive ruins of which can still be seen). In 305 A.D. the rulers of the region were overthrown and replaced by the Afrighids, who built a new capital at Kat, on the Amu Darya about twenty-four miles south of Toprak Qala. After this Khwarezm was subjected to extensive attacks by nomads from the Syr Darya region to the north and infighting broke out among the various factions of the Afrighids.[12]

Thus Khwarezm was in disarray when Muslim Arabs under the direction of Qutaiba Muslim, the governor of Khorasan, invaded the region in 712. Zoroastrianism appears to have remained the dominant religion among the indigenous inhabitants until the end of the century, but eventually the country was Islamized. In 995 the Afrighids, who had ruled since the early fourth century, where overthrown by the Mamun family from Gurganj. Shortly thereafter, in 1017, this family was overthrown by the Turkic Ghaznivids from Khorasan. This spelled the end of the ethnically Persian rulers in Khwarezm. All subsequent rulers of Khwarezm would be Turks, and Turkic language and culture eventually subsumed the indigenous Iranian element. Eventually the Ghaznavids were replaced by the Saljuq Turks, who used Khwarezm as a base for attacks on the pagan Turks in the Syr Darya region and the Kipchaq Steppe to the north. It was here that the Saljuqs captured or recruited many of the men who served them as *ghulam*, or slave-soldiers. As we have seen, the Saljuq appointed a *ghulam* named Anustigin—it is not clears where he was actually from—as governor of Khwarezm in the mid-eleventh century.. His son became the first of the line Khwarezmshahs leading to the Khwarezmshah Mohammad, who now found himself in a war in which he would lose his empire to Chingis Khan.[13]

Although the main objective of the Mongol army was Gurganj, the capital and main city of Khwarezm province, they would have had to pass through numerous cities, towns, and fortresses along the way. Yet Juvaini and the other Persian sources are completely silent about any battles in Khwarezm apart from the big show at Gurganj. Hazarasp, the first major town in Khwarezm, is on the left, or south, bank of the Amu Darya, and if they attacked it they would have had to cross the Amu Darya, always a formidable undertaking, and then recross it to attack Gurganj on the right bank. But there is no record of the Mongols attacking Hazarasp, which leads to the conclusion that like many of the smaller cities along the Royal Road from Bukhara to Samarkand, it may have simply surrendered to the Mongols without putting up a fight (the fortress, now in ruins, in the middle of the modern town dates to the post-Mongol period).

The Mongols did attack Khiva, forty miles west of Hasarasp and like Hazarasp on the south side of the river, so at some point they did across the river. But they also attacked fortresses on the right bank of the Amu Darya directly north of Khiva. Surely they would have wanted to keep river crossings to a minimum. Is it possible that they split up their army after arriving at Hazarasp, with some divisions moving down the right bank and the remainder down the left bank? Or did they proceed first en masse down the right bank of the river and take Gurganj first, then proceed to the other cities and fortresses of Khwarezm in what were essentially mopping-up operations?

Either before or after the fall of Gurganj the ancient city of Khiva was sacked by the Mongols. Khiva, located about twenty-five miles south of the Amu Darya on the edge of the cultivated lands straddling the river, was settled at least 2,500 years ago. Legends to the effect that it was founded by one of the sons of Noah, he of Ark fame, must be dismissed as apocryphal. By the fourth century B.C. the first versions of Ichan Qala, the walled and fortified inner city appeared. At this time the Khwarezmians probably recognized the suzerainty of Persian Achaemenids. Desertification of the area in the second century B.C. led to the abandonment of the city and destruction of the city walls. By first century A.D. the climate had changed yet again, leading to the resettlement of the area and the construction of a new walled and fortified inner city. Around this time the city was probably part of the Kushan Empire centered around Balkh in what is now Afghanistan. Around the beginning of the eighth century Islamic Arab invaders entered Khwarezm, and in 709 the city was largely destroyed by Arab general Qutaiba. With the onset of the Samanid era at the end of the ninth century the now Islamic city flourished once again, soon becoming one of the economic and cultural centers of Khwarezm. With the fall of the Samanids, Khiva fell under the sway of the Qarakhanids, Ghaznavids, and finally the Khwarezmshahs. By 1219 it was a flourishing metropolis centered around the walled and well-fortified Ichan Qala, or Inner City.

The details of the Mongol sack of Khiva are not known. One local

Two of the pillars in the Friday Mosque said to predate the Mongol invasion.

guidebook says only that "it was virtually razed to the ground." The Friday Mosque, constructed in the tenth century in the flat-roofed style common to the Arabian Peninsula, was reportedly burned down during the sack of the city, but a new version was later built on the same site. According to local lore at least seven of the 213 wooden pillars in the current mosque were rescued more-or-less undamaged from the ruins of the mosque destroyed by the Mongols and employed in the rebuilt mosque. These are dated by the tenth and eleventh century Arabic Kufic script carved on them. Some pillars are also slightly charred in places, supposedly from the burning of the mosque in late 1220 or early 1221. The walled inner city, or Ichan Qala, was later rebuilt and eventually became the capital of an independent Khivan state (today the extensively restored Ichan Qala is a world-class tourist attraction).

North of Khiva, on the other side of the Amu Darya, are dozens of fortresses, many of them founded over 2,000 years ago. Most of these strongholds of ancient Khwarezm were abandoned by the thirteen century, but a few were still occupied by the time the Mongols arrived and

Carving on the pillars are said to date from the tenth and eleventh century.

Current-day Khiva.

Ruins of Janpiq Qala.

some attempted to resist. Again, whether the Mongols besieged these fortresses while on their way to Gurganj or returned and seized them after the capital had fallen is unclear. Guldursin Qala, twenty-six miles north of Hazarasp and eleven miles north of the Amu Darya, was reportedly one fortress that resisted. The 1,000 by 750-foot walled city that the Mongols faced had been built by the Khwarezmshahs not long before, in the twelfth century, on the site of a much more ancient fortress. How much resistance the inhabitants of Guldursin Qala offered is unclear. The fortress may have fallen fairly easily, since its walls and towers survived pretty much intact and can still be seen today.

Janpiq Qala, forty miles northwest of Guldursin Qala and a mile and half from the current banks of the Amu Darya, was also attacked by the Mongols. Built in the ninth or tenth century A.D. during an economic boom in Khwarezm, it was situated on the site of an older fortress dating back to the period between the fourth and first centuries B.C. The walled city, measuring 1,500 feet long and up 1,000 feet wide, developed into a substantial craft center with quarters devoted to weaving, stone carving, blacksmithing, and the manufacture of glass and pottery. It was also an important trade entrepôt on the Amu Darya where goods from China, India, Egypt, and the Volga River and Black Sea regions all washed up. Russian researchers have suggested that a breach in the southern wall was made by the besieging Mongols, perhaps with a huge battering ram.

Ruins of Janpiq Qala.

Hole in the wall of Janpiq Qala possibly made by the Mongols.

How much other damage the city suffered at the hands of the Mongols is unclear, but the city did recover and it eventually regained much of its former prominence (the breach in the southern wall was bricked up). The city was probably attacked yet again by Amir Timur (Tamerlane) when he swept through the area in 1388. By the end of the fourteenth century the city was abandoned, but the substantial ruins of the fortress walls and parts of the Citadel have survived to the present day.

Gurganj is situated eighty-five miles west-northwest of Janpiq Qala. What additional fortresses the Mongols may have encountered on the way to Gurganj is unknown, but by the autumn 12020, perhaps in October—the accounts are unclear—the advance units of the Mongol army had reached the outskirts of Gurganj.[14]

Juvaini could just barely restrain himself when eulogizing Gurganj:

> It is the site of the throne of the Sultans of the World and the dwelling place of the celebrities of mankind; its corners supported the shoulders of the great men of the age, and its environs were receptacles of the rarities of the age; its mansions were resplendent with every kind of lofty idea, and its regions and districts were so many rose-gardens through the presence of men of quality, great Sheiks being assembled on one place with the Sultans of the age.

The Afrighids had made Kath in southeast Khwarezmshah their capital, but after the dynasty fell in 995 Gurganj became the most prominent city in Khwarezm. The city soon became an important entrepôt for trade between Inner Asia and the Volga River, at the northern end of the Caspian Sea, which served as the gateway to Russia. Goods arriving from China, India, the Iranian Plateau, Mawarannahr, and elsewhere were transshipped from here by caravans either directly to the mouth of Volga or to the Caspian Sea, where boats carried them north to the Volga.[15]

Gurganj also achieved renown as an intellectual and artistic center. A whole bevy of philosophers, theologians, and poets were either born here or spend time here, including Shahrastanī (1086–1153), the author of The Book of Sects and Creeds, an immense work which attempted to summarize all known religions and philosophies (his even-handed treatment of non-Islamic beliefs earned him the wrath of the Muslim ulama); Fakhr al-Din ar-Razi (1149-1209), author of The Great Commentary, an eight-volume exegesis of the Quran, and a proponent of the "multiverse" theory which maintained that there are either multiple worlds within this universe, or that there exists a multitude of universes outside the known universe; and Ibn Sina, a.k.a. Avicenna, (c. 980–1037), polymathic author of some 450 works on medicine, philosophy, mathematics, logic, physics, astronomy, and much else (he also dabbled in poetry). One of the more famous Sufis of the city, Najm al-Din Kubra 1145-1220) was the founder of the Kubrawiyyah Sufi order which was later to become extremely influential through much of Inner Asia and the Near East. As we shall see, he died during the Mongol attack on Gurganj.

Gurganj may have reached the height of its florescence during the first two decades of the thirteen century. The Syrian geographer Yaqut al-Hamawi (1179–1229), who visited the city in 1219, just prior to the Mongol invasion, deemed it perhaps the richest and most highly developed city he had ever seen.[17] Thus it was only natural that it had attracted the attention of Chingis Khan.

As we have seen, Terken Khatan, the Khwarezmshah's mother and nominal ruler of Khwarezm province, had fled Gurganj several months earlier, leaving a power vacuum in the city. It soon became clear that those who remained behind were neither the best nor the brightest. According to Juvaini, the civil administration of Gurganj was seized by an officer named Ali Durughini, (because of his propensity for lying Nasavi nicknamed him Kuli-Durughan [Mountain of Lies], a play of words on his actual name).[18] This worthy proceeded to loot what he could from what remained in the state treasury kept in Gurganj. He did not, however, make any efforts to rally the 90,000 troops who still remained in the city. Then at some time during the summer of 1220 Temür Malik, the hero of Khujand who had just escaped from Jochi's dragnet on the lower Syr Darya, as described earlier, arrived in town. An experienced commander and obviously a charismatic leader, he rallied a contingent of troops—it's not clear how large—and rode north to attack Jochi's troops who were still on the Syr Darya. He actually managed to seize the city of Yanikent and kill the Mongol governor. Instead of following up on this victory, however, he soon returned to Gurganj with his troops. Apparently there was dissension between him and the military faction which still remained nominally loyal to Terken Khatan, and once again the disputing parties were unable to decide on any concerted approach to the Mongol threat.

In early winter of 1220 two officials who had been in charge of the Khwarezm treasury under Terken Khatan but who had earlier fled Gurganj arrived back in the city. They claimed that they had been in touch with the Khwarezmshah and that they were taking control of the province of Khwarezm on his behalf. The chronology is uncertain, but at this point the Khwarezmshah was probably somewhere in western Iran in headlong flight from Jochi and Sübedei. Whether these two officials were in fact speaking for the Khwarezmshah or simply acting on their own account is uncertain.

Shortly thereafter the situation took a completely different turn. The princes Jalal-ad-Din, Uzlagh Shah, and Aq Shah and an entourage of seventy men arrived in the city with the dramatic news that they had been with the Khwarezmshah when he had died on the island in the Caspian Sea and that they had overseen his burial.[19] Whether they were actually there or not is uncertain. Nasavi implies that they were, but Juvaini does not mention them.[20] In any case, the princes now made a joint announcement proclaiming that before his death the Khwarezmshah had altered his will, making Jalal-ad-Din his heir instead of Uzlagh Shah. Terken Khatan had earlier prevailed upon her son, the now deceased Khwarezmshah, to name Uzlagh Shah as the heir to the throne of the Khwarezmian Empire instead of his older half-brothers Jalal-ad-Din and Rukn al-Din, no doubt because Uzlagh Shah's mother and Terken Khatan were member of the same clan of Qangli Turks.[21] With Uzlagh Shah as the new head of the Khwarezmian Empire the Turkish military faction would at long last gained ascendency over the aristocratic party of the Khwarezmshahs.[22]

Apparently Uzlagh Shah agreed to step aside in favor of his older half-brother and was willing to accept Jalal-ad-Din as the new Khwarezmshah. He was relatively young at the time and as Juvaini notes, "not quick in his studies."[23] The tribal Turkish emirs who had made up the military faction under Terken Khatan could not reconcile themselves with the decision to sidestep Uzlagh Shah in favor of Jalal-ad-Din, however, and soon hatched a plot to eliminate the latter. The leader of the conspirators was one Tuji Pahlawan, who bore the title of Qutlugh Khan. He was considered the leader of the old Turkish military faction which had flourished under Terken Khatan and had probably served as the governor of Jand and Yanikent on the lower Syr Darya before the invasion of the Mongols. He had roughly 7,000 men under his command. Now he and his co-conspirators intrigued to kill or imprison Jalal-ad-Din and put Uzlagh Shah on the throne, presumably as their puppet. Tipped off to the plot, probably by Moghol Hajib, a confederate of the prince who had earlier escaped from the debacle at Bukhara, Jalal-ad-Din and the ever-resourceful Temür Malik along with 300 loyal soldiers fled south to Khorasan.[24] They were probably spurred on by reports that the Mongol armies under Chagaadai and Ögedei were rapidly approaching the city. Apparently the schemes of Tuji Pahlawan to enthrone Uzlagh-Shah fell on deaf ears, since three days later both Uzlagh-Shah and Aq Shah also fled the capital.

Thus at this crucial moment the dead Khwarezmshah's sons abandoned Gurganj and gave up all pretense of leadership in defending the ancient capital of Khwarezm. According to Juvaini, Khumar Tegin, a relative of Terken Khatan's and a leader of the army faction, had elected to remain behind in Gurganj after the princes had fled. With him were other emirs including Moghol Hajib, Er Buqa Pahlavan, Ali "Mountain of Lies" Durughini (his earlier indiscretions now apparently overlooked), and, as Juvaini disdainfully adds, "others of the same sort." Apart from these panjandrums, "there were so many notables of the town and learned of the age as could be neither counted or computed; while the number of inhabitants exceeded that of grains of sand or pebbles."[25] Aware of the threat posed by the Mongols and of the need for a united front, these citizens now rose up and with "one voice" declared Khumar Tegin their new Sultan and "Nauruz King" (King for Day).[26] Thus it was Kumar Tegin who would be tasked with confronting the Mongols who soon appeared outside the walls of Gurganj.

Although all of our Persian sources comment at length on the battle of Gurganj, none of them bother to enlighten us about when the Mongols first arrived at the city walls. Nasavi says the city finally fell on April of 1221. The others say only that the siege lasted anywhere from five to seven months. From this we can conclude that the Mongols appeared before the city in the late autumn or early winter of 1220. A Mongol advance party led by Taji-Beg reached Gurganj first. According to Juvaini, the defenders of the city "beheld a small troop of horsemen like a puff of smoke, who arrived before the gates of the town and busied themselves with driving off cattle. Hereat some short-sighted persons became exultant thinking that they had come in so small a party out of bravado and that they had ventured on such insolence out of sport."[27] Both calvary and foot soldiers rushed out the city gates to confront the Mongols. "The Mongols, like wild game, now startled, now cast a glance behind them and ran." The Khwarezmians pursued them to a place called Bagh-i-Khurram (the Garden of Happiness, according to one rendering), about four miles from the city walls.

It was a trap. A larger contingent of Taji-Beg's men which had been held in reserve suddenly appeared on the flanks of the Khwarezmian party. "They cut off the road before and behind and fell briskly upon them like wolves upon a flock without a shepherd." The fighting continued most of the day and by early evening all the Khwarezmians had been massacred. Both Juvaini and Rashid al-Din (the latter perhaps relying on the former's account) put the death toll among the Khwarezmians at 100,000. This was certainly an exaggeration. Barthold opines that Juvaini must have meant 1,000 and that Rashid al-Din was simply repeating what Juvaini said. In any case, the Mongols, emboldened by this sudden success, proceeded to Gurganj and entered the city via the Qabilan Gate. This daring sortie must have struck terror into the hearts of the populace, but the invaders were still relatively few in number and in no position to hold the city. Fearing that they would get trapped within the city walls they withdrew as night fell. The Khwarezmians did not venture out of the city the next day. The Mongols attacked one of the city gates, but 500 men under the command of Faridun Ghuri, one of the Khwarezmshah's chief generals, managed to repulse them.

At this juncture the main Mongol army began trickling in. Ögedei's corps arrived first, followed by a personal division of Chingis's under the command of Bughurji-Noyon. Last came Chagaadai's corps, under the command of Tulun Cherbi, Ustun-Noyon, and Qadan-Noyon. The amassed Mongol army, including auxiliaries who had rallied to the Mongol cause, may numbered over 100,000. The Mongol chieftains made a show of strength by circling the entire army around the city and then sent in emissaries to demand its surrender and submission. As no answer was immediately forthcoming they prepared for a protracted siege. Mangonels were set up, but since there were no large stones in the area, projectiles had to be made from sections of large mulberry trees that were hardened by soaking them in water. Meanwhile, Mongol envoys continued to cajole the city fathers with "promises and threats, inducements and menaces," all to no avail.[28]

Then Jochi's corps from Jand on the lower Syr Darya arrived on the scene and with their help the Mongols were able to further tighten the noose on the city. Whether Jochi accompanied them is a matter of some dispute. Juvaini implies that he did not.[29] Given his ongoing feud with his brother Chagaadai, he might well have wanted to keep his distance. Other sources, however, say that he did accompany his troops and that he played in crucial role in deciding the ultimate fate of the city, as we shall see.

The investment of the city continued. Levies, presumably seized in Khiva and other cities that the Mongols had already taken in Khwarezm and perhaps brought along with Jochi's corps on the lower Syr Darya, were pushed up to the city walls and made to fill in the moat with rubbish

The 196-foot tall minaret named afer Temür Qutlugh (c. 1370 – 1399), a khan of the Golden Horde. It was probably built in the tenth or eleventh century. It was badly damaged during the Mongol attack on Gurganj and later restored by Temür Qutlugh.

The base of the Temür Qutlugh Minaret

and whatever else came to hand. This operation took ten days, according to Rashid al-Din.[30] Then the prisoners were tasked with undermining the city walls. All the while mangonels hurled hardened sections of mulberry trunks into the beleaguered city. Then the Mongols attacked: "loosing a yell like thunder and lightning they rained down missiles and arrows like hailstones." Terrified by these assaults, Khumar Tegin, the "counterfeit Sultan and leader of the army," as Juvaini styles him, quickly lost heart: "The signs of the Tartar [Mongol] army's victory agreed with his secret surmise." He left his position by one of the main city gates and personally surrendered to the Mongols. His subsequent fate is unknown.

Continuing the assault, the Mongols were soon able to plant their standards on the top of the city walls. But the fight for Gurganj was just beginning. What is now called urban warfare ensued. "The inhabitants opposed them in all the streets and quarters of the town," according to Juvaini, "in every lane they engaged in battle and in every cul-de-sac they resisted stoutly."[31] The Mongols responded by torching whole quarters of the city with naphtha and "sewing the people to one another with arrows." This street-to-street fighting went on for at least two days, during which large sections of the city were completely destroyed.

At this point a rift developed in the Mongolian leadership. The whole point of attacking a city was to seize its wealth. If the entire city was burned to the ground before they had a chance to loot it, all their efforts would have come to naught. "By now," Juvaini explains, "the greater part

This mausoleum is believed to have been built before the Mongol invasion. Who was originally entombed in it is not clear. Some say the Khwarezmshah Arslan (r.1156–1172); others say the theologian and philosopher Fakhr ad-Din ar-Razi (1149-1209), author of The Great Commentary *and many other works. The mausoleum has been heavily restored.*

of the city was destroyed; the houses with their goods and treasures were but mounds of earth; and the Mongols despaired of benefitting from the stores of their wealth." As we have seen, Juvaini maintained that Jochi was not present at the siege of Gurganj. Both Rashid al-Din and Nasavi claim that he was, however, and both maintain that he had serious objections about the scorched earth policy that was obliterating the city. Not only was he concerned about the loss of loot in the short term. Gurganj, the richest city in Khwarezm and one of the richest in Inner Asia, was to be a part of his patrimony when Chingis Khan died. If the battle for the city continued in the same fashion he would inherit nothing but a heap of ashes. According to Nasavi, Jochi himself did everything possible to halt the destruction of Gurganj, including sending numerous envoys to the town fathers seeking their peaceful surrender. Apparently even the Khwarezmshah, in the last days of his life on the island in the Caspian Sea, had sent a letter to the leaders of Gurganj advising them not to oppose the Mongols. Many of the town fathers had advocated coming to terms with the invaders in the hope of saving what they could of their city, but according to Nasavi the "blockheads" among them refused to surrender and in the end these diehards prevailed.[32] Jochi's opponent in this, as might be expected, was his younger brother (half-brother actually) and long-time nemesis Chagaadai. The feud between them, which had come to a head at the conference in 1219 when Chingis Khan had named their younger brother Ögedei to be his successor as Great Khan now flared up again. Chagaadai apparently wanted to press on and take Gurganj by any means possible. If this meant reducing the city to ashes it meant nothing to him.

For the moment Jochi's viewpoint prevailed. According to Juvaini, the Mongols "agreed among themselves to abandon the use of fire and rather to withhold from the people the water of the Oxus [Amu Darya], across which a bridge had been built in the town." This is one of the Persian pen-pusher's more perplexing passages. Clearly the Amu Darya did not run through the city. The main branch of the Amu Darya is now twenty-five miles east of Gurganj, but in the thirteenth century it apparently flowed by right to the south of the city. There were canals leading off the river, but Barthold, who has studied in some detail the layout of thirteenth century Gurganj, maintains that because of a lack of space none of the *ariqs*, or canals, ran through the town in the thirteenth century.[33] So where was this bridge to which Juvaini refers? Barthold does tell us that some 300 feet from the walls of Gurganj a wooden dam had been built to deflect water of the river away from the city. Was this wooden dam the "bridge" to which Juvaini refers? Juvaini implies, however, that the "bridge" was within the city, while the wooden dam was clearly outside the city walls. In any case, the Mongols now attempted to seize the bridge or dam—wherever it might have been—apparently with the intend of destroying it and flooding the city. Here the Mongols suffered a setback. The 3,000 troops devoted to this task were quickly surrounded by the Khwarezmi-

Building believed to the mausoleum of Khwarezmshah Tekish (r. 1172-1200). It was probably built in the early thirteenth century, just before the Mongol invasion. Persian historian Juzjani claimed it was one of the few buildings that survived the Mongol destruction of the city. It has been heavily restored.

ans and massacred.

This fleeting victory in the battle of the bridge emboldened the defenders, but it also hardened the resolve of the Mongols. According to al-Athir, Mongol causalities during the siege had already outnumbered those of the city's defenders.[34] Rashid al-Din claimed that hillocks made of the bones of Mongols killed during the siege were still visible in his time, more than sixty years later. The loss of 3,000 men in one skirmish appeared to weaken the hand of Jochi, who wanted to save the city from total destruction, but apparently he was not yet ready to give in to Chagaadai and the hardliners who wanted to take the city by any means possible. The dissension between the two brothers was finally reported to

Chingis Khan, and he responded by putting the entire army under the command of Ögedei, in effect taking the ever-quarreling Jochi and Cha-gaadai out of the decision-making process. Jochi's attempt to save what he could of the city had failed. Under Ögedei the street-by-street assault on the city resumed. Quarter after quarter of the city fell into the hands of the Mongols until only three remained untaken. The inhabitants of these quarters finally decided to send a local dignitary, Ali ad-Din Khayyati, to Jochi and have him beg for mercy. But their entreaties were too late; not even Jochi could save them now. Sometime in April of 1221 the last resistance was overcome and the city of Gurganj was completely overrun by the Mongols.

The surviving inhabitants were driven out into the surrounding fields. The artisans and others with valuable skills, said to number over 100,000, were separated from the rest and, according to Juvaini, sent off to "Eastern Lands," presumably in China and Mongolia. Juvaini, writing in the 1260s, adds, "Today there are many places in those parts that are cultivated and peopled by the people of Khorazm" (whether the Hui, a sizable Islamic minority now found in China, are the descendants of these forcibly reset-tled craftsmen is a matter of some dispute).[35] The women and young chil-dren were enslaved and parceled out to their new masters. Some skilled men had hidden their talents, believing that instead of being sent off of the East they would be allowed to return to the city as common laborers. They were sorely disappointed. The remaining men were divided among the Mongol troops and each soldier was tasked with executing twenty-four victims.

The Mongols were not yet done with the destruction of Gurganj. After they had looted what they could from the burned out ruins, they decided to flood the city. According to al-Athir:

> They opened the dam which kept the waters of the Oxus away from the city, so that it was completely inundated and buildings collapsed. The site was left an expanse of water. Not one of the populace survived, al-though in other cities some of the people had survived; some hid, some fled, some got out and escaped and yet others threw themselves down among corpses and so were saved. However, from among the people of Khwarazm those who hid from the Tatars [Mongols] were either drowned or died under the rubble. The city became a deserted ruin.[36]

The number who died is uncertain. Juvaini refused to speculate: "I have heard such a quantity of slain that I did not believe the report and so have

not recorded it. 'Oh God, preserve us from the ills of this world and torments of the world to come.'"[37]

Among those who died during the final Mongol assault on Gurganj was
the Sufi saint Abul-Jannab Ahmad b. Omar Najm al-Din Kubra. He was
a native of Gurganj, born there in 1145. Accounts vary as to the source
of his name Kubra. One claims that it comes from the term *al-tammat
al-kobra*, "the overwhelming event". In the Quran, this phrase refers to the
final resurrection, but apparently one of his early teachers gave Kubra this
name because of his ability to overwhelm his opponents in scholarly de-
bates. Another account maintains that his students called him *ayat Allah
al-kobra* (God's supreme sign) and that his name comes from this phrase.
Kubra's parents were textile merchants who engaged in religious studies
on the side. As a child Kubra experienced what he called the "loosening
of the bonds of the intellect." These were apparently mystical experiences
during which he was temporary freed from the bonds of consensual reality. He reined in these impulses and devoted himself to the study of
hadith (sayings of the Prophet Mohammad), a traditional and orthodox
field of scholarship. Intellectually ambitious, he sought out teachers in
Nishapur in Khorasan, Hamadan and Isfahan in Iraq-i Ajam, Mecca, and
finally Alexandria in Egypt. That the son of a textile merchant from Inner
Asia was able follow such an itinerary demonstrates the opportunities
for travel and study that were available to motivated students in the late
twelfth century.

Around the age of thirty-five Kubra became disillusioned with conven-
tional approaches to religion and began to pursue the more mystical path
taught by Sufis. Accounts of where and how Kubra was finally converted
to Sufism vary. One maintains that he moved from Alexandria to Cairo,
where he met a Sufi teacher by the name of Ruzhedan. Under Ruzhedan's
supervision Kubra did several forty-day retreats and engaged in other Sufi
practices. Ruzhedan was so impressed by Kubra's progress along the Sufi
path that he gave him one of his daughters in marriage. Kubra went on
to study with a succession of Sufi teachers in Cairo and Dezful, in Iraq-i
Ajam. While in Dezful one of his teachers, Esmail il-Qadri, declared that
Kubra was qualified to become a teacher himself. He returned to Cairo
to get the blessing of Ruzhedan and then made the long journey back to
Khwarezm, arriving in Gurganj in 1184.

In Gurganj Kubra eventually gathered around him a group of some

sixty devotees, including an inner circle of twelve particularly gifted students. Because of his teaching abilities, his followers gave him the nickname *Shayk-e walitaras*, the "saint manufacturing saint." Among his students was Najm al-Din Razi, mentioned earlier in connection with his
pronouncements about the role of Chingis Khan and the Mongols in the
chastisement of ungodly Khwarezmians. It was long believed that Ba-
haudin Walid, father of the world-famous poet Jalal-ad-Din Muhammad
Rumi (1207–1273), better known simply as Rumi (still one of the biggest
selling poets on amazon.com), and Farid al-Din Attar (1145-1221), the author of *The Conference of Birds* (still in print), were his students; recent
scholarship suggests that these tales are entirely apocryphal.[38]

Kubra's influence extended into the political sphere. Members of the
Khwarezmshah's court, or perhaps Terken Khatan's court, sought him
out, and one of his disciples was the brother of the Khwarezmshah's secretary, providing Kubra with access to official circles. Kubra's relationship
with the Khwarezmshah himself was a bit more rocky. According to one
tale, the Khwarezmshah accused one of Kubra's disciples, Majd al-Din,
of unspecified indiscretions with his mother Terken Khatan (it will be
remembered that Juvaini accused her of indulging in "secret revelries"). In
his anger the Khwarezmshah had Majd al-Din executed. When his passions had cooled the Khwarezmshah went to Kubra to offer blood money
and ask for his forgiveness. Kubra refused to take any money. Instead, he
declared that the blood-price would be lives of the Muslim rulers of various cities and countries. He enumerated these places one after the other,
but just as he was about to conclude with Baghdad, one of his disciples,
frightened by this outburst on the part of his teacher, put his hand over
Kubra's mouth. This pronouncement by Kubra was seen as a prophesy,
since shortly thereafter Chingis Khan invaded Khwarezmia, and indeed,
his grandson would eventually sack Baghdad and kill the last Abbasid
Caliph.[39]

Various stories attest to the belief that Kubra, if not actually encouraged the Mongol invasion of Islamic land, at least acquiesced to it. According to one:

> "there was also the utterance of Shaykh Najm al-Din Kubra . . . One
> day, Shaykh Maslahat Khujandi came to see Shaykh Najm al-Din, who
> was seated with his left leg extended in the direction of Turkistan. The
> holy men [with him] signaled to him, suggesting, 'Is it not contrary to
> protocol to remain seated when a saint enters?' [Kubra] said, 'Very well;
> I have been keeping my foot in a dog's mouth to hold him back, but if

this is the noble opinion of the saints . . . I will stop.' After a few months, the conflict between the Khwarazmshah and Chingiz Khan began."⁴⁰

The "dog" in question here was Chingis Khan.

A similar motif turns up in another version of the story:

"They say that the Shaykh would always sit during gatherings with his leg extended straight out. They would ask him why, and he would say, 'I have kept my foot stuck in the throat of Chingiz Khan.' One day he drew in his leg, and summoned Shaykh Sad al-Din Hammuyi and Shaykh Razi al-Din Ali Lala and the others, and said, 'Go at once to your own countries, for a fire has been kindled in the east that will burn all the way to the west; this is a great calamity, the like of which has never happened in this Muslim community.'"⁴¹

These gnomic utterances seemed to suggest that Kubra through his spiritual power was halting the Mongol advance on Khwarezm. Their import, in the words of Sufi scholar Devin Deweese, was that "Kubra was in full command of the underlying forces of history in his time (and of his own fate), and it was his decision to cease holding back the armies of Chingiz Khan and to let them sweep over the Muslim world."⁴²

Word of Kubra's stature as a holy man eventually Chingis Khan himself. According to one near-contemporary account:

[Chingis Khan] had heard of the Shaykh of Shaykhs and the Pole-star of Saints [Kubra], and knew somewhat of his character [and] he sent him a message that he intended to sack Khwarazm [Gurganj] and massacre its inhabitants, and that one who was the greatest man of his age should come out from it and join him, now that the moment had arrived for the incidence of the catastrophe. 'That I should come forth from amongst them,' replied the Shayk, 'would be an action remote from the way of virtue and magnanimity.'"⁴³

The historian Nur ad-Din Abd ar-Rahman Jamī (1414–1492) tells what happened next:

"When the Tartar heathen reached Khwarazm, the Shaykh [Kubra]] assembled his disciples, whose number exceeded sixty . . . The Shaykh summoned certain of his disciples . . . and said, 'Arise quickly and depart to your own countries, for a fire is kindled from the East which consumes nearly to the West. This is a grievous mischief, the like of which hath never heretofore happened to this people (the Muslims).' Some of his disciples said, 'How would it be if your Holiness were to pray, that perhaps this [catastrophe] may be averted from the lands of

Islam?' 'Nay,' replied the Shaykh, 'this is a thing irrevocably predeter-
mined which prayer cannot avert.' Then his disciples besought him, saying, 'The beasts are ready prepared for the journey: if your Holiness also
would join us and depart into Khurasan, it would not be amiss.' 'Nay,'
replied the Shaykh; 'here shall I die a martyr, for it is not permitted to
me to go forth.' So his disciples departed into Khurasan . . . When the
heathen entered the city, the Shaykh called such of his disciples as remained, and said, 'Arise in God's Name and let us fight in God's Cause.'
Then he entered his house, put on his *Khirga* (dervish robe), girded up
his loins, filled the upper part of his *Khirga*, which was open in front,
with stones on both sides, took a spear in his hand, and came forth.
And when he came face to face with the heathen, he continued to cast
stones at them till he had no stones left. The heathen fired volleys of arrows at him, and an arrow pierced his breast. He plucked it out and cast
it away, therewith passed away his spirit. They say that at the moment
of his martyrdom he had grasped the pigtail of one of the heathen,
which after his death could not be removed from his hand, until at last
they were obliged to cut it off."[44]

So why did Kubra not heed Chingis Khan's advice and flee the doomed
city of Gurganj? His answer might be found in another of the gnomic
pronouncements attributed to him: "'I will attain the blessing of holy war
and martyrdom from you [the Mongols], and you will obtain the blessing
of Islam from us.'" In other words, Kubra himself chose to die as a martyr at Gurganj, and in exchange the Mongols would become Muslims. It
would take several generations, but many of the Mongols who rode west
did finally embrace Islam.

Accounts vary as to the fate of Kubra's body. One claims that it was
never identified among the tens of thousands who were slain during the
attack on Gurganj. Another maintains that his body was identified and
buried amidst the ruins of the Sufi dwelling place that he and his disciples
had occupied.[45] Eventually a mausoleum in his name was built on the
outskirts of Gurganj. It can still be seen there today, but whether or not
his body is actually in it remains a matter of conjecture.

Among the cultural treasures that were lost because of the Mongol invasion of Khwarezm we might mention the library of Shihab ad-Din Khawaqi. This learned scholar was acquainted with all the arts and sciences
and taught at five madrassas in Gurganj. Nasavi, who had visited his library, claimed that he had not seen its like "either before or since."[46] Hearing of the approach of the Mongols, Shihab ad-Din Khawaqi left Gurganj

and fled south to the city of Nisa, near current-day Ashgabad in what is now Turkmenistan, taking the most valuable of his books with him. It proved to be an unsafe haven. Nisa was later sacked by a Mongol raiding party and Shihab ad-Din Khawaqi was killed. His books were pilfered and, according to Nasavi, eventually ended up in the hands of "people of the lowest class." Nasavi himself came from a wealthy family in Nisa. After the Mongol raid on the city he returned there and managed to buy up from these low-lifes the books that had not been destroyed. Nasavi was eventually forced to flee Nisa in advance of another Mongol raid, and he left the books behind in his family's castle. Eventually the castle and all of the other substantial holdings of Nasavi and his family were lost in the upheavals that followed the Mongol invasion of Khorasan. The books originally belonging to Shihab ad-Din Khawaqi disappeared. Nasavi lived in exile for the rest of his life. He finally died destitute in Aleppo, Syria, in 1249 or 1250. He had lost everything he had in Nisa—books, personal possessions, castles, and estates—because of the Mongol invasion, but looking back on his life he reflected: "Of all that I left there I regretted [losing] only the books."[47]

After spending part of the winter rampaging through Badakhstan, in the upper basin of the Amu Darya River, Chingis Khan and his men returned to Termez. Late in the winter of 1220–21 they crossed Amu Darya into Khorasan. After the fall of Gurganj his son Chagaadai and Ögedei and the corps they commanded also crossed the Amu Darya with the intention of linking up with Chingis Khan somewhere in Khorasan. All of Mawarannahr and Khwarezm, including the great cities of Bukhara, Samarkand, Termez, and Gurganj, had fallen to the Mongols. They now controlled all of inner Asia north of the Amu Darya.

Chingis Khan had originally claimed that he was invading the realm of the Khwarezmshah to avenge the deaths of the traders and Mongol envoys in Otrar and the execution of the emissary he had sent to the Khwarezmshah to protest the massacre. He had gotten his revenge. Gayer Khan, the governor of Otrar who had ordered the killings, had been captured, tortured, and executed. The Khwarezmshah himself had been flushed out of his realm and left to die on a remote island in the Caspian Sea, and many members of his immediate family had been executed or enslaved. The Khwarezmshah's mother, Terken Khatan, the second most powerful person in the Khwarezmian Empire, was now a captive of the Mongols. The

Khwarezmians had still not been totally defeated. The Khwarezmshah's talented and ambitious son Jalal-ad-Din and his sizable army were still on the loose in Khorasan and would prove to be formidable opponents. Yet the Amu Darya, at one time seen as the moat that would halt the Mongol advance beyond Mawarannahr, had been breached, and a new phase of the Mongol march west was beginning.

Chingis Khan had also wanted to promote trade with the Khwarezmian Empire. Commerce may have been halted by the wholesale destruction of the great Silk Road trade centers of Otrar, Bukhara, Samarkand, Termez, Gurganj, and others, but in the future there would be nothing to interfere with the free passage of goods from the Pacific Ocean to the Amu Darya. The trade routes between Beijing and Xian in China and Bukhara and Samarkand in Mawarannahr were now controlled by the Mongols. The rough outlines of what would later be called the *Pax Mongolica* were beginning to emerge.

Thus many of Chingis Khan's goals had been accomplished. He and his armies could have returned victorious to Mongolia. Yet Chingis Khan was obviously not through with his march west. Perhaps it was sheer momentum that drove him on. He had a huge army that had to be rewarded with plunder and could not easily be turned around when the rich and fattened cities of Khorasan glittered on the far banks of the Amu Darya. And far off beyond the western horizon was the ultimate prize of the Islamic world: Baghdad. If the Caliphate fell then the approaches would be open to both the Christian lands on the north side of the Mediterranean and the remaining Islamic realms on the south side. Did Chingis Khan envision riding all the way west to the Atlantic Ocean and there, like Alexander the Great on the shores of the Indian Ocean, lament that there no worlds left to conquer? We are not privy to the thoughts of Chingis Khan and so cannot say. We do know that by the late spring of 1221 he and the Mongol army were poised to invade Khorasan, the next stage of Chingis Khan's march west.

ENDNOTES

Chapter 1 — Endnotes

1   Mote, 2003, p. 254, Ratchnevsky, 1991, p. 103-05.
2   See Millward, 2007 pp. 43–50.
3   See Juvaini, 1997, pp. 43–48 for Juvaini's account of the submission of the Uighurs to Chingis Khan.
4   See *Secret History* of the Mongols, §238; Rachewiltz, 2004, Vol. I, p. 163; Vol. II, pp. 845–849; and Ratchnevsky, 1991, pp. 101–102
5   Ratchnevsky, 1991, p. 103.
6   Quoted in Ratchnevsky, 1991, p. 104.
7   Quoted in Ratchnevsky, 1991, p. 105.
8   Morgan, 1990, pp. 63–65.
9   Sinor, 1990, p. 413.
10 Mote, 2003, p. 211–214.
11 Mote, 2003, p. 195.
12 Mote, 2003, pp. 195–198.
13 Ratchnevsky, 1991, p. 9 gives the date; Grousset, 1999, p. 197, gives the place as Beijing. Elsewhere, however Groussett (1966) says the meeting may have taken place in a hunting lodge in Manchuria. Onon, 2001, p. 234, gives the name of the Chin capital.
14 *Secret History*, §53. See also Onon, 2001, p. 52.
15 Juvaini, 1997, p. 21.
16 *Secret History*, §89, 90. Also see Onon, 2001, p. 73–74.
17 Ratchnevsky, 1991, p.50.
18 Mote, 2003, p. 243.
19 Quoted in Grousset, 1994, p. 227. Groussett's sources are not quite clear.
20 Ratchnevsky, 1991, pp. 105–109.
21 Ratchnevsky, 1991, p. 110. Juzjani, 2010 (1881), p. 954–55.
22 Grousset also opines that the mountain was "probably" Burkhan Khaldun. See Grousset, 1966, p. 187.
23 Ratchnevsky, 1991, pp. 109.
24 Juzjani, 2010 (1881), p. 954.
25 Mote, 2003, p. 243.
26 Ratchnevsky, 1991, p. 110.
27 Mote, 2003 #34, p. 244.
28 Ratchnevsky, 1991, p.114. For list of Chin emperors see http://en.wikipedia.org/wiki/Jin_Dynasty_(1115–1234)#List_of_emperors.
29 Quoted in Ratchnevsky, 1991, p. 113.
30 Ratchnevsky, 1991, p. 114.

31 *Secret History*, §248; also Onon, 2001, p. 236.
32 Ratchnevsky, 1991, pp. 114–16, Mote, 2003, p. 245–46.
33 *Secret History*, §252; also Onon, 2001, p. 239.
34 Juzjani, 2010 (1881), p. 965.
35 Rachewiltz, 2004, Vol. II, p. 918.
36 *Secret History*, §252; also Onon, 2001, p. 239.
37 *Secret History*, §252.
38 Ratchnevsky, 1991, pp. 115.
39 Mote, 2003, p. 245.
30 Ratchnevsky, 1991, p. 114.
31 *Secret History*, §248; also Onon, 2001, p. 236.
32 Ratchnevsky, 1991, pp. 114–16, Mote, 2003, p. 245–46.
33 *Secret History*, §252; also Onon, 2001, p. 239.
34 Juzjani, 2010 (1881), p. 965.
35 Rachewiltz, 2004, Vol. II, p. 918.
36 *Secret History*, §252; also Onon, 2001, p. 239.
37 *Secret History*, §252.
38 Ratchnevsky, 1991, p. 115.
39 Mote, 2003, p. 245.

Chapter 2 — Endnotes

1 Cited in Ratchnevsky, 1991, p. 120.
2 Juzjani, 2010 (1181), p. 964.
3 Juzjani, 2010 (1181), p. 964.
4 Barthold, after examining the various sources, concludes that Chingis Khan was still in the vicinity of Beijing when the embassy met up with him (Barthold, 1992, p. 394). But Martin suggests that Chingis left the north China plain for the Mongolia Plateau even before the city had fallen and that the embassy must have encountered him somewhere north of the Great Wall, perhaps in the vicinity of current day Anguli Nuur (Martin's Yü-erh-lo). See Martin, 1977, pp. 178, 226-27.
5 Juzjani, 2010 (1181), p. 966.
6 Quoted in Ratchnevsky, 1991, p.121.
7 Barthold, 1992, p.394.
8 Quoted in Wood, 2002, p. 66.
9 Vaissiere, 2005, pp. 13–41.
10 Juvaini, 1997, p. 77.
11 Juvaini, 1997, p. 78.
12 Barthold, 1992, p. 396.
13 Juvaini, 1997, p. 78.
14 Allsen, 2002, p.   10.

15 Juvaini, 1997, pp. 21–22.

16 See Onon, 2001, pp. 108–110 (*Secret History* §§133 and 135) and Rachewiltz, 2004, pp. 488–498

17 Rashid al-Din, quoted in Allsen, 2002, p. 12.

18 Rashid al-Din, quoted in Allsen, 2002, p. 12.

19 Allsen, 2002, p. 12.

20 Allsen, 2002, p. 14.

21 Barthold, 1992, p. 397. Juvaini, 1997, p. 78, suggests that the Mongol trade mission accompanied the three Muslim traders who had met with Chingis back to Khorezm. Juzjani (2010, p. 966) has Baha al-Din Razi stating that both the Mongol embassy and the trade mission accompanied his own embassy back to Khwarezm. Chingis Khan himself also refers to this in his message sent along with the trade mission to Otrar (Juvaini, p. 79). Since the Mongol mission start did not arrive in Otrar until 1218, both Baha al-Din Razi's embassy and the traders must have hung out in in Chingis's domains for at least a couple of years before returning home.

22 See Barthold, 1992, p. 396, n6.

23 This according to Nasavi's account. See Levi, 2010, p. 125. Nasavi's rhino horns may be the walrus ivory of other accounts. Also see Barthold, 1992. p. 396. Juzjani implies the gold nugget went to the Sultan, but that the rest of items went with the trade mission to Otrar.

24 Levi, 2010, p. 126

25 Levi, 2010, p. 126

26 Levi, 2010, p. 126

27 Barthold, 1992. p.397

28 Another scenario, presented by Nasavi, is that the trade mission did not actually leave for Khwarezm until the three envoys returned to Chingis's court. In this case, Chingis might well have assumed that the peace proposal sanctioned trade. He then dispatched the trade mission. Juzjani says the two missions left together. In this case is it unclear if the trade caravan was aware of the outcome of the diplomatic mission. See Barthold, p. 397.

29 Juvaini, 1997, p. 79

30 Juvaini, 1997, p. 78

31 Juvaini, 1997, p. 79

32 See *Secret History*, §254 and Martin, 1977, p. 229.

33 Rachewiltz, Vol. II, p. 923

34 Rachewiltz, Vol. II, p. 923

35 al-Athir, 2008, p. 225

36 Juzjani, 2010, p. 967.

37 See Martin, 1977, p. 228.

38 Barthold, 1992, p. 394.

39 Browne, 1906, p. 426.

40   Soucek, 2000, pp. 22–23.

41   Abazov, 2008, pp. 20–21.

42   Bosworth, 2002.

43   Jackson, 2000; Barthold, 1992, p. 398; Juvaini, 1997, p. 79.

44   Barthold, 1992, p. 398, citing Juvaini, says he was a Hindu. Juvaini,1997, p. 79, calls him only an Indian, saying nothing about him being a Hindu. Barthold may have just assumed he was a Hindu. He could have been a Muslim from India. In any case, his presence demonstrates that the trade networks of the merchants in the caravan extended into India.

45   Juvaini, 1997, p. 79.

46   Levi, 2010, p. 126.

47   Ratchnevsky, 1991, p. 123.

48   Juvaini, 1997, p. 79.

49   Barthold, 1992, pp. 398–399.

50   Barthold, 199, p. 399.

51   Juvaini, 1997, p. 80; Juzjani, 2010 (1181), p. 967

52   Quoted in Ratchnevsky, 1991, p. 123; apparently a quote from Nasavi through Buniyatov. See another version in Levi, 2010, p. 127

53   Biran, 2005, p. 172.

54   Juvaini, 1997, p. 82

55   Levi, 2010, p. 127.

56   Juvaini, 1997, p. 80.

57   Juvaini, 1997, p. 80

Chapter 3 — Endotes

1   Di Cosmo, 2009, p.23.

2   Biran, 2005, p. 76, n127, Ratchnevsky, 1991, p. 83.

3   *Secret History* §189, see Onon, 2001, p. 167.

4   *Secret History* §117, see Onon, 2001, p. 96.

5   *Secret History* §193, see Onon, 2001, p.70.

6   *Secret History* §194, also see Ratchnevsky, 1991, p. 85.

7   *Secret History* §194, also see Ratchnevsky, 1991, p. 85.

8   *Secret History* §196, See Onon, 2001, p. 177.

9   Gumilev, 1987, p. 203.

10   The *Secret History*, §198, has a different version of these events. It says Chingis attacked the escapees on the Upper Irtysh in 1205. Biran (2005, p. 75) and other modern historians favor 1208. Also see Onon, 2001, p. 181. Bizarrely, Onon places the source of the Irtysh near Ulaangom. If he means the present day capital of Uvs Aimag, he is quite a bit off the mark.

11   See Ratchnevsky, 1991, p. 86 and Biran, 2005, p. 75. Also Juvaini, 1997, p. 61. The eminent Persian historian here makes several mistakes, however.

He states the Khüchüleg was the son of the Ong Khan (Tooril of the Keraits) but then later implies that Khüchüleg was a Merkit!

12 Juvaini, 1997, p. 62.
13 Juvaini, 1997, p. 63.
14 Juvaini, 1997, p. 62.
15 Juvaini, 1997, p. 63.
16 Juvaini, 1997, p. 62, n5.
17 Juvaini, 1997, p. 63.
18 Juvaini, 1997, p. 63.
19 Juvaini, 1997, p. 63.
20 Juvaini, 1997, p. 344, 360. Also see Barthold, pp. 358–59.
21 Juvaini, 1997, p. 345.
22 Juvaini, 1997, p. 346.
23 Juvaini, 1997, p. 348.
24 Biran, 2005, p. 78.
25 Juvaini, 1997, p. 360.
26 Biran, 2005, p. 79.
27 Biran, 2005, p. 80.
28 Juvaini, 1997, p. 64, p. 64, n11, p. 361.
29 Biran, 2005, p. 80.
30 Juvaini, 1997, p. 347.
31 Juvaini, 1997, p. 347.
32 *Secret History*, §209.
33 Martin, 1977, pp. 109, 220.
34 The dating of this episode is a highly contentious issue. Al-Athir, Nasavi, Juvaini, and Juzjani all give widely differing   dates. After examining all the various assertions, Barthold concludes that the Khwarezmshah's confrontation with the Mongols probably occurred in the spring or early summer of 1216. See Barthold, 1992, pp. 369-72. Al-Athir describes the battle in his account of the events of 1220, and implies that it happened after the massacre of the trade caravan in Otrar; this would appear to be a chronological impossibility. His description of the battle, with over 20,000 Muslims killed, is also highly suspect.
35 Quoted in Barthold, 1992, p. 370 and n5, who gives the original Persian text. This quote does not appear in Boyle's (Juvaini, 1997) translation.
36 Juvaini, 1997, p. 69.
37 Quoted in Martin, 1977, p. 225.
38 Quoted in Ratchnevsky, 1991, p. 86.
39 This is Arslan Khan the Younger. His father the Arslan Khan had committed suicide after a dispute with Gür Khan. See Biran, 2005, p. 81 and Juvaini, 1997, pp. 65, 75.
40 Juvaini, 1997, p. 75.

41   Juvaini, 1997, p. 76, Biran, 2005, p. 81.

42   Juvaini, 1997, p. 76.

43   Juvaini, 1997, p. 65.

44   Juvaini, 1997, p. 65.

45   Juvaini, 1997, p. 66.

46   Juvaini, 1997, p. 73.

47   Ratchnevsky, 1991, p. 121.

48   Martin, 1977, p. 230.

49   See *Secret History*, §84–87, for a description of Temüjn's captivity among the Taichuud.

50   *Secret History*, §147.

51   *Secret History*, §147.

52   Martin, 1977, p. 231. Ikh Ulaan Davaa (Big Red Pass) is at N46°35.174' / E092°09.621'.

53   Martin, 1977, p. 231.

54   Juvaini, 1997, p. 66.

55   Juvaini, 1997, p. 67.

56   Biran, 2005, p. 83.

57   Barthold, 1992, p. 403.

Chapter 4 — Endnotes

1   *Secret History*, §254. Also see Rachewiltz, 2004, Vol. I, pp. 181–186 and Onon, pp. 241–245.

2   *Secret History*, §§155, 156. Also see Rachewiltz, 2004, Vol. I, pp. 573–577

3   *Secret History*, §254.

4   *Secret History*, §254. This statement is ambiguous. It could refer to Jochi, as I have interpreted it here; however, Chaagadai could be referring to himself, meaning that he will not waste any more words on the subject at the moment, but he will resort to action at the proper time and place.

5   *Secret History*, §254. Also see Rachewiltz, 2004, Vol. II, pp. 922–931.

6   The Mongols army left from the Saari Steppe; see Rachewiltz, 2004, Vol. I, p. 471, and Vol. II, p. 939.

7   Rachewitz suggests that her absence reinforces the idea that her speech was a fabrication added to the *Secret History* by those with political axes to grind. See Rachewiltz, 2004, Vol. II, p. 939.

8   Rachewiltz, 2004, Vol. II, p. 939. Martin, 1977, pp. 235–36.

9   *Secret History*, §256, Also see Rachewiltz, 2004, Vol. I, p. 189 and Onon, p. 248.

10   Vambery, 1873, p. 122.

11   Barthold, 1992, p. 404.

12   Barthold, 1992, p. 404.

13 Juvaini, 1997, p. 82.
14 Bosworth, 2009a.
15 He reigned as Great Sultan of the Saljuq Empire 1118-57. From 1097-1118 he reigned as sultan of Khorasan.
16 Biran, 2012.
17 Boyle, 1968, p. 6.
18 Bosworth, 2009a.
19 Bosworth, undated.
20 Bosworth, 2001.
21 Bosworth, 2009b.
22 Bosworth, 2001.
23 Bosworth, 2009.
24 Bosworth, 2009c.
25 Juvaini, 1997, p. 465, n2, p. 305, n69.
26 Bosworth, 2009b.
27 Juvaini, 1997, p. 465.
28 Bosworth, 2009a.
29 Bosworth, 1984.
30 Juvaini, 1997, p. 342.
31 al-Athir, 2008, p. 127.
32 Juvaini, 1997, p. 341
33 Bosworth, 2011; Barthold, 1992, p. 354.
34 Juvaini, 1997, p. 341.
35 Juvaini, 1997, p. 341.
36 Narshakhi, 2007, p. 31.
37 al-Athir, 2008, p. 128, Barthold, 1992, p. 360.
38 al-Athir, 2008, p. 128.
39 al-Athir, 2008, p. 132.
40 al-Athir, 2008, p. 132.
41 al-Athir, 2008, p. 133.
42 See Barthold, 1992, p. 354 for a discussion of the marriage matter.
43 Bosworth, 2009c.
44 Bosworth, 2009c.
45 Bosworth, 2009c.
46 Juvaini, 1997, p. 466.
47 Bernard Lewis. 2003, Kindle Locations 988-992.
48 Bosworth, 1984.
49 Bosworth, 2009b.
50 Tekish had fought and defeated the Abbasids before. See Juvaini, 1997, pp. 390, 307.
51 Boyle, 1968, p. 184.
52 Lewis, 2003, Kindle Locations 1035-1037.

53 al-Athir, 2008, p. 205
54 See Howorth, 1876, p.74; also Browne, 1906, p. 436. Barthold, 1992, p.
    400, rejects the accusations of collusion between the Caliph and Chingis
    Khan as "vague rumors."
55 al-Athir, 2008, p. 205.
56 Bosworth, 1984.
57 al-Athir, 2008, p. 206.
58 al-Athir, 2008, p. 206.
59 al-Athir, 2008, p. 206.
60 Levi, 2010, p. 128.
61 Levi, 2010, p. 128.
62 Quoted in Martin, 1977, p. 225.
63 DeWeese, 2006, p. 39-40.

Chapter 5 — Endnotes

1   Juvaini, 1997, p. 82, Levi, 2010, p. 128.
2   Juvaini, 1997, p. 83.
3   Barthold, 1992, p. 404.
4   Juvaini, 1997, p. 83, claims that the army was split up after the siege began.
    Barthold, p. 406, implies but does outright state that the army was divided
    up before it reached Otrar. Also see Juzjani, 2010, p. 975.
5   Barthold, 1992, p. 407.
6   Quoted in Levi, 2010, p. 129.
7   Quoted in Levi, 2010, p. 129.
8   Quoted in Levi, 2010, p. 129.
9   Juvaini, 1997, p. 703.
10 Juvaini, 1997, p. 98.
11 Barthold, 1992, p. 407.
12 Juvaini, 1997, p. 98.
13 Juvaini, 1997, p. 99.
14 Juvaini, 1997, p. 99.
15 Barthold, 1992, p. 407; Juvaini, p. 100.
16 Barthold, 1992, p. 408; Juvaini, 1997, p. 100.
17 Narshakhi, 2007, p. 13.
18 Dayir is the Tayir Bahadur of Juvaini. He is mentioned in the *Secret History*
    (§202) as the commander of a thousand.
19 Juvaini, 1997, p. 102.
20 Barthold, 1992, p. 409.
21 Knobloch, 200, p. 7.
22 Frye, 1996, p. 5.
23 Barthold, 1992, p. 82. The source of the river is said to be at 39°30. N

70°35. E.

24   Barthold, 1992, p. 97.

25   Blair, 1991.

26   Frye, 1996, p. 10.

27   Personal Communication, Dr. Makhsuma Niyazova, Bukhara.

28   Narshakhi, 2007, p. 48.

29   Narshakhi, 2007, p. 14, Barthold, 1992, pp. 98–99, Vambery, 1873, p. xxv.

30   Bosworth, 2011.

31   Narshakhi, 2007, pp. 15–16, Barthold, 1992, p. 99.

32   The 196-foot Kutlug-Timur Minaret in the Khwarezmian city of Urgench is higher, but subject to controversy. Construction on it apparently began in the early eleventh century, but it may not have been completed until the early fourteenth century, during the reign of Kutlug-Timur, a vice-regent of the Golden Horde. Its height at the time of the Mongol invasions is unknown. The minaret still exists among the ruins of current-day Kunye-Urgench.

33   Juvaini,1997, p. 102, says the Mongols arrived at Bukhara at the beginning of March. Al-Athir and Juzjani claim he arrived in early February. Barthold, 1992, p. 409, supports al-Athir and Juzjani.

34   Juvaini, 1997. p. 102.

35   Barthold, 1992, pp. 103, 336.

36   Barthold, 1992, pp. 101–03; Narshakhi, 2007, p. 49. Both accounts are muddled, so say the least. Also see Gaube, 1999, pp. 19–28, Frye, 1996, pp. 9–10, 30, 32, The current city walls, sections of which have been restored, were built by the Shaybanid Dynasty in the sixteenth century and probably rebuilt and repaired in the eighteenth century. How closely this Shaybanid Wall follows the old *Rabad* Wall is uncertain. In any case, these partially restored walls may give a general idea of the appearance of the walls Chingis Khan faced when he arrived on the outskirts of the city in 1220.

37   Nekrasova, 1999, p. 65, Pugachenkova, undated.

38   Barthold, 1992, pp. 100, also n5.

39   Barthold, 1992, pp. 100. The core of the current *Ark*, or Citadel, one of Bukhara's main tourist attractions, dates from the Shaybanid era (1500-98), with some parts probably added later. See Unknown, 1989, Narshakhi, 2007, pp. 29–31, Barthold, 1992, p. 100.

40   Barthold, 1992, pp. 409.

41   Barthold, 1992, p. 409.

42   Ratchnevsky, 1991, p. 89.

43   *Secret History*, §201.

44   Juvaini, 1997. p. 102.

45   Barthold, 1992, p. 410. Al-Athir, 2008, p. 208, says the 11th . Nasavi says the 16th.

46 Gangler, 2004, p. 40.
47 Juvaini, 1997, p.104, Juzjani, 2010, p. 975, n3
48 Ratchevsky, 1991, p. 131, discounts Juvaini's account of the desecration of the mosque.
49 Juvaini, 1997. p. 104.
50 al-Athir, 2008, p. 208.
51 Juvaini, 1997. p. 105.
52 Barthold, 1992, pp. 103.
53 Juvaini, 1997, p. 105.
54 Barthold, 1992, p. 410; al-Athir, 2008, p. 208. It should be noted that al-Athir says this took place after the fall of the Citadel, not before as Juvaini relates.
55 Barthold, 1992, p. 410.
56 Barthold, 1992, p. 411.
57 al-Athir, 2008, p. 208-09.
58 Juvaini, 1997, p. 106.
59 Juvaini, 1997, p. 107.

Chapter 6 — Endnotes

1   Current estimates of the Persian *farsakh* differ from 3.88 miles to 4.18 miles, often rounded off to four miles. See http://www.sizes.com/units/farsakh.htm and http://www.merriam-webster.com/dictionary/farsakh.
2   Barthold 1992, p. 411, opines that the Mongol army did proceed on both the north and south bank of the river.
3   Bretschneider, 2001, Vol. I, p.76.
4   Juvaini, 1997, p. 117.
5   al-Athir, 2008, p. 209.
6   Juvaini, 1997, p. 117; Barthold, 1992, pp. 96-99, discusses the towns of the Zerafshan Valley. See also Buryakov, 1999, p. 43. Buryakov places Dabusiya eighteen kilometers east of Rabat-i-Malik. This is apparently a translation or typographical error.
7   Buryakov, 1999, p. 43.
8   Barthold, 1992, p. 127.
9   al-Athir, 2008, p. 208-09.
10 Barthold, 1992, p. 412.
11 Juvaini, 1997, p.84.
12 Juvaini, 1997, p. 84.
13 Juvaini, 1997, p. 8.
14 Juvaini, 1997, p. 85.
15 Juvaini, 1997, p. 84.
16 Jackson, 2000.

17   Levi, 2010, p. 128.

18   Juvaini, 1997, p. 86.

19   Levi, 2010, p.128.

20   Juvaini, 1997, p.143.

21   Juvaini, 1997, p. 118.

22   Juvaini, 1997, p. 118. Talaqan is a small town thirty-five miles east of Kunduz, Afghanistan. It was apparently visited by Marco Polo, who called it Taican. This Talaqan should not be confused with a town in what is now Turkmenistan which was later destroyed by the Mongols. Khadag Baatar is Juvaini's Ghadag Noyon. See Juvaini, 1997, p. 115. Also see *Secret History*, §§170, 185.

23   al-Athir, 2008, 210.

24   Barthold, 1992. 366.

25   Barthold, 1992. p. 366. Juvaini, 1997, p. 11.

26   Scott C. Levi, 2010, p.127.

27   Barthold, 1992. p. 405.

28   Juvaini, 1997, p. 375.

29   Juvaini, 1997, p. 116.

30   Juvaini, 1997, p. 376.

31   Juvaini, 1997, p. 377.

32   Juvaini says that shortly thereafter news arrived of the fall of Samarkand, p. 378. Later he contradicts himself by stating that the Sultan learned of the fall of Samarkand while in Nishapur.

33   Barthold, 1992, p. 411; Juvaini, 1997, p, 118.

34   Juvaini, 1997, p. 116 and n5.

35   Juvaini, 1997, p. 117 and n7.

36   al-Athir, 2008, p. 209; Juzjani, 2010, p. 779; Barthold, 1992. p. 409.

37   Barthold, 1992, p. 411.

38   Juvaini, 1997, p. 119.

39   al-Athir, 2008, p. 209.

40   al-Athir, 2008, p. 209.

41   Juvaini, 1997, p. 119.

42   al-Athir, 2008, pp. 208-09.

43   Barthold, 1992. p. 86.

44   al-Athir, p.210.

45   Juvaini, 1997, p. 120.

46   Juvaini, p.122. Juvaini's translator says the the 19th. Barthold says the 17th.

47   Barthold, 1992, p. 414; also see Waley, 1931.

48   Juvaini, 1997, p. 122.

49   al-Athir, 2008, p. 210.

Chapter 7 — Endnotes

1   Barthold, 1992, p. 414.
2   The story is hazy, but Asan, a.k.a Hasan Hajji, may have participated in the legendary Baljun Covenant, said to have occurred around 1202, and was thus a witness to Chingis Khan's rise to power in Mongolia..
3   Juvaini, 1997, p. 87.
4   Barchinlighkant is Juvaini's Barligh-Kant. Bretschneider, 2001, Vol. II. p. 95, using Chinese sources, calls the city Ba-rh-ch'i-li-han; also see Vol.I, p. 285, n676. The location of Özkend has baffled even the most determined investigators, including Barthold.
5   Juvaini, 1997, p. 87; for the location see Barthold, 1992, p. 179, n4.
6   The *Encyclopedia Iranica* places it 350 kilometers from the mouth of the Syr Darya, or roughly 35 kilometers below Qyzylorda. See http://www.iranicaonline.org/articles/jand-2.
7   Juvaini, 1997, p. 88.
8   Juvaini, 1997, p. 88.
9   Juvaini, 1997, p. 90; Barthold, 1992, p. 415
10   Juvaini, 1997, p. 90, n12.
11   Barthold, 1992, p. 417.
12   Barthold, 1992, p. 169. The locations are approximate. Apparently Banakat no longer exists.
13   Juvaini, 1997, p. 91.
14   Hitchins, 2009.
15   Juvaini, 1997, p. 92.
16   Juvaini, 1997, p. 92.
17   Juvaini, 1997, p. 92.
18   Juvaini, 1997, p. 92.
19   Juvaini, 1997, p. 94.
20   Juvaini, 1997, p. 94.
21   Juvaini, 1997, p. 94.
22   Juvaini, 1997, p. 94.
23   Juvaini, 1997 p. 95.
24   Barthold, 1992, p. 418.

Chapter 8 — Endnotes

1   Juvaini, 1997, p. 143.
2   al-Athir, 2008, p. 210.
3   Juvaini, 1997, p. 143.
4   Barthold, 1992, p. 72, places the Mela Ford near the mouth of the Vakhsh River, but adds that the ford is eight miles east of Termez, by which he

apparently means old Termez. The Vakhsh River flows into the Amu
Darya about fifty miles east of old Termez. It is possible Barthold confused
the Vakhsh River with the Surya Darya, which runs into the Amu Darya
near Termez? Also see Juvaini, 1997, p. 144 and p. 144, n3.
5   al-Athir, 2008, p.210.
6   Barthold, 1992, p. 421.
7   Barthold, 1992, p. 420.
8   Quoted in Barthold, 1992, p. 423.
9   Juvaini, 1997, p.144.
10 Juvaini, 1997, p.144.
11 Juvaini, 1997, p.379.
12 Juvaini, 1997, p. 179.
13 Juvaini, 1997, p. 380.
14 Juvaini, 1997, p. 380.
15 Juvaini, 1997, p. 181.
16 Juvaini, 1997, p. 381.
17 Barthold, 1992, p. 421.
18 Barthold, 1992, p. 423.
19 Juvaini, 1997, p. 145.
20 See remarks of Barthold,, 1992, p. 424, and Boyle, 1968, p. 310.
21 Cited in Barthold, 1992, p. 423.
22 Barthold, 1992, p. 424.
23 Juvaini, 1997, p. 145, says Sübedei "proceeded to Tus by way of Jam"; n10
    states that the ruins of Tus, or Tabaran, are a few miles north of Meshed.
24 Willey, 2005, p. 153.
25 Quoted in Barthold, 1992, p. 422.
26 Juvaini, 1997, p. 387, n77.
27 Juvaini, 1997, p. 387.
28 Juvaini, 1997, p. 466.
29 Juvaini, 1997, p. 382.
30 Juvaini, 1997, p. 383.
31 Juvaini, 1997, p. 383.
32 Juvaini, 1997, p. 147, p. 384.
33 al-Athir, 2008. p. 213.
34 al-Athir, 2008. p. 214.
35 Sujas is said to be near the town of Sultaniya. See Juvaini, 1997, p.1 47, n22.
36 Juvaini, 1997, p. 179.
37 Barthold, 1992, p. 425.
38 Boyle, 1968, p. 311.
39 Juvaini, 1997, p. 467; Barthold, 1992, p. 431. Al-Athir, 2008, however,
    relates a completely different version of Terken Khatan' capture; see p. 213.
40 Juvaini, 1997, p. 387.

41   Barthold, 1992, p. 426.
42   al-Athir, 2008, p. 214.
43   Juvaini, 1997, p. 468.
44   al-Athir, 2008, p. 215.

Chapter 9 — Endnotes

1   Barthold, 1992, pp. 137-38, p. 427; Juvaini, 1997, p. 128.
2   Quoted in DeWeese, 2006, p. 36.
3   Quoted in DeWeese, 2006, p. 34.
4   Quoted in DeWeese, 2006, p. 32.
5   Quoted in DeWeese, 2006, p. 26.
6   DeWeese, 2006, p. 52.
7   DeWeese, 2006, p. 23.
8   Soucek, 2000, Kindle Edition Location 143-145.
9   Juvaini, 1997, p.129.
10   Juvaini, 1997, p.129.
11   Juvaini, 1997, p. 124.
12   Rapoport, 2011.
13   Bosworth, 2011a
14   Barthold, 1992, p. 437.
15   Soucek, 2000, Kindle Version: Locations 200-203.
17   Barthold, 1992, p. 147
18   Juvaini, 1997, p. 124; Barthold, 1992, p. 431.
19   Juvaini, 1997, p. 401; Barthold, 1992, p. 432.
20   Barthold, 1992, p. 432.
21   Bosworth, 2009a.
22   Juvaini, 1997, p. 402.
23   Juvaini, 1997, p. 401.
24   Barthold, 1992, p. 431; Juvaini, 1997, pp. 124, 158 n17.
25   Juvaini, 1997, p. 124.
26   Juvaini, 1997, p. 124.
27   Juvaini, 1997, p. 125.
28   Juvaini, 1997, p. 126.
29   Juvaini, 1997, p. 124 n4.
30   Barthold, 1992, p. 434.
31   Juvaini, 1997, p. 126.
32   Barthold, 1992, p. 434.
33   Barthold, 1992, p. 147.
34   al-Athir, 2008, p. 227.
35   Juvaini, 1997, p. 128.

36   al-Athir, 2008, p. 228.
37   Juvaini, 1997, p. 128.
38   Algar, 2009.
39   DeWeese, 2006. p. 47.
40   DeWeese, 2006. p. 50.
41   DeWeese, 2006, p. 50.
42   DeWeese, 2006, p. 51.
43   Browne, 1906, p. 492
44   Browne, 1906, p. 493
45   Algar, 2009
46   Barthold, 1991, p. 429.
47   Barthold, 1991, p. 429.

BIBLIOGRAPHY

Abazov, R. (2008). *The Palgrave Concise Historical Atlas of Central Asia*. New York, Palgrave MacMillan.

Ahmed, S. (2012). Hadith i. A General Introduction. Encyclopedia Iranica Online: http://www.iranicaonline.org/articles/hadith-i-intro, www.iranicaonline.org.

al-Athir, I. and D. S. Richards (2008). *The \Chronicle of Ibn al-Athir for the Crusading Period from al-Kamil fi'l-Ta'rikh Part 3*. Surrey, Burlington VT, Ashgate.

Algar, H. (2009). Kobrawiya i. The Eponym. Encyclopaedia Iranica: http://www.iranicaonline.org/articles/kobrawiya-i-the-eponym.

Allsen, T. T. (2002). *Commodity and Exchange in the Mongol Empire*. Cambridge Cambridge University Press.

Barthold, W. (1992). *Turkestan Down to the Mongol Invasion*. New Delhi, Munshiram Manoharlal Publishers Pvt Ltd.

Biran, M. (2005). *The Empire of the Qara Khitai in Eurasion History: Between China and the Islamic World*. Cambridge, Cambridge University Press.

Biran, M. (2012). Joči. Encyclopaedia Iranica: http://www.iranicaonline.org/articles/joci.

Biran, M. (2012). Ilik-Khanids. Encyclopaedia Iranica: http://www.iranicaonline.org/articles/ilak-khanids

Bolshakov, O. G. (1999). Central Asia Under the Umayyids and the Early Abbasids: Part Two. *Central Asia Under the Early Abbasids. History of Civilizations of Central Asia, Vol. 4*. Delhi, Motilal Banarsidass Publishers.

Bosworth, C. E. (1984). Ala-al-Din Mohammed. Encyclopædia Iranica: http://www.iranica.com/articles/ala-al-din-abul-fath-mohammad-b.

Bosworth, C. E. (2001). Ghurids. Encyclopaedia Iranica; http://www.iranicaonline.org/articles/ghurids.

Bosworth, C. E. (2002). Otrār. Encyclopedia Iranica: http://www.iranicaonline.org/articles/otrar, www.iranicaonline.org.

Bosworth, C. E. (2008). Jalal-al-Din Khwarazmsah i. Mengübirni. Encyclopaedia Iranica:http://www.iranicaonline.org/articles/jalal-al-din-kvarazmsahi-mengbirni.

Bosworth, C. E. (2008a). Jand. Encyclopaedia Iranica: http://www.iranicaonline.org/articles/jand-2.

Bosworth, C. E. (2009a). Khwarazmshahs: i. Descendants of the line of Anuštigin. Encyclopaedia Iranica: www.iranica.com/articles/khwarazmshahs-i.

Bosworth, C. E. (2009b). Tekis b. Il Arslan. Encyclopaedia Iranica; http://www.iranicaonline.org/articles/tekis-b-il-arslan.

Bosworth, C. E. (2009c). Terken Katun. Encyclopaedia Iranica: http://www.iranicaonline.org/articles/terken-katun.

Bosworth, C. E. (2011). Al-e-Borhan. Encyclopaedia Iranica: http://www.

iranicaonline.org/articles/al-e-borhan

Bosworth, C. E. (2011a). Chorasmia ii. In Islamic times. Encyclopædia Iranica: http://www.iranicaonline.org/articles/chorasmia-ii.

Bosworth, C. E. (2012). Jand. Encyclopaedia Iranica: http://www.iranicaonline.org/articles/jand-2.

Bosworth, C. E. (undated). Bukhara ii. From the Arab Invasions to the Mongols. Encyclopedia Iranica Online: http://www.iranicaonline.org/articles/bukhara-ii.

Bosworth, C. E. and O. G. Bolshakov (1999a). Central Asia Under the Umayyids and the Early Abbasids. Part One: The Appearance of the Arabs in Central Asia under the Umayyads and the Establishment of Islam. *History of Civilizations of Central Asia, Vol. 4*. B. A. Litnikov. Delhi, Motilal Banarsidass Publishers.

Boyle, J. A., Ed. (1968). *The Cambridge History of Iran: Vol. 5. The Saljuq and Mongol Periods*. Cambridge, Cambridge University Press.

Bretschneider, E. (2001). *Medieval Researches From Eastern Asian Sources: Fragments towards the Knowledge of a Geography and History of Central and Western Asia from the 13th to the 17th Century*. New Delhi, Munshiram Manoharlal.

Browne, E. G. (1906). *A Literary History of Persia: Volume II. From Firdawsi to Saadi*. New York, Charles Scribner's Sons.

Browne, E. G. (1969). *A Literary History of Persia. Vol. 1: From the Earliest TImes until Firdawsi*. Cambridge, Cambridge University Press.

Browne, E. G. (2009). *A Literary History of Persia. Volume III: The Tartar Dominion (1265–1502)*. Cambridge, Cambridge University Press.

Buryakov, Y. F., et al. (1999). *The Cites and Routes of the Great Silk Road*. Tashkent, Chief Editorial Office of Publishing and Printing Concern "Sharj".

Christian, D. (1998). *A History of Russia, Central Asia and Mongolia*. Oxford, Blackwell Publishers.

Chuvin, P. (2001). *Samarkand, Bukhara, Khiva*. Paris, Flammarion.

Cosmo, N. D., et al., Eds. (2009). *The Cambridge History of Inner Asia: The Chinggisid Age*. Cambridge, Cambridge University Press.

Davidovich, E. A. (1999). The Karakhanids. *History of Civilizations of Central Asia, Vol. 4*. B. A. Litnikov. Delhi, Motilal Banarsidass Publishers.

DeWeese, D. (2006). "Stuck in the Throat of Chingiz Khan": Envisioning the Mongol Conquests in Some Sufi Accounts from the 14th to 17th Centuries. *History and Historiography of Post-Mongol Central Asia and the Middle East: Studies in Honor of John E. Woods*. J. Pfeiffer and S. A. Quinn. Wiesbaden, Harrasowitz Verlag.

Dughlat, M. H. and t. N. Elias (1895). *Tarikhi-i-Rashadi: A History of the Moghuls of Central Asia*. London, Sampson Low, Marston and Company.

Frye, R. N. (1996). *Bukhara: The Medieval Achievement*. Costa Mesa, Mazda Publishers.

Frye, R. N. (1999). How Old is Bukhara? *Bukhara: The Myth and the Architecture*.

A. Petruccioli. Cambridge MA. Aga Khan Program for Islamic Architecture at Harvard University and the Massachusetts Institute of Technology.

Frye, R. N. (undated). Bukhara i. In Pre-Islamic Times. Encyclopaedia Iranica http://www.iranicaonline.org/articles/bukhara-i.

Gangler, A., et al. (2004). *Bukhara—The Eastern Dome of Islam.* Stuttgart, London, Edition Axel Menges.

Gaube, H. (1999). What Arabic and Persian Sources Tell Us about the Structure of Tenth-Century Bukhara. *Bukhara: The Myth and the Architecture.* A. Petruccioli. Cambridge, MA, Aga Khan Program for Islamic Architecture at Harvard University and the Massachusetts Institute of Technology.

Gibb, H. A. R. (1923). *The Arab Conquests of Central Asia.* New York, AMS Press.

Golden, P. B. (2011). *Central Asia in World History.* Oxford, New York, Oxford University Press.

Golden, P. B. and C. E. Bosworth (2012). Gozz. Encyclopedia Iranica Online: http://www.iranicaonline.org/articles/gozz, www.iranicaonline.org.

Grousset, R. (1966). *Conqueror of the World: The Life of Chingis-Khan.* New York, The Viking Press.

Grousset, R. (1999). *The Empire of the Steppes: A History of Central Asia.* New Brunswick, Rutgers University Press.

Hansen, V. (2012). *The Silk Road:A New History* (Kindle Edition), Oxford University Press.

Hitchins, K. (2009). Khujand. Encyclopedia Iranica: http://www.iranicaonline. org/articles/khujand-city-in-northwestern-tajikistan.

Howorth, H. H. (1876). *History of the Mongols from the 9th to the 19th Century: Part 1, The Mongols Proper and the Kalmyks.* New York, Cosimo Classics.

Howorth, H. H. (2008). *History of the Mongols from the 9th to the 19th Century: Part 3, The So-Called Tartars of Russia and Central Asia.* New York, Cosimo, Inc.

Jackson, P. (2000). Gāyer Khan. Encyclopedia Iranica Online: http://www. iranicaonline.org/articles/gayer-khan-, available at www.iranicaonline.org.

Jailov, A. H. The Arab Conquest of Transoxania Part II. *History of Civilizations of Central Asia, Vol. 3.* B. A. Litnikov. Delhi, Motilal Banarsidass Publishers.

Juvaini and J. A. Boyle (1997). *Genghis Khan: The History of the World-Conqueror.* Seattle, University of Washington Press.

Juzjani, M. a.-S. (2010 (1181)). *Tabakat-i-Nasiri: A General History of the Muhammadan Dynasties of Asia including Hindustan . . . Vol. II.* Delhi, Low Price Publications.

Knobloch, E. (2001). *Monuments of Central Asia: A Guide to the Archeology, Art and Architecture of Turkestan.* London, New York, I. B. Tauris.

Levi, S. and R. Sela, Eds. (2010). *Islamic Central Asia: An Anthology of Sources.* Bloomington and Indianapolis, Indiana University Press.

Lewis, B. (2003). *The Assassins* (Kindle Edition). New York, Basic Books.

Litvinsky, B. A. (1999). Historical Introduction. *History of Civilizations of Central Asia, Vol. 3.* B. A. Litnikov. Delhi, Motilal Banarsidass Publishers.

Litvinsky, B. A. (1999b). The Hephthalite Empire. *History of Civilizations of Central Asia, Vol. 3.* B. A. Litnikov. Delhi, Motilal Banarsidass Publishers.

Litvinsky, B. A., et al. (1999a). The Arab Invasions. *History of Civilizations of Central Asia, Vol. 3.* B. A. Litnikov. Delhi, Motilal Banarsidass Publishers.

Marshak, B. I. (1999). Sogdiana. *History of Civilizations of Central Asia, Vol. 3.* Delhi, Motilal Banarsidass Publishers.

Martin, H. D. (1977). *The Rise of Chingis Khan and His Conquest of North China.* New York, Octagon Books.

Millward, J. A. (2007). *Eurasian Crossroads: A History of Xinjiang.* New York Columbia University Press.

Morgan, D. (1990). *The Mongols.* Cambridge MA and Oxford, Blackwell.

Mote, F. W. (2003). *Imperial China 900–1800.* Cambridge MA and London Harvard University Press.

Muqaddasi (2001). *The Best Divisions in the Knowledge of the Regions,* Ithaca Press.

Narshakhi (2007). *The History of Bukhara.* Princeton, Markus Wiener Publications.

Negmatov, N. N. (1994). States of North-Western Central Asia. *History of Civilizations of Central Asia, Vol. II.* Paris, UNESCO.

Negmatov, N. N. (1999). The Samanid State. *History of Civilizations of Central Asia, Vol. 3.* B. A. Litnikov. Delhi, Motilal Banarsidass Publishers.

Nekrasova, E. G. (1999). Lower Levels of Bukhara: Characteristics of the Earliest Settlements. *Bukhara: The Myth and the Architecture.* A. Petruccioli. Cambridge, MA, Aga Khan Program for Islamic Architecture at Harvard University and the Massachusetts Institute of Technology.

Onon, U. (2001). *The Secret History of the Mongols: The Life and Times of Chinggis Khan.* Richmond, Surrey, Curzon Press.

Pugachenkova, G. A. and E. V. Rtveladze (undated). Bukhara v. Archeology and Monuments. Encyclopædia Iranica: http://www.iranicaonline.org/articles/bukhara-v.

Rachewiltz, I. d. (2004). *The Secret History of the Mongols: A Mongolian Epic Chronicle of the Thirteenth Century.* Leiden, Boston, Brill.

Rapoport, Y. A. (2011). Chorasmia i. Archeology and pre-Islamic history. Encyclopædia Iranica: http://www.iranicaonline.org/articles/chorasmia-i.

Ratchnevsky, P. (1991). *Genghis Khan: His Life and Legacy.* Oxford, Blackwell Publishers.

Sevim, A. and C. E. Bosworth (1999). The Seljuqs and the Kkwarazm Shahs. *History of Civilizations of Central Asia, Vol. 4.* B. A. Litnikov. Delhi, Motilal Banarsidass Publishers.

Shuptar, V. (2008) The History of Ancient Otrar. http://www.discovery-kazakhstan.com/archive/2008/10_15.php

Sinor, D., Ed. (1990). *The Cambridge History of Early Inner Asia.* Cambridge Cambridge University Press.

Sinor, D. (1999). The Kitan and the Kara Khitay. *History of Civilizations of Central Asia, Vol. 4.* B. A. Litnikov. Delhi, Motilal Banarsidass Publishers.

Soucek, S. (2000). *A History of Inner Asia.* Cambridge, Cambridge University Press.

Vaissiere, É. d. l. (2005). *Sogdian Traders: A History.* Leiden, Boston, Brill.

Vaissière, É. d. l. (2004). Sogdian Trade. Encyclopaedia Iranica: http://www.iranicaonline.org/articles/sogdian-trade.

Vaissière, É. d. L. (2011). Sogdiana iii, History and Archeology. Encyclopædia Iranica: http://www.iranicaonline.org/articles/sogdiana-iii-history-and-archeology.

Vaissière, É. d. l. (undated) Sogdians in China: A Short History and Some New Discoveries. http://www.silkroadfoundation.org/newsletter/december/new_discoveries.htm

Vambery, A. (1873). *History of Bokhara: From the Earliest Period Down to the Present, Composed for the First Time after Known and Unknown Historical Manucripts.* London, Henry S. King & Co. .

Waley, A. and L. Chih-Ch'ang (1931). *The Travels of an Alchemist: The Journey of the Taoist Ch'ang Ch'un from China to the Hindukush at the Summons of Chingiz Khan.* London, George Routledge & Sons, LTD.

Willey, P. (2005). *Eagle's Nest: Ismaili Castles in Iran and Syria.* London, New York, I. B. Tauris.

Notes

Typeset in Adobe Jenson Pro 11/13

Made in the USA
Middletown, DE
25 August 2022

72254242R00125